Metaphor in educational discourse

Advances in Applied Linguistics

General editors: Christopher N. Candlin and Srikant Sarangi

This series offers a number of innovative points of focus. It seeks to represent diversity in applied linguistics but within that diversity to identify ways in which distinct research fields can be coherently related. Such coherence can be achieved by shared subject matter among fields, parallel and shared methodologies of research, mutualities of purposes and goals of research, and collaborative and cooperative work among researchers from different disciplines.

Although interdisciplinarity among established disciplines is now common, this series has in mind to open up new and distinctive research areas which lie at the boundaries of such disciplines. Such areas will be distinguished in part by their novel data sets and in part by the innovative combination of research methodologies. The series hopes thereby both to consolidate already well-tried methodologies, data and contexts of research and to extend the range of applied linguistics research and scholarship to new and under-represented cultural, institutional and social contexts.

The philosophy underpinning the series mirrors that of applied linguistics more generally: a problem-based, historically and socially grounded discipline concerned with the reflexive interrogation of research by practice, and practice by research, oriented towards issues of social relevance and concern, and multi-disciplinary in nature.

The structure of the series encompasses books of several distinct types: research monographs which address specific areas of concern; reports from well-evidenced research projects; coherent collections of papers from precisely defined colloquia; volumes which provide a thorough historical and conceptual engagement with key applied linguistics fields; and edited accounts of applied linguistics research and scholarship from specific areas of the world.

Published titles in the series:

Multimodal Teaching and Learning: The Rhetorics of the Science Classroom, Günther Kress, Carey Jewitt, Jon Ogborn and Charalampos Tsatsarelis
Language Acquisition and Language Socialization: Ecological Perspectives, edited by Claire Kromsch

Metaphor in educational discourse

Lynne Cameron

LONDON • NEW YORK

Continuum
The Tower Building, 11 York Road, London, SE1 7NX
370 Lexington Avenue, New York, NY 10017-6503

First published 2003
© Lynne Cameron 2003

All rights reserved. No part of this publication may be reproduced or transmitted in any form or by any means, electronic or mechanical, including photocopying, recording or any information storage or retrieval system, without permission in writing from the publishers.

British Library Cataloguing-in-Publication Data
A catalogue record for this book is available from the British Library.

ISBN   0-8264-4939-5 (hardback)
         0-8264-4940-9 (paperback)

Library of Congress Cataloging-in-Publication Data
Cameron, Lynne.
  Metaphor in educational discourse/Lynne Cameron.
    p. cm.—(Advances in applied linguistics)
  Includes bibliographical references and index.
  ISBN 0-8264-4939-5—ISBN 0-8264-4940-9 (pbk)
  1. Metaphor. 2. Language and education. 3. Discourse analysis. I. Title.
II. Series.

P301.5.M48 C36 2002
808'.001'4–dc21

2001054274

Typeset by YHT Ltd, London
Printed and bound in Great Britain by MPG Books Ltd, Bodmin, Cornwall

Contents

Foreword *by Christopher N. Candlin and Srikant Sarangi*	vi
Acknowledgements	x
1 An applied linguistic approach to metaphor in discourse	1
2 Talking, thinking and learning: theoretical background	27
3 Researching metaphor in classroom discourse	51
4 The linguistic form of metaphor in classroom discourse	86
5 Deliberate and conventionalized metaphor in classroom discourse	100
6 Metaphor in classroom activity	120
7 Researching metaphor interpretation	144
8 Metaphors in text 1: 'The Ozone Layer'	167
9 Metaphors in text 2: 'The Heart'	200
10 Systematicity, metaphor and metonymy	239
11 Metaphor in educational discourse: review and discussion	265
Appendix 1 Linguistic metaphors and grammatical analysis in the geology lesson	272
Appendix 2 Linguistic metaphors and teaching sequences in the geology lesson	275
References	278
Index	291

Foreword

Lynne Cameron's *Metaphors in Educational Discourse* is the third title in the *Advances in Applied Linguistics* series. Partly by coincidence and partly by design, Cameron's book, which explores how children make sense of scientific phenomena and the role metaphor plays in this sense-making, marks a continuation of the first title in the series, *Multimodal Teaching and Learning: The Rhetorics of the Science Classroom* (Kress, Jewitt, Ogborn and Tsatsarelis, 2001). While Kress *et al.* emphasize the need for a multimodal approach in the educational setting which takes us beyond language as such, Cameron's focus remains on language, but her analysis is far from being merely linguistic, as she deals with the use of the figurative/metaphorical language in the teaching/learning context. In a sense, language becomes conceptualized as a multimodal phenomenon, embodying different layers of interpretive practices.

Another point of departure for the present book can be located in how the research came about. Unlike the Kress *et al.* volume, which arose from a funded team-based, interdisciplinary project, Cameron's book is an example of long-standing doctoral and post-doctoral research at an individual level. One of the founding goals of this series was to disseminate different kinds of research in the field of applied linguistics. As we see it, Cameron's book serves as an excellent example of doctoral research which offers considerable scope for emulative studies by herself and by others, in different disciplinary fields, and in different educational settings across different cultures. Although the data are drawn from a single site, the richness of the data and the sophisticated nature of the data analysis make up for any lack of breadth in the corpus; it persuades the reader of the generalizability of the findings.

Cameron takes a broad view of metaphors: she describes them as 'the introduction of a centrifugal force into the dynamics of discourse' and argues her case around the notion of 'alterity' – where metaphors can create, reduce or resolve discoursal and/or conceptual alterities. This book thus goes beyond being a study of metaphors or, for that matter, the language of metaphors. The analytic chapters focus on the

Foreword

'talk *around* metaphors', with the explicit purpose of teaching and learning science. Theoretically, Cameron takes a constructionist approach to metaphor. For her, 'metaphors are not only linguistic devices to help explain concepts, but actually structure the concepts themselves'. This is true of the environment of learning science. It is this reconstructionist approach which can account for potential misunderstandings in the transfer of meaning. In other words, metaphors can fail to communicate. Cameron's very last words are a good way of articulating the complexities involved: '[Metaphor] is at once both true and false, both disjunctive and connecting, ordinary and yet surprising.'

The book offers a good blend of theoretical connections, as linguistic and cognitive models of metaphor theory become reassessed in light of complex systems theory and the Vygotskyan concept of zones of proximal development. In so doing it makes a connection, from an applied linguistic perspective, with language education (see, for instance, Larsen-Freeman's [1997] work on chaos theory and the ecology of language acquisition; Lantolf [2002] on social construction-ism and language learning; and Kramsch [2002] on the linkage between language acquisition and language socialization). Indeed, what stands out in Cameron's research is the application aspect – how metaphors manage to play a significant role in learning and understanding concepts. Through her analysis, Cameron illustrates that different texts/authors use metaphors to different effect. She takes to task those text writers who might inadvertently introduce metaphors as part of their writing style, but fail to develop them, and thus leave open the possibility of unintended consequences. This line of argument follows neatly from a constructivist view of language more generally.

Also important for Cameron's purpose is to explore the relation between understanding and learning. She very convincingly shows how metaphors both contribute to and limit understanding, and thus play a gatekeeping role in learning. We can think here of the perils of everyday metaphors when trying to explain scientific or professional knowledge. The misalignment between technical meaning and intended meaning can be counter-productive and lead to confusion. But ultimately it shows the power of metaphors in understanding. Metaphors have the potential for causing misunderstanding, especially when there are mismatches between a text writer's intentions behind a metaphor use and the worldly knowledge that students bring to their classroom learning environment. The topic knowledge that learners may have at a given time and the metaphors they are presented with can override linguistic knowledge, for example, that of syntactic and logical relations. A misunderstanding triggered by a metaphor can have knock-on effects on how the rest of the text is processed. The detailed analysis of the two classroom texts – The Ozone Layer and The Heart – despite their differential use of metaphors drive this point home rather elegantly.

There are practical lessons here for textbook writers and teachers. It is not only that different texts and authors make differential use of metaphors. At the micro-analytic level, Cameron shows how different kinds of metaphors are processed differently by readers of texts. In the educational setting which is our focus here, nominal metaphors are processed differently from verb metaphors – indeed the latter are more likely to go unnoticed, or become interpreted non-metaphorically. Perhaps there is something here to pause and think about. How much of what Cameron finds in her empirical studies could be of direct relevance to students themselves? As applied linguists, we have not that often addressed ourselves directly to students. If we were to take this challenge seriously, it would be parallel to current debates about the role of social scientists in the area of public understanding of science.

It is necessary to consider the important role that metaphors take on, in addition to being markers of exclusiveness and inclusiveness. The issue of sharedness remains paramount: the gap between text-writers' use of metaphors and the learners' level of world knowledge index a lack of in-groupness, which consequently may lead to non-learning or wrongful learning. The problem is not limited to which metaphors to use or not use, but is extendable to which ones should be interpreted metaphorically and which should be allowed to operate non-metaphorically. As Cameron puts it: 'Children need to learn to recognize when a metaphorical interpretation is not appropriate.' This level of discrimination in the judging of what is or is not metaphorically interpretable then becomes an indication of novice/expert identities vis-à-vis one's membership in different communities of practice. This takes one beyond the act of classifying metaphors as simply dead or alive! Metaphors are certainly available to learn by, but they remain also to live (or die) by.

From a textual interactional perspective, Cameron shows how different texts and interactional episodes may come not only with different types of metaphors, but also with different distribution patterns. For instance, in the classroom setting, metaphors seem to cluster in summarizing sequences and in agenda organization sequences. Such clustering offers considerable additional arguments for the strength or weakness of the generic integrity of particular genres.

There is, however, more to counting and noticing of metaphors in science talk and text. For many of us, the languages of science and of metaphor are perhaps too disparate to come together. Cameron draws our attention to 'an interesting paradox or conflict between the needs of science texts to inform accurately, and the inaccuracy prompted by the use of metaphors employed to inform effectively'. This points to the element of inexactness in science, which justifies the use of metaphorical resources. Managing this inexactness metaphorically is at the heart of current attempts to explain inherent fuzziness in scientific accounts. Although Cameron's book is firmly sited in the school setting, the focus on 'discrepancies in understanding' suggests much wider contextualization. In particular, it offers ways in which describing and accounting for the management of alterity can provide insights into what is distinctive about professional practices and the expertise of those engaged in them. Alterity can, after all, be used strategically, to flush out opinion, compel people to be clearer, to be more precise, to lay bare positions. Such strategic use of alterity can of course be realized differently, especially in terms of interpersonality. It can be adversative, as in courts of law, or non-adversarial, as with psychotherapists and their clients. Alterity management, and the role played by metaphor in that, is thus a professional accomplishment (Candlin 2002).

A further comment relates to the mediating role of the researcher in empirical/observational studies (Sarangi 2002; Sarangi and Candlin 2001). Cameron finds herself in a situation which demands her practical, pedagogical involvement. Her talk with the children then acquires the status of relevant data. Increasingly we have to learn to live with this reality of applied linguistics research.

References

Candlin, C. N. (2002) Alterity, perspective and mutuality in LSP research and practice, in M. Gotti, D. Heller and M. Dossena (eds), *Conflict and Negotiation in Specialised Texts*. Bern: Peter Lang, 21–40.
Kramsch, C. (ed.) (2002) *Language Acquisition and Language Socialization: Ecological Perspectives*. London: Continuum.
Kress, G., Jewitt, C., Ogborn, J. and Tsatsarelis, C. (2001) *Multimodal Teaching and Learning: The Rhetorics of the Science Classroom*. London: Continuum.
Larsen-Freeman, D. (1997) Chaos/complexity science and second language acquisition. *Applied Linguistics* **18** (2), 141–65.
Lantolf, J. (2000) *Socio-cultural Theory and Second Language Learning*. Oxford: Oxford University Press.
Sarangi, S. (2002) Discourse practitioners as a community of interprofessional practice: some insights from health communication research, in C. N.

Candlin (ed), *Research and Practice in Professional Discourse*. Hong Kong: City University of Hong Kong Press.

Sarangi, S. and Candlin, C. N. (2001) 'Motivational relevancies': some methodological reflections on the social theoretical and sociolinguistic practice, in N. Coupland, S. Sarangi and C. N. Candlin (eds), *Sociolinguistics and Social Theory*. London: Pearson, 350–88.

Acknowledgements

I would like to thank the following people who have contributed to the development of my metaphor work, from doctoral thesis to this book: Gerard Steen, Guy Cook, Graham Low, Ray Gibbs, Alice Deignan. My sons have grown up with metaphor; their continuing interest in what I bring home to talk about has inspired and supported me. My parents have never stopped encouraging me and have provided support in ways too many to list. Freda Waldapfel has provided the believing friendship that I needed to push through to a completed manuscript.

Thanks are due to 'Louise', who cheerfully acted as major participant in the research study, to her friends, and to their headteacher who generously welcomed me into the school. Some institutional support for the research and writing was given by the College of Ripon and York St John, and the School of Education, University of Leeds.

We are grateful to the copyright owners for permission to use the following texts:

Anne Michaels and Bloomsbury Publishing for the extract from *Skin Divers*, Chapter 1

Dorling Kindersley/Pearson for 'The Heart' from *The Body and How It Works* by Steve Parker, published by Dorling Kindersley Ltd. © 1987 Dorling Kindersley Ltd, London, Chapter 9

We were unable to trace the copyright owner of 'The Ozone Layer' text in Chapter 8.

1 An applied linguistic approach to metaphor in discourse

Introduction

Poetry has long been seen as the paradigm site for metaphor, as in the opening lines of the poem *Skin Divers* by Anne Michaels:

> Under the big-top
> of stars, cows drift
> from enclosures, bellies brushing
> the high grass ready for their heavy
> festivities. Lowland gleams like mica
> in the rain. Starlight
> soaks our shoes.

Michaels stretches our imaginations; she creates new images for us, as she describes the night sky as a circus tent, and compares the moonlit sheen of the fields to 'mica in the rain'. We can only make sense of the last sentence through a figurative interpretation, as the poet skilfully constructs a complex metaphorical image with the simplest of syntax and lexis.

However, metaphor is not just the property of poets; they merely use it better than the rest of us. It has become an accepted tenet in metaphor studies that metaphor is found throughout everyday language (Gibbs 1994). This extract from a letter from my mortgage company includes metaphors of growth, performance and targets:

> We wrote to you in January to update you on how mortgage endowments generally were performing in the light of lower future inflation and likely lower future investment growth. We now enclose the information we promised you. It gives you a detailed update on the progress your Plan is making towards reaching its target amount.

The extract also contains a metaphorical phrase: 'in the light of', and a metaphorical description of my financial plan that has it 'making progress towards a target', like an animate being or perhaps a guided missile.

It is this claim for the 'ubiquity of metaphor' (Paprotté and Dirven 1985) that brings metaphor within the scope of applied linguistics. If, as cognitive linguists now hold, metaphor is not just a surface ornamentation of language but a phenomenon of human thought processes, then metaphor in real-world language becomes an important investigative focus. Understanding how metaphor is used may help us understand better how people think, how they make sense of the world and each other, and how they communicate. Metaphor would therefore seem to deserve the attention of applied linguists.

To date, metaphor has received rather more attention from literary theory, philosophy and cognitive psychology than it has from linguistics or applied linguistics. In literature, metaphor is one of the major tropes, or 'figures of speech', creating poetic effect through language that brings together ideas and images in unexpected conjunction. In philosophy, metaphor provides a challenge to logic by appearing to state an untruth that has some truth, or to compare two things that are dissimilar. Linguistics has preferred to work with literal meanings, and has generally found no place for metaphor in semantic theories of language, relegating it to the backwaters of pragmatics. In recent years, accounting for metaphor has led to new collaborations across these various theoretical fields, supported by work in cognitive psychology. The new discipline of 'cognitive linguistics' has grown up with metaphor as an underpinning construct, providing a foundation for thought and conceptualization. Cognitive linguistics has shifted the locus of attention from metaphor in language to metaphor in the mind, or 'conceptual metaphor'.

Choice and use of language has not been a central concern of cognitive linguistic approaches to metaphor, but it seems likely that language does affect how we construct our conceptualizations and therefore the nature and use of conceptual metaphor. A central principle of the applied linguistic approach to metaphor developed here is that metaphor must be investigated in *both* language and mind, and that it is important to bring the two realms together, in theory and in analysis.

The studies reported in this book investigate metaphor in educational discourse, where thinking, conceptualizing and understanding each other are particularly crucial. The research aimed to find out more about how metaphor is used in classrooms, how students understand the metaphors they encounter and how metaphor can contribute to learning.

Investigating metaphor in everyday educational discourse required the development of specific identification procedures and analytic methods. Theoretical ground-clearing and development have been needed to operationalize metaphor in spoken discourse and to develop a framework to link language use, understanding in situated talk, and learning. Both the theory and the research methods have relevance for other applied linguistic studies that include a focus on metaphor, within the specific context of formal education and in other social contexts. In this first chapter, the empirical studies are sited within current and historical developments in metaphor theory. The next section develops implications for adopting a discourse perspective on metaphor. The components of metaphor are then described and labelled, and a historical overview of metaphor theory is presented, in order to site the studies. By the end of the chapter, we will have established basic principles for an applied linguistic approach to metaphor, an outline of the central construct and a diachronic perspective on the work reported here.

Taking a discourse perspective on metaphor

<u>Discourse</u> is taken here as 'language in use'. Language in use, including metaphor, always occurs <u>in a specific context</u>, where it is produced and made sense of, by specific people. A discourse perspective attempts to keep metaphor contextualized.

Some examples from the data may help the reader to get a first hold on the idea of metaphor, and to highlight issues that a discourse approach to metaphor needs to deal with.

(Note: samples of real discourse are given in italics. Metaphorical words and phrases are also underlined.)

(1) *you're <u>on the right track</u>*
 a teacher in a mathematics lesson to a child who offered an incorrect answer to her question.
(2) *you are <u>spokes in a wheel</u>*
 a teacher to children practising a country dance, to help them visualize the shape of their formation.
(3) *a noun which is <u>talking about</u> more than one thing (is plural)*
 a teacher during an English lesson.
(4) *this printer is <u>playing up</u>*
 written notice on a computer printer in the classroom.
 when you try to work on it, it <u>goes mad</u>.
 spoken explanation of the notice by pupil to researcher.
(5) *The atmosphere is the <u>blanket</u> of gases that surrounds the earth.*
 from a book on the ozone layer written for children.

Each of these extracts includes a word or phrase (underlined) that is somehow incongruous in its situation of use – this is the core of the metaphor. The incongruity or anomaly exists because we can find some other way of interpreting the word or phrase that contrasts with the discourse-appropriate interpretation: a *track* (1) is found in an athletics stadium not a maths lesson; there is no concrete *wheel* in the dance practice (2), only the idea of one; nouns do not *talk* (3), and printers do not *play up* or *go mad* (4), people do; a *blanket* belongs on a bed (5), not in space.

The incongruity between the content of the discourse context and the content of the item signals the possible presence of metaphor. A further requirement for the presence of metaphor is that some resolution can be found to this incongruity that makes sense of this 'double semantic content' (Kittay 1987). These necessary conditions for metaphor create a rather broad and inclusive category, which will later be narrowed down.

Metaphor and discourse context

Applied linguists, with their concern for 'language in use', must recognize and deal with the situatedness of discourse; context has to be taken account of both in theory and in analysis (Duranti and Goodwin 1992). The context of discourse both constructs and constrains what is done with language, including the use of metaphor (Cameron 1996).

The broad context for the studies in this book is formal education, with data collected in an English school classroom with pupils aged between 9 and 11. However, context works at many levels of detail. Rather than seeing it as a kind of backdrop to language use, as in a play in a theatre, we can think of language use as embedded in nested series of contextual frames that radiate outwards from any specific use of language.

Contextual frames involve (at least) physical, social, interactional or linguistic factors:

- physical: relating to the setting in which the discourse takes place
- social: relating to participants in the discourse, their relationships, membership of social groups, etc.
- interactional: relating to processes of communication and interaction within the discourse
- linguistic: relating to uses of language in immediately previous and subsequent talk
- conceptual: relating to ways of thinking and knowing, concepts of participants.

An applied linguistic approach

If we consider the context of example (2), the teacher's description of how the pupils should move in a country dance, we can identify aspects of the immediate contextual frame:

- **physical**: in the school hall on a day in late April, preparing for a May Day celebration, with tape-recorded music
- **social**: particular children, particular teacher, with their particular school-based relationship, friendship groups, peer groups, etc.
- **interactional**: the immediately previous and subsequent organization of the lesson, interaction between teacher and pupils, and pupils and pupils
- **linguistic**: the immediately previous and subsequent language used by teacher and pupils
- **conceptual**: teacher's and pupils' concepts of *spokes* and *wheel*, and of the dance

By moving outward in time we can locate these factors in their historical development. It might, for example, be relevant to take account of the pupils' experience of watching the same dances when they were younger, and how this has made them eager to dance well now that they are the oldest pupils in the school, allowed to try the most complicated formations. When we come to explore metaphor in conceptual development, it will be important to consider how children use previous knowledge, for example gained from watching television programmes.

Moving outwards in space, both geographic and social, locates the classroom talk in the broader contexts of the school as educational institution and as located in an area that can be described, both socially and geographically, as 'middle England'. The children can be viewed as members of their families, villages, socio-economic class, and nation.

There is no end to context. The artificial (and metaphorical) construct of nested frames imposes some order and constraint on the infinite amount of possible detail, but it remains an organization by the analyst.

Discourse context is important because it helps both analysts and discourse participants to decide whether an utterance should be interpreted as metaphor. The metaphorical meaning of *you're* <u>*on the right track*</u> (example 1) will be recognized partly because it was produced in the physical context of a maths lesson in which there was no 'track' involved; if it had been spoken to pupils doing athletics and referred to the literal track they were to run on, a non-metaphorical sense would have been relevant.

The social context of educational discourse, with its asymmetric power relations between teacher and pupils, will be used to help describe and explain the affective impact of metaphor in educational discourse. Interactionally, it is important to know that the comment *on the right track* occurred in response to a child's incorrect answer to a teacher's question. Together, these social and interactional contextual factors around the utterance suggest that the metaphor may work to deflect possible loss of face for the child.

An applied linguistic investigation of metaphor use in discourse cannot proceed without taking account of the different types and levels of contextual factors. The idea of contextual frames will contribute to identifying such factors and including them in the analysis.

Degrees of metaphoricity

The examples in the previous section include metaphors that are quite 'strong', although not very creative, such as <u>blanket</u> (5), and metaphors that somehow seem 'weaker', such as <u>talking about</u> (3) or <u>playing up</u> (4), because they are more conventional or less visual. The intuitive notion of metaphor strength is difficult to operationalize. It will need attention though, because answering apparently reasonable questions such as 'How much metaphor does a teacher use in a lesson?' requires the construction of a bounded category of metaphor. Decisions will need to be made about whether idioms and conventional ways of talking warrant labelling as metaphorical (Cooper 1986: 137; Toolan 1996: 90). Chapter 3 deals with this problem in some detail.

My starting point is to take a broad and inclusive approach to metaphor rather than a narrow view that requires it to be novel and creative (as does Goatly 1997). I adopt a prosaic approach to metaphor rather than a poetic one. The next section explains the origin and extension of prosaics as an approach to discourse analysis of language use.

A prosaics of metaphor

Prosaics is concerned with the ordinary rather than with the special or artistic use of language. The term was coined by Morson and Emerson (1990: 15) to capture Bakhtin's ideas about the importance of everyday language and events:

> Prosaics encompasses two related, but distinct, concepts. First, as opposed to 'poetics', prosaics designates a theory of literature that privileges prose in general and the novel in particular over the poetic genres. Prosaics in the second sense is far broader than theory of literature: it is a form of thinking that presumes the importance of the everyday, the ordinary, the 'prosaic'.

Bakhtin rejected the Saussurean abstraction of language from context, that leaves aside instances of talk (*parole*) in order to study and systematize decontextualized language (*langue*) (Bakhtin 1981). He believed that, in the process of abstraction, essential aspects of 'the original cultural process . . . their "eventness"' was lost (Morson and Emerson 1990: 39). The prosaic for Bakhtin is the site of linguistic creativity. Creative acts take place in ordinary events working with the raw material of the everyday, not just in the special exceptional events that are labelled 'creative'.

Bakhtin warns of both the importance of trying to study everyday events, and the difficulty of doing so: 'A model of language . . . is nothing unless it can help us appreciate the overlooked richness, complexity, and power of the most intimate and the most ordinary exchanges' (Morson and Emerson 1990: 34).

If we are to see how metaphor contributes to that complexity and power, we must take a prosaic approach to metaphor in discourse, exploring metaphor in its 'most ordinary' guises, as well as in its more poetic forms.

While Bakhtin holds that special acts of creativity are 'extensions and developments of the sorts of activities we perform all the time' (Morson and Emerson 1990: 187), the precise relation between the creative and the conventional remains in need of explication. It seems unlikely to be one of straightforward continuity, as is suggested by the contemporary pragmatics theory of relevance in which metaphors are seen as 'simply [sic] creative exploitations of a perfectly general dimension of language use' (Sperber and Wilson 1986: 237).

A concern with the everyday and the ordinary in language use does not, contra Sperber and Wilson, lead to the simple, but rather to the complex. Bakhtin's focus on the prosaic and on heteroglossia, the many different forces on language use (Bakhtin 1981), projects the complex as normal, and the simple as unusual, the result of labour, and therefore deserving of explanation (Morson and Emerson 1990: 31). The apparently simple poetic metaphor in Michaels' poem quoted at the beginning of the chapter, 'starlight soaks our shoes', is the result of much conscious work with the conventional and prosaic possibilities of the language. Such creative metaphors are summits of achievement with language, worthy of study in their own right, but, in the study of metaphor in discourse, poetic metaphors should not be taken as paradigms or prototypes (also Black 1979). The lowlands of prosaic discourse are our site of investigation, with metaphor in everyday talk and text as our starting point for empirical study.

As noted in the introduction, it is not controversial today to claim that figurative language is widely used in everyday language. However, a prosaics of metaphor does not make this type of 'downwards' claim for figurative language; the everyday, rather than the creative, is taken as starting point. Prosaics is concerned to explore the everyday in its own right, rather than as a dilution of the poetic and creative. Further, a prosaic approach will attempt to explain the poetic by starting from the prosaic, seeing how creative uses of metaphor arise from everyday uses.

The dynamics of metaphor in discourse

An applied linguistic approach to metaphor that uses discourse as data is unavoidably dynamic, in that it is concerned with changes in language and in thinking that take place over time. Changes can occur on various timescales that we shall be concerned to interrelate.

If metaphor affects understanding and thinking, then we would expect, on a micro-level or immediate timescale, to see changes in understanding happening as the discourse progresses. For example, pupils may come to know more about the atmosphere as a result of encountering the *blanket* of *gases* metaphor in the text. Such micro-level changes occur within a particular child's mental development, and contribute to a larger change on a longer developmental or ontological timescale.

When we look at metaphor from a language perspective, we also want to see it as dynamic across discourse events and across the evolution of the language. Although four of the example metaphors were given as single sentences, many of the metaphors found in the classroom data were used several times across lessons, or in the same stretch of talk. Example (4), *This printer is playing up. When you try to work on it, it goes mad*, shows two connected metaphors about the same topic, one written and one spoken. A dynamic approach will describe not just individual instances of metaphor, but how the metaphors across discourse are connected, and how the impact of metaphor is built up through interactional dynamics.

Summary: epistemic commitments of the studies

These introductory sections have set the scene for the applied linguistic investigation of metaphor. In summary, the approach is interactional, contextualized, prosaic and dynamic.

These epistemic commitments influence the evaluation and choice of theoretical frameworks, research methods and analytic tools. Theory is needed to define categories and processes, and to produce coherent explanations of what happens. Theory is always open to question and to development, as new empirical evidence is added or as new ideas are formulated that question the logic or coherence of existing theory. An empirical investigation needs a theoretical framework that supports, in the sense of giving coherence to and justification for, the asking of particular research questions. A coherent theory will also help decide the research methods: what data to collect, how to collect the data, how to analyse the data. Trying to answer the research questions may in turn produce results that undermine parts of the theory and lead to revisions. In this way, a field of study develops and changes.

Metaphor as a field of study is complicated because there are several contributing disciplines and paradigms, each with its own guiding principles of theory and research. However, that is frequently the case in applied linguistics. Without the luxury of an established single paradigm and set methods for investigation, applied linguists have further work to do to make the contributing theories and research methods fit together without contradiction. By establishing epistemic commitments at the start, we have a baseline against which we can check the suitability and compatibility of the frameworks and tools that are selected and adapted.

Components of metaphor

In this section, some basic terminology is introduced that will be used throughout the book. So far we have said of metaphor that it brings together two potentially incongruous ideas. Metaphor works on both the linguistic and the conceptual plane, and so we need terms to describe both the language components and the conceptual components of metaphor. The key pairs of terms are focus/frame, and Topic/Vehicle. The first makes a semantic contrast and the second refers to lexis and conceptual domains.

Focus and frame

The linguistic presence of metaphor is signalled by a lexical item that can have an interpretation which is incongruous with the discourse context, or with the meaning created by the co-text. So, in example (5), *the atmosphere is a blanket of gases*, the lexical item *blanket* links to a different semantic field or conceptual domain from that intimated by *atmosphere, gases, Earth*, etc. The lexical item *blanket* is the focus of the metaphor, or the Vehicle term, and the rest of the phrase or sentence, against which it appears incongruous, is called the frame of the metaphor (Black 1979).

In traditional theories (see pp. 13–18), written text was the source of metaphor, and the sentence was taken as the unit of analysis within which an incongruity was evident. To work with spoken discourse and texts longer than the sentence, the notion of metaphor frame needs to be widened to something like 'a complete metaphorical utterance' (Kittay 1987: 65), which would be a minimal unit of discourse against which the focus term appears incongruent. Kittay notes that 'metaphorical completeness need not be coincident with syntactic completeness'. However, for samples of real discourse rather than constructed short examples, this unit is very difficult to operationalize in terms of both minimality and completeness. Even in a written sentence, such as *the atmosphere is the blanket of gases*, the focus term is clearly *a blanket*, but there are several possible candidates for the frame:

- the whole clause *the atmosphere is (the blanket) of gases*
- the beginning of the clause *the atmosphere is (the blanket)*
- the noun phrase *(the blanket) of gases*.

Neither simple minimality nor completeness will suffice to identify just one frame; in addition, if our concern is with the processing of information at discourse level, then the syntactic structure of both the phrase and the whole clause would seem to be important since the information available to a receiver derives not just from the independent lexical items, but also from the particular way in which they are collocated, the 'local contexts of other utterances', which go to make up the 'emerging context' of the discourse (Schiffrin 1994: 416).

In a discourse approach, the metaphor frame needs to be reconceived from a single stretch of language to a series of frames that work outwards from the focus across the discourse. There may thus be an immediate, syntactically minimal frame, consisting of the clause or phrase element at the next level, of which the focus would be a constituent element. In the example of *the atmosphere is the blanket of gases*, the 'immediate linguistic frame' would be *(the blanket) of* gases, determined as the Noun Phrase of which the focus would be an immediate constituent. Beyond that, there may be further frames at clause level, at sentence or utterance level, at the level of section of a text or a turn or exchange in spoken English, and at the level of discourse event. Such a set of nested Linguistic Frames may eventually encompass the whole of the discourse, and can be seen as linked to underlying Conceptual Frames which encapsulate the world knowledge brought to processing of the discourse by participants.

In some instances, there may be no Linguistic Frame within a turn: for example, imagine a car runs out of petrol because the driver had not filled the tank. A passenger in the car might comment on the situation using the proverb *A stitch in time saves nine* as a complete turn. The proverb is a metaphorical focus in the frame of the discourse situation. In such cases, a 'default' frame (Kittay 1987; Steen 1989) is said to apply, in the sense of a shared but unspoken understanding of what the focus is metaphorical against. Default frames are brought into play in discourse processing as and when needed, constructed by participants who use their background knowledge and the disambiguating information available in the discourse context to make sense of the metaphor.

The identification of a possible metaphorical focus in talk or text is the first step in identifying the presence of a metaphor (Steen 1999a).

Topic and Vehicle

The metaphorical focus is also known as the Vehicle of the metaphor, in contrast to the Topic which is the content of the on-going discourse, and which, as we have seen with the *stitch in time* example, may or may not be actually present as a lexical item. The immediate linguistic frame of the Vehicle will usually contain items that help identify the Topic of the metaphor.

The terms Topic and Vehicle are commonly used to refer both to lexical items and to the content domains that they label. If we are to investigate how language use impacts on thinking, then it is important to know which is being referred to. I will use 'Topic domain/Vehicle domain' whenever I am referring to conceptual or content domains, and 'Topic/Vehicle' to refer to lexical items. The terms will be used with initial capitals to distinguish this technical use from non-technical uses. Alternative labels for Topic and Vehicle are Target and Source domains. The term Tenor is sometimes used as an alternative to Topic.

The term 'domain' is used, often rather loosely in much of the literature, to refer to the ideas or semantic field referred to by a lexical item. It is important to establish that a domain is not just a collection of concepts or entities, visualized as nodes that can be labelled nominally, but also the relations between the entities – relations of cause and effect, composition, contrasts, etc. As an example, the domain of *blanket* would include concepts such as *bed, wool, duvet, pillow, warm* and relations between these such as *blankets are made of wool, blankets keep people warm in bed*. Some of the debates in metaphor theory arise from differences in opinion as to the nature of the domains involved (see Cameron 1999a) and from the analyst's process of inferring from the surface of the discourse how to describe the underlying conceptual domains. It is important for the approach developed here to note that the actual concepts and relations activated in discourse will vary with individuals and their previous experience and knowledge (Barsalou 1989).

Linguistic metaphor and process metaphor

If Topic and Vehicle, or focus and frame, are the components of metaphor, is a metaphor just the combination of the components? Here we should note the distinction between 'metaphor' as an uncountable noun which often refers to a process of mapping across domains (Lakoff and Johnson 1980) or, more traditionally, a figurative device (Burke 1945), and the countable noun 'a metaphor' which refers to a linguistic expression consisting of the focus placed within its immediate frame (although, as usual this only works straightforwardly with the simplest examples). We can highlight this important distinction by labelling such expressions 'linguistic metaphors' (Steen 1994; Cameron 1999b).

Linguistic metaphors can be contrasted with 'process metaphors', which are linguistic expressions that do actually activate two domains in the mind of a discourse participant, and that lead to the noticing of incongruity, the resolution of which results in the construction of a meaning for the expression.

That it is crucial for a discourse approach to separate process metaphors from linguistic metaphors can be illustrated by two examples from the data. In the first example, a linguistic metaphor used by a child could not be understood because of lack of domain knowledge on my part. He wrote about a football match: *the tenshun [sic] was as great as Indianapolis.* I later learnt that *Indianapolis* refers to the Indianapolis 500, the annual international car race. So although the linguistic form suggested a metaphorical simile (see below), I was unable to interpret it as a process metaphor.

A second example shows the converse effect: a 7-year-old interpreted a phrase heard on the television as a process metaphor, even though it had not been intended as such. He said: *Weather men use metaphors. When they say there will be a hot spell . . . like a witch's spell.* The word *spell* had functioned for him as a metaphorical focus in the frame of weather forecasting, as he had interpreted the lexical item as belonging not to the Topic domain of weather but to a Vehicle domain of witches. The resulting incongruity had led to an actively metaphorical interpretation.

These examples illustrate the need to remove speaker intention and hearer interpretation from criteria for metaphoricity. They also create an intractable problem: how to identify ambiguities that offer the possibility of metaphorical (mis)interpretation and so can be labelled as linguistic metaphors. The analyst is forced, sooner or later, to make some judgement as to which ambiguities or instances of polysemy have a reasonable probability of being interpreted as such. This is what

I had to do in analysing classroom discourse data (further justification and method are discussed in Chapter 3), and, in reality, this is what any analyst is required to do when identifying metaphor in text (e.g. Low and Cameron 2002).

Metaphor theory: an historical overview

So far in this chapter, we have begun to see some of the features of metaphor in discourse and how they might be dealt with. This section will place such discussion in an historical context and evaluate previous work for its relevance to an applied linguistics approach. A full review of the literature on metaphor is impossible, simply because of the sheer quantity since Aristotle's writings on metaphor in the fourth century BC. Instead, I review in some detail three major 'schools' of metaphor theory: Aristotelian, traditional, and cognitive. I then summarize the shifts in views on the nature and function of metaphor, and gather together what is useful in a study of metaphor in educational discourse. On the way, I will identify some of the gaps in theory and research that appear when available theory is held up against the epistemic commitments developed above.

Aristotle and metaphor

It is worth briefly revisiting Aristotle's thinking on metaphor, because it is the source of most of what has developed since, and also in order to correct some of the misunderstandings of his original ideas (see also Mahon 1999).

For Aristotle, successful metaphor in rhetoric or speech-making combined 'clarity, pleasantness and unfamiliarity', and, when used appropriately, could act conceptually to produce new understanding. In addition to its rhetorical function, he also recognized the cognitive function of metaphor that has risen to dominance in the last two decades.

Although Aristotle has become associated with seeing metaphor as a renaming or substitution of one term by another (for example Black 1979; Aitchison 1987; Gibbs 1994), he in fact articulated a much more complicated view of the nature and function of metaphor than he is often credited with. For example, Ricoeur (1978: 47) suggests that Aristotle gave primacy to nouns used metaphorically, but in *The Art of Rhetoric*, examples are given of phrase and word length metaphor Vehicles, including nouns, verbs and adjectives used metaphorically. Aristotle also describes the relation between metaphors and similes, and discusses the particular force of metaphors based on analogy. In an analogical metaphor, two terms in the Topic domain stand in the same relation to each other as two terms in the Vehicle domain. Analogy directs attention to these relations in the two domains that the metaphor brings together:

> the youth killed in the war had so disappeared from the city
> as if someone had taken spring from the year

The removal of *the youth killed in the war* from *the city* in the Topic domain is linked to the removal of *spring* from *the year* in the Vehicle domain. Through the juxtaposition of the two acts of removal in the metaphor, the horror of the war is given a new force.

Aristotle described the process of understanding metaphor as finding similarities within differences (Kittay 1987), and suggested that, in order to reach an interpretation, hearers would need to draw on shared cultural understandings or 'endoxa'. In this, Aristotle was making a point that some later philosophers (e.g. Saddock 1993; Searle 1993) chose to ignore: that metaphor is not a matter of semantics or pragmatics, but of both. The discourse context and background knowledge of discourse participants contributes to the meaning of a metaphor.

For Aristotle, who was describing deliberate stylistic effects in political rhetoric, the use of metaphor was always intentional and the study of metaphor was firmly based in discourse context. In taking his ideas out of their particular context of use and applying them to metaphor in general, much of the precision of Aristotle's theory has been lost.

A further contributing factor to the distortion of Aristotle's work in later centuries is the range of the term 'metaphor'. In classical Greek, the term had much wider reference. It was used to refer to any type of expression which substituted for another, including diminutives and euphemisms, and to ways of talking about a Topic domain that had not previously existed (also termed 'catachresis') for which there could be no literal equivalent. It may be that theory was transferred inappropriately from the broad Greek concept of metaphor to the much narrower concept of later theorists. As we will see in the next section, there is a problem in the reverse direction, when theory developed for a very narrow view of metaphor is applied to a wider range of language use. A broad view of metaphor, such as the one adopted in this book, is again becoming more common, as the underlying process of metaphor is seen at work across various aspects of language (e.g. Goatly 1997).

Aristotle's work on metaphor in his study of Poetics and Rhetoric generated many of the basic ideas that still hold sway in the study of metaphor. At the same time, his work left open a range of avenues for exploration by future scholars who, despite taking metaphor study forwards in quite differing directions, refer to him as their academic ancestor.

Substitution, Comparison and Interaction views of metaphor

By-passing important work in metaphor across the centuries, such as that of Quintillian in the second half of the first century AD, Tesauro and Vico in the seventeenth and eighteenth centuries, Rousseau (see Kittay 1987) and Nietzsche (Cooper 1986), we move to the twentieth century to examine three influential theories of metaphor that, despite the present dominance of cognitive linguistics, still hold some value for metaphor researchers.

These three theories work with restricted views of metaphor and of language, influenced by the rise of logical positivism in philosophy, which postulated not only the possibility of literal language, but also its primacy. Metaphor then was said to exist, in contrast to literal language, as decoration or ornament, and to be constructed deliberately for poetic effect. Aristotle's broad view of metaphor is thus reduced to a much narrower concern with metaphors that are clearly figurative, new and active, and that a receiver will have no difficulty in noticing and recognizing as metaphor. Metaphor, as 'a figure of speech', is primarily a linguistic phenomenon. All linguistic metaphors are presupposed to function as process metaphors, so that the two categories are collapsed into one.

SUBSTITUTION THEORY

The Substitution theory of metaphor, often claimed to be directly descended from Aristotelian theory, but, as I have suggested, actually a misrepresentation of it, characterizes metaphor as 'renaming' of the Topic by the Vehicle:

> Metaphor is the application to one thing of the name belonging to another. (Aitchison 1987: 144)

> Metaphor: A rhetorical figurative expression of similarity or dissimilarity in which a direct, nonliteral substitution or identity is made between one thing and another. (Myers and Simms, *Longman Dictionary of Poetic Terms* 1982)

The Substitution theory would thus see the example *the atmosphere is a blanket of gases* as a renaming, or substitution, of *atmosphere* with the term *blanket*. The idea of mapping across conceptual domains is reduced to the linking of concepts or entities, with the relations in the domains left out of the picture.

In this simplified view of how metaphor works, the sentence containing *blanket* is held to be replacing some set of literal sentences (Black 1979: 27). The principle that a literal equivalent of a metaphor can be found and will work as a paraphrase of it, also entails that metaphor is decorative and can be dispensed with, without any loss of meaning. For those who see metaphor as creative and essentially irreducible, this principle and its entailments lie at the heart of the weakness of the Substitution theory. It is further weakened if metaphor is characterized as renaming, which focuses attention on nominal metaphors to the neglect of other types, particularly verb metaphors.

COMPARISON THEORY

Metaphor as Implicit Comparison is a special case of metaphor as Substitution, in which the literal equivalent to the metaphor is held to be a comparison, or a statement of similarity (Black 1979). In this view, a metaphor is seen as a reduced simile. So a metaphor such as Shakespeare's *Juliet is the sun* can be expanded into *Juliet is like the sun*, and the finding of similarities between *Juliet* and *the sun* will lead to the meaning of the metaphor. Inherited from the Substitution view is the problem that the theory suggests there should be a literal equivalent to every metaphor, since the similarities generated by the metaphorical comparison are held to be accessible to full literal explication.

Both Comparison and Substitution theories appear inadequate for all but the most obvious metaphors. However, they can be rescued to some extent by the realization that it is necessary to distinguish clearly between the task of an analyst and that of a user of metaphor (Winner 1988). While an analyst may expand a metaphor by finding similarities through a process of comparison, a particular individual user of metaphor in discourse may do something quite different, producing creative interpretations that draw on personal experience as well as on culturally shared knowledge. Keeping separate the processing work of analyst and user is crucial to theory development. Although a metaphor analyst can proceed from a linguistic analysis, the further work of describing how individuals in discourse contexts proceed to comprehension of metaphor requires us also to draw on theory and empirical research from psychology and text processing that can help us understand how conceptual domains are activated and used. I have called for theory to reflect the state of our knowledge of real on-line processing as closely as possible (Cameron 1999a); at the very least, processing as implied by a theory of metaphor must not be incompatible with empirical findings.

Many poetic metaphors do take a nominal form and offer themselves to a Comparison or Substitution analysis: *The world is an unweeded garden* (Shakespeare); *My love is like a red, red rose* (Burns). So do pet names and insults, which may be one of the contexts in which children first encounter metaphor (Marjanovic-Shane 1989): *Don't eat like a pig; You're my little honey pot; Who's a sweety pie?*

INTERACTION THEORY

The Interaction theory of metaphor was developed by Black to account for the creation of new understandings through metaphor (Black 1962, 1979/93). Black built on ideas from Coleridge, and later I. A. Richards, for whom metaphor was a process of the imagination that could ignite or fuse images and perspectives into a creative and new whole. In the Interaction view, a mental process linking Topic and Vehicle generates new and irreducible meanings rather than activating pre-existing similarities, as in the Substitution and Implicit Comparison theories. Black proposed that a listener or reader would bring to metaphor interpretation a 'system of associated commonplaces', somewhat akin to Aristotle's endoxa, and later reworded, after criticism from Ricoeur (1978: 88), as an 'implicative complex' of understandings and beliefs (Black 1993: 28). The two complexes interact through mental processes of selection, mapping and organization, to produce a new understanding that cannot be paraphrased with literal equivalents.

Black's work brought the cognitive role of metaphor back to centre stage after long periods when metaphor had been reduced to mere linguistic decoration. However, Black was only concerned to construct theory around novel and strongly active metaphors, the poetic rather than the prosaic. By choosing to work only with active metaphors, Black continued the conflation of linguistic metaphors and process metaphors. He explicitly recognized the limitations of this approach when he wrote: 'It may well be a mistake to treat profound metaphors as paradigms' (Black 1993: 21).

Elsewhere (Cameron 1999b), I have analysed the assumptions about speaker and listener that underpin Black's theory and suggested that, in only working with strong poetic metaphors, three possible criteria for metaphoricity are conflated: etymology, discourse norms and individual processing. Etymology can be used to rule out the possibility of metaphor, as when Black contends that *falling in love* originated as catachresis rather than as metaphor (1993: 26). Conversely, tracing the original meanings of Topic and Vehicle terms can produce evidence of metaphorical extension of meaning at some time. For example, 'salary' originated from the Latin word for 'salt' which was given to Roman soldiers as part of their pay, and thus it might be said that, etymologically, salary is metaphorical. Since most participants in prosaic discourse have little access to etymological information, I prefer as an analyst not to make use of it, but to try to work from current use of words, or discourse norms, to identify linguistic metaphor. What counts as evidence for current norms remains at issue.

The key development offered by the Interaction theory was the notion that Topic and Vehicle are systems of ideas, knowledge and beliefs that interact, rather than just names or features of concepts that are simply 'transferred'. It has been criticized for not sufficiently accounting for how particular aspects of the systems are selected and used in the interaction of domains (Johnson 1987; Kittay 1987). The 'perspectival theory' of metaphor (Kittay 1987) addressed this criticism by highlighting the importance of semantic relations in the two systems, such as contrasts and affinities, and suggesting that the interaction involved a restructuring of the Topic system in terms of the relations operating in the Vehicle domain. Again, Kittay is offering an analytically coherent theory rather than a process-compatible theory.

More recent work on visual metaphor (Forceville 1994) adopts the Interaction theory as underpinning framework, and sees as a strong point in its favour the place it has for connotations and other culturally shared beliefs to be mapped across domains, as well as more concrete properties. If we are to have a theory of metaphor in prosaic discourse that is compatible with processing research, then we need it all: a domain linked to a lexical item needs to be seen as containing all that might be activated by an individual participating in discourse, including images, knowledge, beliefs, connotations, feelings, and memories of previous experience.

Cognitive theories of metaphor

Lakoff and Johnson took metaphor study in a new direction with the publication in 1980 of their book *Metaphors We Live By*. Schön and Reddy had already begun to use metaphors in language as a clue to people's thinking and conceptualizing (Schön 1979; Reddy 1979). Reddy's work in particular has importance for applied linguistics because he peels back the metaphors underlying a 'conduit' model, which sees communication as the 'transmission' of information through 'channels'. He offers an alternative metaphorical understanding of communication, 'the toolmakers' paradigm', in which we each attempt to make sense of other people's meanings from within our own context (Reddy 1979). Lakoff and Johnson took the idea that metaphors hold together a view or model of an aspect of the world a step further. They suggested that metaphor is a basic mental operation by which we understand the world through mapping from known domains to unknown domains, and that some conceptualizations are metaphorically structured in our minds (Lakoff 1993). This idea is the starting point for a 'cognitive theory of metaphor' and has generated much work on the link between metaphor and thought.

For cognitive metaphor theory, 'The language is secondary. The mapping is primary' (Lakoff 1993: 208). The primacy of the mind is reflected in terminology: the term 'metaphor' is reserved for conceptual mappings, and 'metaphorical expression' is the term for the linguistic manifestation of the mapping (what we have called linguistic metaphor). A 'conceptual metaphor' is a mapping of domains (Topic and Vehicle), and is conventionally written in small capitals, e.g. LOVE IS A JOURNEY. The mapping produces a range of metaphorical expressions in the language that retain systematicity in language as a result of their mental links, e.g. *We've hit a dead-end street. We can't turn back now. Their marriage is on the rocks* (all examples from Lakoff 1993: 208–9).

The enduring influence of traditional theories of metaphor can be seen in the adoption of the nominal form for conceptual metaphors. A case can be made for alternative formulations to reflect the role of the verb in English and in metaphor.

The terminological distinction is not always maintained, and even the most devout of cognitive metaphor theorists sometimes find themselves talking about 'metaphors' in language. One reason may be that Lakoff's wish to make language secondary is in conflict with the reliance of cognitive theorists on language as evidence for their theories. It is, furthermore, to hand, whereas conceptual mappings are well hidden and require careful psycholinguistic empirical work to extract and analyse them (see the work of Gibbs e.g. 1994). Systems of metaphors in language provide evidence to support claims about conceptual metaphor (but see discussion in Chapter 11), and the idea of conceptual metaphor can explain how we make sense of novel metaphors in language as extensions of existing conceptual metaphors (Lakoff 1993). Language and thought needed to be separated in order to develop the cognitive theory and to highlight its departures from 'traditional' metaphor theory, but they are not perhaps as separable as some of the programmatic statements and claims suggest.

A strong view of the role of conceptual metaphor in structuring thinking has developed that builds on the idea that 'metaphors may create realities for us, especially social realities' (Lakoff and Johnson 1980: 156). Work in this area proceeds by identifying metaphorical expressions in language, using them to reconstitute conceptual metaphors and then analysing the conceptual mappings for limitations or built-in assumptions. For example, as well as Reddy's analysis of metaphors of communication, Sontag (1991) has deconstructed metaphors of illness; Novek (1992) examined metaphors of literacy; Cortazzi and Jin (1999) and Oxford (2001) collected metaphors of language teaching and learning; and Ellis (2001) and Block (1999) explore the metaphors of second language learning. Fairclough (1989, 1992) includes the analysis of metaphors in particular discourses as part of critical discourse analysis. This mode of research has also begun to ask whether metaphor does not perhaps offer a tool for changing behaviour and thinking, through conscious unveiling and readjustment of metaphors (Gibbs 1999a). Criticism has been justly levelled at methods of data collection which in the early days amounted to little more than armchair reflection by native speakers, gathering together all the examples that could be recalled. Later studies use respondents to produce metaphors that will be used as data, but this also needs to be done with care (see discussion in Low 1999). Corpus techniques appear to offer a further valuable contribution (Deignan 1999a, b).

While cognitive metaphor theory locates metaphor in the head, there are those who argue that the ontological impact of cultural constructs on our mental maps cannot be ignored and may occur prior to metaphor in influencing concept formation (e.g. Keesing 1987; Quinn 1991; Gibbs 1999b). This consideration is of importance for applied studies, particularly if we are concerned with how the metaphors of other languages and cultures can be understood or learnt.

Recent work suggests that some 'primary conceptual metaphors' may be so basic to human experience that they occur in all or most cultural contexts, and may serve as foundational to other metaphors (Grady 1999). For example, many cultures and languages make a correspondence between size and importance: *the big man* is often the boss or leader. (We should note that this only applies to the male of the species: *the big woman* does not seem to work in the same way!) The word for *big*, when translated into other languages, will work as a metaphor for *important*.

It seems likely that transferability of metaphors across cultures may be limited to this relatively small group of primary conceptual metaphors, and that the metaphors of different languages will vary with cultural factors, as well as with social and other factors. A conceptual metaphor may be similar in two cultures but expressed differently in the languages. Pupils in Bangladesh would find *the atmosphere is the blanket of gases* difficult to understand, but the same idea might be accessible as *the atmosphere is the canopy of gases* because it links to experience of how the rainforest canopy works.

Deignan *et al.* (1997) provide a similar example for the idea of *interrogating a suspect*. In English we talk of *grilling a suspect*. The Polish equivalent is *mangling*. This is a striking example of how a mistranslated conventional idiom becomes vivid and, in this case, unpleasant. Since both cultures presumably 'grill' and 'mangle', there is in this case no obvious cultural reason why the linguistic expressions have developed in different ways.

There is surprisingly little interest in the ontogenetic development of conceptual metaphor. Cognitive theory seems to posit individual minds as ready-formed adult thinkers, rather than as individuals whose minds develop through social interaction in particular sociocultural contexts. Given the focus on embodied experience as generative of metaphorical thinking (Lakoff and Turner 1989; Gibbs 1999a), the neglect of childhood experience in conceptual development is the more surprising. From a sociocultural perspective, the acquisition and use of the metaphors is of empirical interest, and we will see how metaphor repertoires are developed through participation in social action and interaction.

Cognitive theory sees metaphor as a process and a product of mapping across concept domains. The mapping does not necessarily happen on-line, since conceptual metaphors will not necessarily be activated during discourse processing. So, although the theory recognizes the distinction between linguistic and process metaphors, it is not really concerned with it. Traditional metaphor theory, which was only concerned with active metaphoric processing, adopted a three-step model of processing in which literal meaning was held to be activated first, then seen as inappropriate, and then replaced with metaphorical meaning. Empirical evidence has shown that on-line comprehension of metaphor need take no longer than comprehension of non-metaphorical language (Janus and Bever 1985; Vosniadou 1989; Chandler 1991; Cacciari and Glucksberg 1995; Gibbs 1994). Gibbs stresses that there are different levels of metaphor understanding: 'comprehension' may take place in real time without 'recognition' of the presence of metaphor happening or without further 'interpretation' of metaphor through activation of entailments of the conceptual link (Gibbs 1994: 117).

Blending theory has been put forward as a processing theory for cognitive approaches to metaphor (Fauconnier and Turner 1996, 1998). In this framework, domains are replaced by 'mental spaces' as the unit of cognitive organization, and they are held to be constructed on a temporary basis when processing linguistic metaphor. Rather than two domains, of Topic and Vehicle, blending theory requires four spaces: two input spaces, associated with the Topic and Vehicle, a 'generic space' which contains what is shared by the two inputs, and the 'blended space', where the ideas combine and interact (Grady *et al.* 1999). The notion of a blended space is to account for meanings that can emerge from a metaphorical interpretation without pre-existing (compare Black's view of metaphor as interaction). Blending theory is more concerned than conceptual metaphor theory with how we create meaning from novel blends. However, conceptual metaphors are seen to contribute to the blending process because they are stable structures available in memory. Blending theory has been used to explain not only metaphor but other cognitive operations that involve the combining of concepts, including the most prosaic of language processing.

Shifts in the study of metaphor: summary and evaluation

This necessarily brief historical review demonstrates how views of metaphor have shifted over the centuries, with some shifts being repeated over shorter periods too. Metaphor, at its narrowest, has been seen as mere ornament, a decorative use of language that adds to style and impact but that is removable. As such, it was ignored as largely irrelevant to the study of language and the development of semantic theory. In the contemporary cognitive paradigm, metaphor is seen as fundamental to thinking and concept formation, systematically pervading our language and our thinking, and even, at its strongest, controlling our minds and actions. Cognitive linguists, in their desire to take the study of metaphor out of the realm of language, are, I suggest, overoptimistic about the feasibility of separating human thought from human language use. Cognitive linguistic analysis of conceptual metaphor depends heavily on metaphorical expressions in language that are collected, analysed and offered as supporting evidence for metaphorical thinking. Furthermore, 'language' from which metaphors are mined is usually the abstracted system of 'langue', or a set of linguistic resources generalized across the speech community, rather than actual use or discourse. If evidence found in language is abstract or generalized, then care is needed when theory developed from that evidence is reapplied. On this basis, some of the stronger claims of contemporary metaphor theory about the mental processes of individuals must be resisted (Gibbs 1994). The fact that metaphors are used in particular ways 'in the language' does not entail that every 'individual mind' thinks metaphorically using the same conceptual metaphor.

In earlier work I made a distinction between 'levels' of analytic work carried out in metaphor studies (Cameron 1999a: 7). It seems important to acknowledge that different analysts come to the study of metaphor with different epistemic commitments, and this is perhaps especially true in this field where analysts may be members of academic traditions as distinct as those of philosophy, literary studies and cognitive psychology. Work at 'theory level' (or Level 1) would include that of philosophers and linguists whose epistemologies require commitment to system, abstraction, argument using formal logic, and elegance of theory. They are not obliged in their work to account for adequacy in the way theories and procedures fit with the empirical reality of discourse or mental processing. Work at 'processing level' (or Level 2), in contrast, attempts to develop theories and procedures that do fit with what is known about human language use and mental processes. The work reviewed in this section has been Level 1 work, while the applied linguistic approach I adopt in this book clearly sites itself within Level 2. Level 1 work has not generally felt the need to theorize or investigate the use of metaphor in social interaction, and it remains to be seen how far Level 2 work will need to develop its own categories and explanatory theories. A good example of the type of difficulties that can arise when Level 1 work is used in analysis at Level 2 is the problems experienced when Level 1 definitions of metaphor were used in the Level 2 work of identifying instances of metaphor in spoken discourse (this is discussed further in Chapter 3). Meanwhile, there is some Level 2 work that deals with metaphor as a social phenomenon and that is reviewed next.

The affective dimension of metaphor

It is often suggested that a major function of metaphor is ideational, helping to explain something abstract or complicated in terms of something more familiar or concrete (e.g. Lakoff and Johnson 1980: 33; Kittay 1987). Example (5), *the atmosphere is the blanket of gases*, demonstrates this 'ideational' function. However, we also noted that *you're on the right track* (Example 1) may have had an 'affective' function, in deflecting the impact on a child's confidence of producing an incorrect answer in public. If we are to investigate the multiple functions and impacts of metaphor in discourse, we need to address affective functions that metaphor might play in situated discourse.

In educational research, the affective dimension of classroom discourse is often neglected, and deserves more attention for its role 'in motivating and integrating learning and development' (Chang-Wells and Wells 1993: 85). In metaphor studies, on the other hand, there has been some recognition of the affective or interpersonal impact of metaphor, rather eclipsed by recent cognitive concerns. Cooper (1986) focused on the interpersonal as providing an answer to the question of why a speaker or writer might choose to employ metaphor, and developed Cohen's idea that an important role of metaphor is the 'cultivation of intimacy' (Cooper 1986: 153; Cohen 1979). Intimacy can be both taken for granted and enhanced through the use of metaphor, which brings with it attitudes to the topic that are assumed to be shared, or are then available to be shared, between discourse participants. In an extension of this idea, sub-groups in society can be seen as using metaphor to establish in-group language and identity. Individuals can make use of shared repertoires of metaphor to obtain membership themselves and to exclude others; they may deliberately deviate from shared norms to express individuality or disaffiliation. It is possible then that metaphor use in educational contexts may play a role in inducting children into various groupings, both sociocultural, as members of a school and community with particular values, and technical, in various academic subject disciplines, e.g. as children learn to be 'mathematicians' or 'historians'.

Two sets of empirical studies emphasize the relevance of the affective or interpersonal impact of metaphor (Drew and Holt 1988, 1995, 1998; Strässler 1982). Drew and Holt (1988) used conversation analysis techniques to investigate the use of idioms, many of which are metaphoric, in complaint sequences. They showed that expressions such as *It was like banging my head on a brick wall* often work ideationally to summarize the details of a complaint, while at the same time working interpersonally to indicate the speaker's attitude to the seriousness of the complaint. Interactionally, such idioms regularly occur at the end of a sequence of details and serve to initiate topic change. The figurative nature of an idiomatic expression, and, importantly, the recognition by participants of that figurative nature, serve to 'remove the complaint from its supporting circumstantial details' (406). A consequence of this distancing from detail is to render the idiomatically formulated utterance less open to question by other speakers. Drew and Holt suggest that such distancing through metaphor represents a seeking for affiliation in potentially hostile situations, where, for example, the other speaker has not sided with the complainant as explicitly as desired. The placing of the expression in the interaction suggests that the idiom serves to 'bring speaker and recipient into some kind of alignment before changing the topic' (412).

Strässler's study of idioms in English talk and texts (1982) found that idioms are mostly used to refer to people or objects in the third person, as in the Drew and Holt example above. He too argues that in using an idiom a speaker conveys much more than ideational content. For example, in discourse contexts where there is a large power differential between participants as in a client–therapist relationship, the lower status participant is less likely to use third-person idioms and is restricted to first-person idioms; use of second-person idioms appears to establish superiority. Idioms are seen as particularly amenable to use for evaluation in talk, combining summarizing with conveying attitude, in line with both Drew and Holt's conclusions and with Ortony's compactness thesis (Ortony 1975). Strässler comments on how use of idioms may also carry a risk to interpersonal relations because they can be inappropriately strong in formulation.

These findings about the use of idioms extend to metaphor as defined here, to the extent that they signal affective features worthy of close attention when classroom discourse is analysed. Attention needs to be paid to the content and sensitivity of choice of metaphor in terms of mediating attitudes and values.

An applied linguistic approach to metaphor in discourse: summary

How then will this study make use of the ideas from theories of metaphor, bearing in mind the epistemic commitments?

The scope of metaphor

Three categories – linguistic, process, and conceptual – will form a basis for thinking about metaphor in discourse. Exploration of the relations between the categories will contribute to a re-uniting of thought and language.

The category of linguistic metaphor will be established through the potential for incongruity between two domains to be interpreted from surface lexical content. Neither metaphorical intention nor metaphorical interpretation will be necessary conditions for membership. Adopting this broad category of linguistic metaphor allows a prosaic approach, as discourse is trawled for possible metaphor using a net with small holes.

The language of metaphor

Language in use is the site of investigation of metaphor, and linguistic metaphors will be the primary data. Since one side of metaphoricity lies in mental mapping across incongruous domains, the category of linguistic metaphor will include language forms that bring together lexis to suggest such incongruity. Obvious inclusions in this broad category will be some similes, but only those where dissimilar domains are linked, e.g. *the atmosphere is like a shield*, and hyperbole.

Metaphor in thought

Metaphor may involve any of the cognitive processes described in the overview of theories: renaming, substitution, comparison, interaction, structure mapping, conceptual mapping or conceptual blending.

The study will keep active the possibility that concepts may be structured (and restructured) through metaphorical mappings, and that they therefore may develop through metaphor, so that a process of readjusting a metaphorical model may be an important part of learning, in school and beyond.

The notion of 'domain' or 'space' used to describe mental organization will be informed in this study by current research in cognitive psychology that is shedding light on how concepts are processed.

Systematicity of metaphor

If conceptual metaphors are part of our sociocultural inheritance, then learning in childhood will include the acquisition of metaphorical mappings for certain concepts. Discourse data from classrooms might be expected to show evidence of the systematic use of metaphors in language and of the acquisition of metaphors through participation in discourse.

In conclusion, we have seen that the recent shift in metaphor studies – from language to thought – may downplay the interrelatedness of language and thought. A process study into the use of metaphor cannot do so, and needs a theoretical framework to support the study of metaphor as a phenomenon of language in use for mental and interpersonal action. Talking and thinking are not to be seen as individual, separated and abstracted, but on-line, in the moment and jointly constructed. The next chapter takes on the task of developing the theoretical tools to serve this perspective of the study.

2 Talking, thinking and learning: theoretical background

Introduction

The previous chapter questioned the separation of language and thought that pervades the literature on metaphor, and suggested that the separation was a convenient artifice that would assist some approaches to theory construction but which is untenable for an applied linguistic approach concerned with the use of metaphor in discourse. What we need is not two separated concepts but an overarching concept that captures what happens when people attempt to share ideas and understandings in ongoing talk.

A prosaic approach (Chapter 1; Bakhtin 1981; Morson and Emerson 1990) does not see a metaphor as a static piece of language that is used and reused, but sees each use of metaphor as unique, and as arising from the particular communicative needs of the specific discourse participants at the moment when the metaphor is used. Metaphors, like any other use of language, can bring to a discourse event traces of previous uses and of previous discourse events. Description of metaphor in use then requires attention to the context of use, such as the institutional nature of the setting, and to the sociocultural histories of those involved and their previous discourse encounters (Bakhtin 1981, 1986; Vygotsky 1962). If we are concerned to investigate how metaphor use contributes to learning, then a further ontogenetic timescale, on which changes in individual or shared understanding may be observed, is of interest. The theoretical framework developed in this chapter links ideas from complex systems theory with Vygotskyan and Bakhtinian constructs around language and thought in order to take account of the dynamics of discourse on these different but linked timescales.

Slobin (1996: 75), in a recent reworking of the Whorfian hypothesis about the links between culture and language, offers a suggestion in relation to individual processing: 'a special kind of thinking that is intimately tied to language – namely, the thinking that is carried out, on-line, in the process of speaking'. He suggests that the structures of a language impact on thinking at this micro-level timescale, and that, to reflect this, we should use the '*dynamic* entities: *thinking* and *speaking*' (Slobin's emphasis) rather than the traditional terms 'language' and 'thought' .

To move from the individual 'thinking and speaking', to jointly constructed interaction, we turn to sociocultural theory, which offers 'mediated action' as a unit of thinking and speaking (Wertsch 1991, 1998). Sociocultural theory also provides a link between the micro-level timescale of ongoing interaction and a longer timescale in which learning might be said to take place. Useful ideas from sociocultural theory are described in the next section; they are then complemented by work from complex systems theory to take fuller account of the dynamics of thinking and speaking on varying timescales.

Sociocultural theoretic approaches to language and thought

Language as psychological tool; metaphor as technique for tool-using

Vygotsky saw language as a psychological 'tool', the acquisition of which dramatically alters the course of a young child's mental development (Vygotsky 1962). Language offers the possibility of symbolic representation and manipulation of ideas, and of shared interaction about ideas. From the beginning of a child's life, she or he is involved in communication with others, and this social interaction pushes forward cognitive development.

Within this Vygotskyan view of language as 'psychological tool', how should we see metaphor? Perhaps it might be conceived of as one tool within a larger 'toolkit' (Wertsch 1991), since, at an abstract level at least, metaphor assists thinking through particular uses of language (Lakoff and Turner 1989). The notion of 'tool' suggests something more static and fixed than metaphor turns out to be in discourse; as the examples in Chapter 1 showed, although we do find metaphors in discourse, we more often find people using language metaphorically. So metaphor (or 'metaphorizing') may be better pictured as a technique or 'means' (Wertsch 1998) for using the tool of language, and empirical investigation may reveal the extent to which metaphor can be identified as a single, unified technique in educational discourse and how it might be described.

Mediation and internalization

Both tools and other people can act to 'mediate' activity. When a concrete tool, rather than a psychological or symbolic tool, mediates activity, it serves to make the activity more efficient in attaining particular goals, for example when a bird smashes a snail against a (mediating) rock. In analogy with this concrete use of tools, language is seen as able to mediate thinking, and one individual can mediate the behaviour of another through language or through action. Adults have a key role in children's development through their mediation of behaviour and of thinking. Vygotsky suggested that interaction mediates thinking and learning when children internalize what has first happened in social interaction with an adult or peer. He wrote of development as a movement from the '*inter*mental' to the '*intra*mental', and held that what a child can do with the mediation of a helpful adult predicts what that child will soon be able to do alone. The gap between solo action or thought and mediated action or thought is called the 'zone of proximal development'. Internalization is not a linear process in which concepts are transferred from adult to child, but a process of reconstruction in the child's mind that makes use of the experience of interaction with the adult, and that can be adjusted through further interaction.

Researchers investigating how caregivers interact with toddlers in two different communities describe the mediation they observed as 'guided participation' (Rogoff *et al.* 1993). In both contexts, caregivers adjusted their discourse to create links between what the children knew and new ideas, and used collaborative structuring of steps towards the joint solution of problems. Teachers in classrooms develop forms of mediation or 'mediated activity' (Wertsch 1991), just as parents do with younger children, but in somewhat different ways. Tharp and Gallimore (1988) list seven ways in which teachers mediate performance and facilitate learning in classrooms, including modelling, giving feedback and questioning.

Vygotsky wrote about how participants in talk construct transient and contextualized understandings that are continually shifting (1962). He used the Russian word 'smysl', translated into English as 'sense', to capture this, and distinguished sense from 'meaning' (decontextualized dictionary-type full meanings), and from 'reference', which indicates objects through direct connections (Vygotsky 1962; Frawley 1997). In discourse, the 'sense' that participants construct, their personal and variable understandings, are active and in flux. Work in this paradigm, backed by child language research, shows that children can participate in talk that is ahead of their comprehension (Frawley 1997; Chang-Wells and Wells 1993; Locke 1993). The move from partial understanding, supported by participation in discourse, to fuller understanding is seen as a main driving force in the development of understanding through internalization.

When researchers examine discourse, can they claim to find evidence of thinking as well as speaking? Wells (1999) reminds us of the need for caution. We never have access to people's minds, only to what is said. Discursive psychologists (e.g. Edwards 1997) go further, and insist that what we see is what there is. Using conversation analysis as a research instrument, they not only require that evidence of understandings be found in discourse data, but go further in (apparently) denying the existence of inaccessible mental processes and seeing 'mind as a discursive process' (Roebuck 2000).

At this point, we find ourselves between two extremes. At one end, the idea of discourse as mediated activity is helpful in conceptualizing how learning might be supported through talk, but it is still quite fuzzy in how it describes mental activity. At the other extreme, discursive psychologists claim that we should not attempt to describe mental activity other than as it is verbalized in discourse. I want to push a little further in describing how minds can be changed through participation in discourse, and pursue this with some additional Vygotskyan ideas.

Intersubjectivity and alterity

Intersubjectivity and alterity are different ways to describe and explain what it is that people share when they are engaged in social interaction, and in jointly constructing discourse and ideas. They are concerned with the deep problem of how, from our individual minds and realities, we reach out to others, using language to try to share our thoughts.

Intersubjectivity refers to a shared focus of attention and perspective that is constructed between participants in discourse (Rommetveit 1979; Rogoff 1990; Smolka *et al.* 1995; Wertsch 1998). We might see intersubjectivity between teacher and pupils around a scientific concept as a goal of an educational discourse event, and some investigators have used increases in intersubjectivity as a measure of learning on microgenetic and ontogenetic timescales (Tharp and Gallimore 1988; Wertsch 1998). Intersubjectivity can be conceived of as intramental, or it may be seen as located and managed in discourse (e.g. Edwards 1997).

The notion that thoughts, concepts or understandings can be passed to other people invokes a communication, or 'conduit', model of language use, in which a 'message' is 'transmitted' from sender to addressee (Reddy 1979). Both Vygotsky and Bakhtin rejected this model and emphasized the continual construction and reconstruction of meaning that takes place in discourse, and that disallows the possibility of one person ever perfectly understanding another. For Vygotsky, words can give only imperfect access to another's thoughts through the contextualized meanings that are constructed in on-line discourse. Bakhtin saw discourse as involving a dialogic, back-and-forth using and choosing of words to try to be understood by 'the other', so that what a speaker says is continually affected by the listener and by the speaker's perception of the listener's understanding. Each person's understanding of the words of the other is mediated by his or her sociocultural history, including previous discourse history.

If we accept that we deal in continuously shifting approximations, then intersubjectivity becomes theoretically untenable. Wertsch (1998) sets out two ways forward. The first is that suggested by Rommetveit (1979), accepting that pure intersubjectivity (complete understanding of 'the other') is not possible but retaining intersubjectivity as a motivating objective that generates a force towards mutual understanding in discourse. The alternative is to take up a construct from Bakhtin – 'alterity' or 'other-ness'. In doing so, we reject the possibility of a perfect convergence of understanding by participants in discourse and focus on the inevitability of difference. Alterity, as differences in understanding and perspective, is not merely to be lamented, but to be understood and worked with. I suggest that alterity, the somewhat neglected, dialogic counterpart of intersubjectivity, offers a key construct for analysing metaphor in educational discourse at several levels.

First, alterity describes the continually shifting baseline from which teaching and learning move on. Using alterity, or discrepancies in understanding, has been characteristic of skilful teaching since Socrates. Skilled teachers are able to estimate alterity accurately and to select from a range of teaching strategies to deal with it. 'Prolepsis' is a teaching technique that works from alterity, deliberately creating omissions or discrepancies in discourse to create learning opportunities (van Lier 1996: 161). We can focus then on how alterity is made visible in discourse and how it is managed. In adopting alterity, it is not necessary to drop intersubjectivity altogether; when straightforward ideas are to be learnt, alterity may reduce to a simple set of propositions that are known by one person and are to be understood by the other. Those propositions that all participants understand then represent intersubjectivity, and it may be feasible to measure its increase. Usually though, learning is less simple, and alterity will be present in the diverse or discrepant understandings of participants. In most educational discourse, alterity is managed with the objective of reducing it towards compatible, if not identical, understandings. As such, the mediation of alterity (or more precisely, of perceived alterity) may drive discourse between teacher and pupils.

Second, metaphor works through alterity in the thinking and speaking of on-line interaction. In its strong form, metaphor imports an incongruous Vehicle term into the ongoing discourse, thereby opening up alternative meanings and interpretations around the Topic term. One of the questions that has concerned metaphor researchers is how the risk of misunderstanding that is created in this process is contained (Goatly 1997). Effective use of strong metaphor in educational discourse must address this issue of risk, and in empirical investigation we will be interested to search for evidence of alterity around metaphor use, and thus of risk of misinterpretation, and to analyse how such alterity is managed in the discourse.

Spontaneous and scientific concepts in educational discourse

In his experiments into concept development, Vygotsky discovered differences in thinking between children and adults. In later work he explored how concepts develop over the longer term through the particular types of social interaction that occur in formal institutional settings, such as schools. He made a distinction between 'spontaneous concepts' and 'scientific concepts' (Vygotsky 1962) that will be useful in this study to describe changes in understanding that take place on a more macro-level timescale.

Spontaneous and scientific concepts may relate to the same real world phenomenon in quite different ways, deriving as they do from different sources and in response to different goals. Spontaneous concepts develop through everyday experiences with the concrete and the real, and are highly contextualized and experiential. Scientific concepts originate in, and are characteristic of, formal education. They do not necessarily relate to science, but have 'scientific' organization in that they are formal, logical, hierarchical and decontextualized (Kozulin 1990). For example, we see the sun rise and set over the horizon every day and build up a spontaneous concept from this experience, but we also learn the scientific concept that the earth is revolving around the sun. Learning the scientific concept does not lead to abandoning the spontaneous concept. We work quite happily with two different and contradictory conceptualizations of the relation between the earth and the sun, moving between the concepts as the occasion warrants.

When children participate in formal education they are required to develop scientific concepts; they bring to this learning process the spontaneous concepts they have already acquired. A theory of the developmental relationship between spontaneous and scientific concepts must acknowledge their differing sources and nature. Spontaneous concepts do not necessarily evolve into scientific concepts, since there may be discontinuities between them, as between the two concepts of how the earth moves relative to the sun. Scientific concepts are not just learnt as pre-formed wholes but are 'changeable dynamic structures' (Kozulin 1990: 169) that a child must (in Piagetian terms) accommodate and assimilate into existing concepts. The introduction of scientific concepts, which often happens through spoken discourse, will have an effect on existing spontaneous concepts, starting a process of adaptation and interaction between the two (Vygotsky 1962).

By distinguishing spontaneous and scientific concepts, Vygotsky provided a theoretical base for describing key aspects of classroom subject learning. Similar ideas underpin later views of learning as developing 'expertise' in a move from 'novice' to 'expert' (Wood 1998) or as the refining of 'naive theories' (Carey 1985). Recent work within cognitive psychology into 'explanation-based', or 'theory-based', concepts is revealing how individuals conceptualize, classify and store information from their experience in ways that organize and structure the information, both internally and in relation to other world knowledge, through 'explanatory theories' (Ross and Spalding 1994; Keil 1989). In this terminology, learning is the accumulation of information that leads to 'restructuring' of mental organization. Such restructuring may be weak, as new categories are added, or it may be strong, when more dramatic recategorization is accompanied by the development of new explanatory theories (Carey 1985). Vygotskyan theory adds the sociocultural dimension to these Piagetian ideas; individual learning is embedded in contextualized interaction and mediation.

When we move from theory to empirical investigation, we are prompted to look for ways in which the development of formal or scientific concepts is mediated through the use of metaphor in educational discourse of various types. For example, teachers may make explicit links between spontaneous and scientific concepts in spoken classroom discourse, while textbooks and more formal lessons may include metaphorical explanations of scientific concepts. In each of these instructional settings and discourses we will investigate how metaphor operates to mediate thinking and learning.

Mediated action: a sociocultural discourse unit

The final theoretical construct that we need for classroom discourse comes from activity theory, which is a more recent development in sociocultural theory (Leont'ev 1978; Wertsch 1991, 1998; Lantolf and Appel 1994; Engeström 1996; Scollon 1998; Wells 1999; Lantolf 2000). Activity theory, as its name suggests, places human activity at its core. It makes a three-level distinction between 'activity', 'action' and 'operations'. Although these can be seen as hierarchical distinctions, in that an activity may include several actions, which are in turn realized through various operations, the three levels also take a different perspective on the same event. Activity prioritizes the socially constituted aspects of the context that influence behaviour; action highlights activity driven by conscious and concrete 'goals'; operations are the procedures that lead to the accomplishment of goals, and are often automatized or routinized.

What happens in classrooms, including discourse, can be seen as 'mediated activity' (Wells 1999), described through nested contextual frames. Episodes of classroom discourse in which metaphor may impact on understanding and learning can be described as 'mediated action' (Wertsch 1998). I suggest, however, that there is a problem with the need for action to be led by conscious and concrete 'goals'. This teleological requirement is probably part of the Marxist inheritance of sociocultural theory (Thelen and Smith 1994) and sits somewhat uncomfortably with other aspects of the theory as it has been developed beyond its originating contexts. Identifying participants' goals in talk is not straightforward. Different participants may have different goals, and, in the case of adult–child talk, may have different possibilities of making them 'conscious' – goals are likely to shift and change as the talk proceeds, and as alterity and intersubjectivity change. In these studies, the 'goals' of discourse are taken to be what they are manifested as in the talk and in participants' behaviour. For example, if the teacher explains an idea to the class, then the goal of the teacher's talk is taken to be explanation.

Constructs from sociocultural theory: summary

Vygotskyan theory suggests that thinking and learning may be explored through investigation of educational discourse as mediated action in which participants attend to and manage perceived alterity. In episodes of talk we can investigate how differences in meaning are negotiated, and over the longer term, we are interested in how scientific concepts develop and connect with spontaneous concepts.

Each notion that has been discussed in this section has been dynamic and dialogic. In the final section of the chapter, the theory of complex systems is introduced. I will suggest that not only is it compatible with sociocultural theory, but that it offers additional ways of thinking about and investigating the talking and thinking processes that are our central concern. Before moving to complex systems theory, the next section brings metaphor back into the picture and reviews empirical studies on using and learning from metaphor.

Understanding and learning from metaphor

Making sense of metaphor

A Vygotskyan perspective on understanding metaphor is compatible with the idea of ad hoc concepts or mental spaces activated in discourse and made coherent in a continuously developing way. It also emphasizes the delicate interplay of language and thought in the ongoing processes in constructing and expanding the 'sense' of words and concepts (Vygotsky 1962; Wertsch 1985). 'Sense', as a translation of the Russian 'smysl', is the 'overall, cultural, psychological and personal significance' of a word for an individual (Frawley 1997: 28), i.e. its conceptual content as activated in on-line discourse. Sense thus serves as a link between speaking and thinking, and understanding metaphor is the process of 'making sense', of activating the sense of Topic and Vehicle words in their discourse context in moves between thought and language:

> The relation of thought to word is not a thing but a process, a continual movement back and forth from thought to word and from word to thought. In that process the relation of thought to word undergoes changes which themselves may be regarded as development. Thought is not merely expressed in words; it comes into existence through them. Every thought tends to connect something with something else, to establish a relationship between things.
> (Vygotsky 1962: 125)

Metaphor understanding is then a process of making sense and constructing coherence through the dynamics of the 'social mode of thinking' (Mercer 1994: 95), which we may call, after Slobin, 'talking-and-thinking'.

If we turn from understanding to learning, a Vygotskyan view would lead to the expectation that evidence of metaphor in effecting cognitive change might be seen intermentally in advance of its internalization and intramental use (Vygotsky 1962). In other words, the construction of shared understanding of, or through, metaphor in discourse may be an important step on the way to the construction and restructuring of an individual child's own understanding. The negotiation of shared understandings towards group norms may make use of metaphor to negotiate understanding, as for example when one participant uses metaphor to link new knowledge to existing knowledge (Rogoff 1990), or when the negotiation of metaphors themselves is involved (Roschelle 1992).

Metaphor and learning

How then may metaphor contribute to intramental development or learning? Vosniadou suggests that 'metaphorical thinking may play an important role in the child's attempts to acquire new knowledge' (1987a: 882). The simplest view of how learning happens would be the transfer of conceptual information or structure from Vehicle to Topic domain through analogy. More radical learning might involve the collapse of existing spontaneous conceptual structure in the Topic domain and the rebuilding of more 'scientific' conceptual structure that incorporates information from the Vehicle concept, in a process of 'restructuring' (Carey 1985). Metaphor may play other roles in cognitive change. For example, by being a vivid use of language, a particular metaphor may be stored in episodic memory along with the information it carries, and serve to facilitate future recall. In this section, I highlight several ways in which it has been suggested that metaphor may contribute to cognitive change, both constructively and negatively.

Development in understanding of concepts may sometimes be viewed as the adoption by the learner over time of increasingly complex sets of metaphors. For scientific metaphors, this development is also from concrete and specific to abstract and general. Strong cognitive change is particularly relevant for students in formal education, who are likely to be in the process of moving from their 'spontaneous' concepts to the 'scientific' concepts of the adult world (Vygotsky 1962: 84), through a series of conceptual restructurings (Carey 1985). Kittay (1987: 75) suggests that metaphors can help to bring about restructuring, but they may also have a weaker role in learning by contributing to the assimilation or accumulation of propositional or other information about a Topic, through the transfer of attributes from the Vehicle concept domain.

In a study of university students of statistics, Evans and Evans (1989) compared the learning outcomes of listening to statistics lectures, some of which used metaphor and some of which avoided metaphor. Learning outcomes were tested through the students' ability to transfer their understanding to solve three types of problems: in a domain close to the original, in a familiar but unrelated domain, and in an unfamiliar and unrelated domain. On the first two types of tasks, no differences were found, but in the 'general transfer' case, to an unfamiliar and unrelated domain, students who had been taught through metaphor performed better than the control group; they made fewer conceptual errors. Evans and Evans suggest that students switched to a metaphor-using strategy when confronted with a novel situation, and that their results support the theoretical view of metaphor as contributing to learning through the transfer of relational structure between distant, unrelated Vehicle and Topic domains.

Vosniadou (1989) and Brown (1989) both emphasize that children are cognitively equipped to make analogical transfers between Vehicle and Topic domains, and thus to learn from them, and that failures are more likely to be due to lack of domain knowledge rather than to problems with the analogical process. Gentner and Toupin (1986) report a study in which 4- to 6-year-olds and 8-year-olds were compared on their ability to transfer the plot of a story from one set of characters to another, with variation in the transparency of the mapping required. The study showed that all the children could perform such transfers, but that the older children became more skilled and more able to be independent of surface similarity through the use of higher order connecting relations. Thus for children, the probability of cognitive change via encounters with metaphor is likely to be affected by age and domain knowledge.

Developmental complexification of metaphors can take place over quite a short period of time for a particular concept, and a study by Roschelle (1992) illustrates how peer interaction is one discourse mode in which this can happen. The study investigated processes involved in the negotiation of metaphorically expressed understandings as two 15-year-olds completed tasks on a computer program designed to teach them about vectors of velocity, force and acceleration. One of the core processes found was the gradual sharing, justifying and refining of the girls' 'theory-constitutive metaphors', lexicalized as 'pulling/adding/travelling/hinging', to become more complex (Roschelle 1992: 237).

The potential cognitive role of metaphor goes beyond structuring concepts to the prompting of conceptual restructuring, the use of analogy in problem-solving, and assisting recall of information. The use of metaphor brings an alternative conceptualization, that of the Vehicle term, into the discourse, perhaps producing conflicts with aspects of the Topic domain that may prompt 'noticing' of gaps in understanding (Schmidt 1994), new explanations, and/or restructuring of concepts. Through the comparison or transfer between structures of Vehicle and Topic, gaps in the structure of the Topic domain may be revealed, leading to a search for new information and understanding, and to knowledge accumulation.

Studies of case-based or exemplar-based problem-solving (Dreyfus and Dreyfus 1986; Medin and Ross 1989) provide a further scenario in which metaphor may play a key role. Problem-solving is 'often based on specific examples rather than abstract principles' (Medin and Ross 1989: 217), with features of a current problem prompting recall of earlier experiences with similar problems and the generation of solutions through analogy. Adults have been shown to use analogy effectively for problem-solving (Gick and Holyoak 1980); and Gentner and Gentner (1983) demonstrated that making a guided analogy with a familiar domain could help adults understand unfamiliar concepts such as electricity. That children can make positive use of analogy has been shown in the learning of early literacy (Goswami 1991) and in problem-solving (Holyoak *et al.* 1984). The latter study compared how pre-school and 11-year-old children applied information presented in a story analogically to a physical problem. The older children, like adults in other studies, failed because they did not notice the possibility of solution by analogy, rather than because they did not understand how to make links between the domains; they sometimes needed the possibility of mapping to be made more explicit. Younger children, on the other hand, required the mapping between original and new to be completely explicit, otherwise they could not understand how to make use of the analogy. This points again to the delicacy needed in selecting Vehicle domains, and suggests that the open-endedness of metaphor may sometimes not function well for younger children.

Metaphor may help learning by working as a mnemonic for how concepts are connected, extending the capacity of memory (Sticht 1993) and acting as one of Bruner's 'prosthetic devices by which human beings can exceed or even redefine the "natural limits" of human functioning' (Bruner 1990: 21). However, I have not been able to find much empirical evidence to support a claim for a positive role for metaphor in remindings. Winner (1988) finds only one study, by Arter (1976), that shows metaphorical language use giving advantages in recall.

Research on children's understanding of metaphorical language has consistently highlighted how metaphor may only be partially understood because of their partial or inaccurate domain knowledge. Adults too may also bring partial or inaccurate domain knowledge to their understanding of metaphor. There are further potential dangers in the use of metaphorical language which have been empirically demonstrated not to be restricted to children's learning, and which derive from the very same properties of metaphor that contribute positively to cognitive change. Research carried out with medical students demonstrates how initially helpful analogies may 'become serious *impediments* to fuller and more correct understandings' (Spiro *et al.* 1989: 498), as they fail to serve the need to complexify the students' understandings of the workings of the human body. Most problems with metaphor seem to arise through reliance on just one analogy that is useful initially, but which is too simple or inaccurate to allow for the complex understandings required for more advanced study. The power of the original analogy for the individual is such that it is not easily jettisoned or replaced. Metaphor may contribute negatively to cognitive change by

- providing a false sense of understanding and thus disallowing access to alternative structures;
- providing concept domain structuring that is too simple or partial;
- leading to inappropriate transfers of attributes or relations.

(based on Spiro *et al.* 1989)

Spiro *et al.* note that a further cause of problems can be the use of everyday language terms in technical discourses, transferred via analogy, but with their everyday meanings and/or connotations transferred inappropriately. They suggest that there are several sources of misleading but 'seductive' analogies:

- simplified metaphors from teachers or textbooks
- misconceptions in teachers or textbooks
- learners' own metaphors

(Spiro *et al.* 1989: 510)

The solution proposed by Spiro *et al.* for over-reliance on too simple a metaphor is to 'combat the power of a limited analogy with *another powerful analogy* that counteracts the limitations of the earlier one' (Spiro *et al.* 1989: 514). It is recommended that instruction make use of integrated multiple analogies (or metaphors) which have been specifically chosen to correct the negative aspects of the original analogy, along with explicit discussion about the shortcomings of each, including the original. This strategy will require of the teacher or the textbook writer an awareness of the limitations of basic metaphors and analogies.

Understanding and learning from metaphor: summary

A theoretical model of understanding metaphor in discourse includes the activation of mental spaces related to Topic and Vehicle, and the construction of coherence in conceptual content and (internal) explanatory theories. Empirical findings do not give a picture of uncomplicated benefits from metaphor use. Rather, they suggest that use of metaphor can contribute to learning by complexifying concepts through analogy and through prompting restructuring. Metaphor can help recall of information and can help apply what is known to new contexts. The nature and content of individual instances of metaphor and the discourse context of use, including the previous knowledge of discourse participants, will clearly be significant in whether learning opportunities are opened up or limited.

By examining metaphor in the discourse of the classroom, we can identify the learning opportunities, or 'affordances' (van Lier 2000), that are created. The empirical challenge undertaken in the second half of the book will then be to access comprehension and interpretation of metaphor through on-line talking-and-thinking, and to make justifiable inferences from evidence of joint talk to individual cognitive development so that pedagogical implications can be drawn. Theoretically, empirical evidence of metaphor interpretation in discourse will allow testing of the Interaction theory and the theory of Conceptual Blending for their adequacy in accounting for what happens in language use.

Complex systems theory

This section draws on recent developments in the natural sciences to help develop, at a macro level, the integrated epistemological and theoretical framework required to deal holistically with the mediating role of prosaic metaphor in the dynamics of contextualized interaction.

I am not alone in finding the existing tools of applied linguistics sometimes inadequate for such holistic enterprises; across the discipline there are symptoms of a search for a new paradigm. Recent conference papers and articles in key journals have begun to suggest the limitations of the traditional reductionist scientific paradigm, and have tried out other possibilities for underlying perspectives (Rampton 1995; Block 1996; Lantolf 1996; Swain and Lapkin 1998), while those working happily within the traditional scientific paradigm, for example within second language acquisition, still defend their values and results. In these debates, the changes taking place within science, and the paradigm shifts being experienced in mathematics, biology and physics, seem to have gone largely unmentioned. In fact, the debates within science express concerns that parallel those of applied linguists: how to take account of context; how to work with non-simple, non-linear systems without neglecting or underestimating key factors; how to explain similar phenomena with apparently disparate causes.

The theory of complex systems, which has been developing rapidly over the last 10 to 15 years, seems to offer a way forward. Complex systems theory now brings together chaos theory, catastrophe theory and complexity theory, with particularly exciting applications developing in evolutionary biology (e.g. Casti 1994; Cohen and Stewart 1994; Goodwin 1997; Kauffman 1993, 1995). Complex systems theory has been applied in psychology (Bütz 1995; Clark 1997; Port and van Gelder 1995), to economics, and, in somewhat looser applications, to fields such as management (Battram 1998). The potential for applied linguistics was recognized in a paper by Larsen-Freeman (1997). Detailed application of methodology has not yet been published, but, in fields that share some commonalities with applied linguistics, such as developmental and cognitive psychology, initial work has been carried out to demonstrate that cognition, including aspects of first language learning and memory, involves complex dynamic systems (Elman 1995; Petitot 1995; Thelen and Smith 1994; van Geert 1995, 1998; van Gelder and Port 1995).

I suggest that applied linguistics can draw analogically on this new direction in science for ways of conceptualizing language in use; a longer term aim will be to see whether language in use may actually work as an example of a complex system, as technological evolution is now held to (Kauffman 1995; Knudsen and Cameron 2000). For this study, complex systems theory appears to offer helpful ways of describing metaphor at work in discourse as both conceptual and linguistic.

I next outline what a complex systems view of language in use might look like, and then go into further detail about the nature of complex systems and the implications for the studies in this book.

Discourse as a complex adaptive system

A complex system contains 'a huge number of elements with many degrees of freedom' (Mainzer 1996: 3). The elements of the system, which may themselves be systems, can interact in many different ways (Waldrop 1992: 11). A forest is an example of a complex system, since it includes different species of flora and fauna interacting with each other and with the climate and soil. Other examples are a city and the human body. Because of the many, and many types of, interactions between elements, complex systems are nonlinear. A linear system is one in which elements act independently of each other, with the whole system amenable to straightforward analysis and explanation as the sum, or superposition, of analysis of its parts, in traditional reductionist ways (Waldrop 1992: 64; Mainzer 1996: 3). In nonlinear systems, elements are not independent, and alterations to one element can have knock-on effects on other elements.

We might choose to view discourse as a complex system, formed by the interrelation of complex subsystems that represent individual participants in the discourse, as a forest is formed by the interrelation of its subsystems. If we then consider discourse as not just language but as talking-and-thinking-in-interaction, then each individual participant can be seen as bringing to discourse interrelated systems of language, of knowledge and understanding, of attitudes and values. Each of these 'mental resource systems' also possesses features reminiscent of complex systems in biology and physics:

- they are *not independent of context*, in that they are influenced by the nature and goal of the event, and/or context-based processing constraints;
- they are *nonlinear*, in that they link into other, interactional and cognitive, resources;
- they are *adaptive*, in that individual contributions to the event are adjusted as the interaction proceeds, in order to take account of misunderstandings, interruptions, and other internal or external problems.

Mental resource systems interact in the on-line processes of talking-and-thinking, adapting to each other and to the cognitive and linguistic environment produced by the preceding discourse. Setting up this analogy between discourse and complex systems allows a move away from an idealized, reductionist situation, in which the 'whole' of language use is broken down into 'parts', either parts as individual language use, or parts as separation of context from language.

Having established an outline of the discourse–complex systems analogy, I now go into more detail about the properties of complex systems so that the links in the analogy can be tightened. We can then proceed to explore possible implications for metaphor in educational discourse that arise from the analogy, given our current knowledge about the behaviour of complex systems.

Properties of complex systems

All complex systems are dynamic and nonlinear, and all biological complex systems, as well as many physical and chemical systems, are also open (Thelen and Smith 1994: 53). Each of these properties is now explained in turn.

A dynamic (or, more accurately, dynamical) system is one that changes continuously over time, with future states depending on earlier ones. In a complex system, not only does the state of the elements change over time, but the nature of the relations between elements also changes. An obviously dynamic system is the growing city, where development of edge-of-town shopping malls can have knock-on effects on city centre shopping and road use. In a complex systems perspective, mental resources are not seen as static representations, as in traditional cognitive science, but as a dynamic system which 'is always on the move' (Thelen and Smith 1994: 244). Every use of the resources changes them, and the changed resources are then brought to the next discourse episode or event. A complex systems perspective on discourse as dynamic works with the prosaic approach which sees every use of metaphor as a unique occurrence, affected by previous uses and by discourse context. We may also note that intersubjectivity and alterity are dynamic.

Complex systems are nonlinear in the way they and their elements change over time. In mathematics, linear change is that which is strictly proportional and when displayed on a graph produces a straight line with an equation of the form $\{y = mx + c\}$. Nonlinear equations have powers of x greater than 1, and a system is nonlinear if change does not happen in simple, proportionate ways. Nonlinear change is common in human systems. For example, when a new motorway was built around London, the increase in road space did not result in a lower density of traffic, as a linear relationship would have predicted, but instead, traffic density increased, as local people used the road for short journeys. Before the advent of powerful computers, physicists and mathematicians had no easy ways to work with nonlinearity, and so very often carried out idealizations to simplify relations in order to produce linear equations that could be solved. Once nonlinear equations could be tackled through recurrent numerical calculations, descriptions of nonlinear behaviour became available. Nonlinear change characterizes developing language resources, for example when vocabulary growth shows sudden spurts in early childhood (Snow 1996).

Nonlinear change in a system can be brought about by co-adapting subsystems, which are themselves complex dynamic systems. In the forest example, a climbing plant may use a tree for food and as a place to grow, but the tree may be affected by this process: the tree and the climber co-adapt. Trees use sunshine to grow, but as they grow, they gradually block out sunshine from the forest floor, creating different types of micro-climate in a process of co-adaptation. Many types of subsystems interact and change each other in a continual process of co-adaptation, and we can look at discourse in this light, with individuals co-adapting in their talking-and-thinking-in-interaction: the sociolinguistic phenomenon of 'accommodation' in language use, in which various aspects of language shift in use (Coupland and Giles 1988; Locke 1993), would appear to describe co-adapting complex dynamic systems. The construct of co-adaptation can be applied to individuals talking-and-thinking within collaborative discourse.

Some complex systems are not closed systems, which are restricted in how they can change because they obey the second law of thermodynamics; rather, they are open to new inflows of energy and influence from the environment or ecology of the system. An implication of the openness of complex systems is a requirement to consider both internal and external interactions, i.e. the components of both the system and the ecology, and how they affect each other through processes of adaptation. Returning to previous examples, we can see that a forest is an open system, as when it is vulnerable to international market forces that encourage logging, and that a city is open to the impact of changes in business or political climate. In line with sociocultural theory, an individual's mental resources are open to influence and mediation by other people or by the uses to which they are put. Discourse is an open system since ideas and input to the ongoing talk may be contributed from individuals and may change the dynamics of the discourse.

When mental resources, including language, are put to use in discourse, they will be adapted and selected for the particular demands that the discourse content and other participants exert. Change in complex dynamic systems occurs through processes of selection and adaptation in the context of specific discourse settings. In our analogy, we might expect to find change in language, and cognitive and affective resources occurring as a result of selection and adaptation in talking-and-thinking-in-interaction. These changes may manifest themselves in various ways but they are our objects of concern in this study. We are concerned with the development of scientific concepts first as cognitive change, with changes in metaphor use and understanding; and second as affective change with changes in attitudes and values. Change in complex systems can be continuous or it can involve sudden and dramatic shifts (Cohen and Stewart 1994), just as conceptual change can be slow and continuous or show more dramatic restructuring.

Returning to discourse, we can put into action the analogy of a changing complex system. In this analogy,

- each individual has complex dynamic systems of mental resources: linguistic, cognitive, affective;
- resources are brought to talking-and-thinking-in-interaction, which produces a context or ecology for the use of participants' resources;
- the resource systems of participants interact and co-adapt in talking-and-thinking;
- use of resources requires adaptation and selection;
- continued adaptation and selection over time causes the system to change in various ways;
- changes in the systems are what we label 'learning' or conceptual development.

This complex systems view of discourse and learning as change in mental resources occurring in talking-and-thinking-in-interaction over time is compatible with the Vygotskyan view of learning through social interaction that was developed earlier. The compatibility, at least in principle, between complex systems theory and Vygotskyan theory has been noted by Thelen and Smith (1994) and Frawley (1997); van Geert (1995, 1998) attempted to operationalize the link. Morson and Emerson (1990) noted similarities between some of Bakhtin's ideas and early versions of chaos theory. In fact, much more of Bakhtin's thinking aligns itself with complex systems theory, as we will see later.

Having set out key features of the analogy between discourse and complex dynamic systems, we can now proceed to develop it by examining what is known about the behaviour of complex systems in other fields and seeing how this can be applied to talking-and-thinking-in-interaction. In doing so, I will suggest how metaphor and the mediation of alterity can be analogized and what is implied for a prosaic approach to studying metaphor in discourse.

The behaviour of complex systems

A battery of mathematical constructs and methods has been developed to describe the way complex systems evolve and change. These make use of a branch of mathematics called topology, which deals with the geometry of surfaces. Topology lends itself to visualization, through the use of graphs, landscapes, and diagrams. These spatial constructs and visualization techniques can be applied descriptively to systems of language in use.

The 'state' of a system is its collective state, the position or state of each element and relation at a particular point in time; the 'initial state', or 'initial dynamics', is the system's state at time zero. As the system changes over time, it is seen as moving from one state to another, tracing a path over time that is called its 'trajectory'. Change in systems can be continuous, or it can be discontinuous and sudden. The set of all possible states of the system is an abstract space called the 'state space' (sometimes 'phase space') of the system. Kauffman describes the state space as 'the mathematical universe in which the system is free to roam' (1995: 75), and it is also described as a landscape of possibilities of the system. These spaces are often drawn as two or three dimensional landscapes across which the system moves.

The mathematics of change in complex systems shows it to be characterized by certain important general trajectory patterns. Some places in the state space of a system are like valleys so deep that the system, once having entered, cannot immediately escape. Such trajectories are called 'attractors'. An attractor from which the system cannot move on is a 'fixed point attractor': we can think of a destroyed forest or of fossilization in language learning. Two other types of attractor have been found in the change of complex systems: limit cycle attractors and strange (or chaotic) attractors. Systems can escape from limit cycle attractors, but tend to return to them after a period of time. A forest under traditional slash-and-burn agriculture exemplifies this. In chaotic attractors, systems appear to behave in random and unpredictable ways, but mathematically such behaviour has underlying patterns. It is not random. However, the behaviour is unpredictable, and also very sensitive to initial conditions of the system. The progressive states of a system vary in stability. Fixed point and limit cycle attractors represent periods of stable behaviour; with chaotic attractors, the system is extremely unstable.

Important work by Kauffman (1995) is revealing how complex systems appear to organize themselves into certain trajectories in the vicinity of attractors. A system seems to tend to move near to, but not actually into, chaotic attractors. In this edge of chaos state, a system has many dramatically different possibilities as to its future state, and the system changes both rapidly and effectively. There is an intriguing parallel between the edge of chaos and Vygotsky's zone of proximal development, although the poetic label 'edge of chaos' may perhaps generate more parallelism than is strictly appropriate. The most interesting place for researchers and teachers in both systems may be at the edge of chaos, where the system has a degree of variability but also some stability, and where there is the largest potential for change and co-adaptation.

In a complex systems description, learning can be seen as the cognitive resources system moving from one stable path or state to another via a series of fixed point attractors. On a micro-level timescale, during a discourse event, the behaviour of an individual's mental resource system may be less than stable, and even move towards chaotic behaviour. Over a longer developmental timescale, shifts in the resource system may be evidenced initially by increased variability around a stable attractor that represents a new state of knowledge. A cognitive attractor may be a new concept, explanatory theory, or contextualized understanding. The degree of stability or variability of resources in and around an attractor state can be seen as representing how well understood some aspect of knowledge is.

I want also to consider the possibility that metaphors may function as combined linguistic, conceptual and affective attractors in the trajectory of talking-and-thinking-in-interaction. A metaphor attractor would be a particular linguistic form that carries a particular conceptual understanding for users. While contemporary metaphor theory emphasizes embodiment as driving the use and development of conceptual metaphor (Gibbs 1994, 1999), it still needs to develop explanatory theories of the ontogenetic or sociohistorical development of linguistic metaphors related to conceptual metaphors.

So, while the general physical reality of the conceptual metaphorical mapping MORE IS UP can explain how we understand the examples from Chapter 1: *investment growth/reaching its target*, we also may wonder how it is that only certain linguistic forms have come to be conventionally used to express the ideas. An evolutionary analogy, in which the co-adaptation of systems results in the development of certain forms rather than others, may help. Rorty (1989), and Nietszche before him, claimed metaphor as a major force in the generation of new ways of using language. In the ontogenetic development of scientific concepts, metaphors may act as attractors that help crystallize interim understandings within a child's zone of proximal development.

To pursue the hypothesis that metaphors can act as attractors in the dynamics of discourse, we need to look at the behaviour of complex systems to see what might constitute evidence. Attractors in trajectories are permanent or temporary stabilities in the system. Their stability is indexed by two measures: variability and resistance to perturbation. When systems are in transition, variability increases and small perturbations or changes to the system will disrupt the trajectory much more than before or after the transition. Examination of discourse data will reveal what variability around metaphor use looks like, and may also demonstrate the effect of perturbations to the system of evolving talk-and-thinking.

Alterity as driving talking-and-thinking

The changing trajectories of complex systems are described in biological and psychological studies by collective variables. A collective variable in a complex system condenses the degrees of freedom of the system and acts as a dependent measure of change in the system (Thelen and Smith 1994: 251). The trajectory and phase shifts of the system through its state space can be graphically represented by the successive values of the collective variable, which is identified through empirical work.

In developmental psychology, studies using complex systems theory (again analogically) in the detailed empirical investigation of how young children learn to reach and grasp, identified hand speed as a collective variable; control of hand speed served as a parameter for overall reaching (Thelen and Smith 1994). Another example of finding a collective variable to describe change in a complex system comes from a study by Kelso (1995) into rhythmic finger moving, reported in A. Clark (1997). The study investigated what happened when subjects were asked to move their two index fingers rhythmically, like windscreen wipers on a car. There are two comfortable or stable ways of moving the fingers: either in phase and parallel, or in anti-phase, starting at right angles to each other. (Try it!) The stable anti-phase movement only works for low frequencies of oscillation. If subjects begin in anti-phase mode and are asked to move their fingers gradually faster, there is a critical frequency at which a switch occurs and the fingers shift into phased oscillation, rather like a horse switches suddenly rather than gradually from a trot to a canter. The collective variable that best described the finger moving turned out to be the difference between the phases, which stays constant for a wide range of different frequencies of finger movement but then suddenly changes at the critical point. It is a collective variable because 'it cannot be defined for a single component (fingers) but only for the larger system' (Clark 1997: 117).

The power of the phase differential to act as a collective variable to describe the changing complex system in the finger movement suggests a further analogy that might be applied to educational discourse: that the trajectory of talking-and-thinking in classrooms might be driven by alterity and by participants' tendency to reveal, manage and reduce it. Alterity may act as a collective variable to describe how the system of talking-and-thinking-in-interaction moves across its state space from one attractor to the next. Some of these attractors may be metaphors.

Emergence

Emergence is described as the appearance of simplicities from lower-level complexity: 'regularities of behaviour that somehow seem to transcend their own ingredients' (Cohen and Stewart 1994: 232). As examples, we can take colour, which cannot be traced into any particular component of something possessing colour, e.g. a flower; or life 'emerging from chemistry by way of DNA'. The importance of such emergent simplicities presents a clear and intriguing parallel with Bakhtin's concerns about the importance, and difficulty, of explaining the simple in language use (described in Chapter 1). In the quote that follows, Cohen and Stewart (1994: 222) reflect on the nature of scientific enquiry and what it has tried to explain. They use the term 'complexity' here with its everyday meaning of 'complicatedness', rather than the more precise mathematical meaning:

> Scientists have been asking the wrong question.
> They have focussed upon complexity, and they have taken simplicity for granted. The answer to complexity turns out to be fairly obvious and not, in itself, especially interesting. If you have a lot of simple interactors, and let them interact, then the result can be rather complicated.
> The interesting question is precisely the opposite, the question that most scientists never thought to ask because they didn't see that there was a question to ask. Where does simplicity come from?

An emergent phenomenon results from the nonlinear interactions of parts in a system; it cannot be explained by breaking the system into its parts. It is a 'whole' that is somehow more than the 'sum of parts'. We might think of new understandings that arise from participating in discourse as 'emergent', and a particular linguistic metaphor may usefully be conceived of as an emergent simplicity of the interacting complexities of language in use.

Complex systems and metaphor in discourse: summary

In this section of the chapter, I have developed at some length the analogy between educational discourse and complex systems. The analogy provides an alternative vocabulary to describe metaphor in discourse, but it is potentially much more than that. It offers a radically new way of conceptualizing what happens when people participating in discourse use metaphor, deliberately or otherwise, in their talking and thinking.

As the empirical studies are reported, I shall attempt to apply the principles of a complex systems analysis of findings alongside the use of more conventional applied linguistic methods. Since the studies reported here were not designed as complex systems investigations, my aim is to develop the analogy so that it may later be tried as theory. Two hypotheses have been generated in connection with the complex systems analogy: that metaphors may act as attractors in the discourse, and that alterity may serve as a collective variable to describe how the discourse proceeds and how learning is promoted. Clearly, these notions need much more detailed operationalization to be useful, and this will be built up from the discourse data. If feasible, they may then be used in future studies that work within a complex systems paradigm.

Conclusion: research aims and questions

The research aims formulated at the end of Chapter 1 can now be turned into research questions using the theoretical frameworks of this chapter. The empirical studies that will be described in the rest of the book explore:

- how metaphor is used in educational discourse;
- how students understand the metaphors they encounter;
- how metaphor contributes to learning.

The research questions that structured the empirical work are:

1. What is the nature of metaphor in educational discourse?
2. What opportunities does metaphor offer for the mediation of thinking, learning, affect and action?
3. What helps or prevents students taking advantage of the opportunities offered by metaphor?

Chapter 3 describes the educational context in which these questions were investigated and operationalizes the key constructs.

3 Researching metaphor in classroom discourse

Introduction

The metaphor literature reviewed in Chapter 1 embodies a view of metaphor as pervasive in language use and conceptually important. A sociocultural view of learning holds that the interaction between adults and children is crucial for conceptual development. Together, these views would indicate an important pedagogic role for metaphor in discourse. To research how metaphor mediates thinking and action in educational discourse, a two-pronged empirical investigation was undertaken: the first study examined the use of metaphor in discourse from a classroom, while the second study explored children's understanding of metaphors in text. The two types of investigation worked with the same student participants but used different methods of data collection and analysis. The first study addresses research question 1 and provides some answers to 2 and 3; the second provides more detailed answers to questions 2 and 3.

The chapter begins by describing the sociocultural context in which the investigation took place, the school, the key participants and the process of collecting the spoken classroom discourse data. A review of other empirical studies of school discourse produces some figures for comparison, but also many inadequacies. The rest of the chapter is concerned with analysis of the spoken discourse data. The initial step of identifying linguistic metaphors is far from simple. I describe how problems were resolved and discuss the implications for theories of metaphor. Once the data set of linguistic metaphors was assembled, various forms of analysis were applied. These analyses of metaphor as a 'product' of discourse were then complemented by 'process' analyses. The final section shows how the ideas of complex systems theory helped to design analysis of the discourse as mediated action, so that the pedagogic role of metaphors could be described.

The context of the research

The discourse data for both studies were collected in a small primary (elementary) school in the UK. The school is situated in a small village in a rural northern county. Most of the children are from reasonably affluent families; all are white and used English as their first language. The school had just three classes, each with children from more than one year group. The data were collected in the third class of the school, which at the time had 15 children aged between 9 and 11. In UK primary schools, a class is usually taught by one teacher for all, or most, subjects. In this small school, the class teacher was also the headteacher, and she was replaced in the classroom for two mornings a week by a regular part-time teacher (also a woman). A third teacher also had occasional contact with the class.

The class was organized into four groups, each group sitting round a set of tables. The teaching was a mix of whole class and group work. In the group work, the children worked on the same subject area, but not necessarily collaboratively. There was a relaxed but hard-working atmosphere in the class and the school, and my subjective perception that, by and large, the children were well-behaved is supported by the few occasions that the data include behaviour control incidents.

To add validity to the linking of the studies, the same child served as a focus for data collection in both. In the first, classroom study, data were collected about her experience of metaphor in the daily discourse of the classroom. The second, a think-aloud study, explored the sense that she was making of the metaphor around her.

Louise (the pseudonym chosen by the child for herself) was 10 years and 7 months old at the beginning of the study, the oldest of two children in her family. She was selected by the teacher to participate in the research on the grounds that she was 'sensible' and likely to be communicative. She was a fluent reader, having completed the structured reading scheme used by the school, and could write competently, although not quickly. Cognitively, the teacher described her as able and poised for a period of rapid development.

The age and academic skills of the participants (Louise and some of her classmates) place them at the end of childhood. They were in the final year of primary school. In language skills they resemble many adults, being well past the major stages of first language acquisition. They are functionally literate. Conceptually, they can reason logically and have accumulated a rich store of experiential knowledge, but there are also many ideas that are in the process of being understood and developed, and, in some areas, they have restricted experience and knowledge. In their mid-way position between childhood and adulthood, they provide a rich ground for researching language and thinking, with the opportunity to see how concepts develop through both social interaction and formal education.

Louise's participation in the study was discussed and agreed with her parents. Louise herself collected the data by wearing a tie-pin microphone which was connected to a small audio cassette recorder that she carried around or hung on the back of her chair. The microphone picked up all the classroom talk that was addressed to the whole class or to her, as well as much that was addressed to other pupils but that she could have overheard. It also collected talk between Louise and her peers, particularly her close friend Ellen.

Although this method of data collection was not as discreet as we might have wished, it produced adequately clear recordings of talk involving Louise. She herself quickly became used to the recording, as did the class teacher. The part-time teacher seemed to be more conscious of it. However, as with any recording of an event, the extent to which the apparatus ultimately affects the discourse is impossible to assess.

I made nine visits to the school for the two studies. Visits lasted for half or more of the school day in each case, and a good relationship developed between myself as researcher and Louise as participant as the studies progressed. For this first classroom study, recordings were made over four school days, yielding about ten hours of usable data. Louise and I had several informal conversations to clarify points of information. As researcher, I was present in the classroom during the recordings, observing and writing timed field notes. I also copied down board work, and collected copies of all the texts and worksheets that Louise used during the data collection periods.

I transcribed the recorded data orthographically, producing about 27K words of transcribed data. This amount is a reasonable sample across a range of classroom discourse events, and is probably at the limit of what one person can transcribe and analyse manually, but it does have limitations once we move to work with the metaphors. With an expected frequency of around 20 to 50 metaphors per 1K words (see p. 57), we would predict having around 500 to 1000 metaphors to work with. Any generalizations from such a sample will need to be done very carefully, and the major role of findings may be to suggest further, more focused or more extensive empirical studies. The absence of similar studies in the published literature justified starting in this way.

The nature of the classroom events recorded

Language use in a primary classroom is complex and varied in mode, style and register, and in participants and purposes. Participants in the ongoing interaction vary in number and in the roles they are assigned or choose to adopt in different discourse contexts. The classroom was typical in the way physical settings contributed to creating discourse contexts, for example when children working in a group around a table talked to neighbours doing individual work on tasks, or when pupils waiting in line to talk to the teacher at her desk talked about their work or their out-of-school lives. The teacher spent a considerable proportion of her time in one-to-one discussions with pupils about their work, but these interactions could become input for other pupils who could hear them and might 'tune in' for a few minutes, perhaps then discussing what they heard with other children standing or sitting nearby. Another apparently straightforward type of interaction, the teacher addressing the whole class in more formal delivery of subject matter, also had attached to it other separate but motivated interactions, as when pupils might pick up on an unusual word or idea and share their amusement or interest with a friend or when they tried to make sense of something the teacher said that contradicted their own knowledge. In more informal teacher–class interaction, the teacher used questions and prompts in shared problem-solving activities.

An initial division of the data was made by discourse events, using where possible the school label. A 'discourse event' is a unit of mediated activity or social interaction that has a wholeness about it, signalled by a label or by a clear start and finish. It is used as a discourse parallel to the notion of 'speech event' (Hymes 1972). Nearly half of the recorded talk took place, not in specific and demarcated lessons, but while the children worked individually on tasks that the teacher had set. During this time, the teacher monitored their work, intervened to help, or carried out a range of other activities with the children such as listening to them read aloud or correcting writing. This activity is labelled 'class work'. The full range of discourse events that were recorded is listed in Table 3.1.

Review of research into metaphor in classroom discourse

Teachers' use of metaphor in spoken discourse

It initially seems a reasonable question to ask how much metaphor is used in classroom discourse, but turning to published studies about what might be called 'metaphor density' in text and talk quickly reveals that this is not a straightforward measurement, and, as we move to discuss procedures for identifying metaphor in data, the reasons will become obvious. A quick survey of studies gives some indication of the wide range of figures and the problems caused by discrepancy in the units of analysis chosen by researchers. The units

Table 3.1 Discourse events recorded and transcribed as data

Discourse event	Type of activity	Teacher	Length of discourse event (minutes)	No. of words in transcript
Class work				
1 Class work 1	Children working on tasks that the teacher set in advance. Teacher monitors, intervenes or pursues a range of other goals unrelated to the tasks such as correcting work, listening to reading	T1	260	8723
2 Class work 2		T2	12	636
3 Geology lesson	Teacher-led lesson on three types of rocks	T1	30	2578
Maths work				
4 With teacher T1 (math1)	Joint problem-solving between teacher and class	T1	38	2203
5 With teacher T2 (math2)	Return of a maths test, with demonstration of correct answers. Maths problems given orally or in writing	T2	50	4547
6 Lesson on apostrophes (apost)	Teacher explanation of how to use apostrophes, and exercises	T2	65	2831
7 Maypole dancing (dance)	Teacher-led dancing practice in the school hall	T1	70	3179
8 TV programme (TV)	A schools programme and follow-up discussion, in the school hall	T1	18	1916
Totals			543 minutes	26,613 words

used by different researchers have to be related to the broad unit 'linguistic metaphor' used in this book.

A study by Pollio *et al.* (1977) measured how many 'figures of speech' per minute of talk were produced by teachers, and found that, over 12 hours of talk, on average four were produced per minute. A definition of 'figure of speech' was not given, but it is likely that it approximates to a strong linguistic metaphor. My recordings suggest that teacher talk runs at about 70 words per minute, which gives a figure of 4 metaphors in 70 words. Extrapolating to a unit of 1000 words, we have a metaphor density of 57 metaphors per 1000 words.

In a study of figurative speech in college lectures, Corts and Pollio (1999) counted an average rate of one 'figure' in every 4.8 'sentences', where 'figure' includes 'metaphor, hyperbole, irony, and so forth' (84). If we assume that a spoken 'sentence' at this level contains 10 words, the density of figurative language is around 21 instances per 1000 words. Interestingly, they also found 'bursts' of metaphor during the lectures, in which the use dramatically increased to an equivalent of around 100 per 1000 words.

Other studies investigate the use of 'idioms', again variably defined. Lazar *et al.* (1989) measured the proportion of idioms in 5400 'utterances' by teachers in Grades K–8 (children aged 5 to 13) and found 'at least one' idiom in 12 per cent of utterances, with more in upper grades. Idioms here were conventionalized expressions with multiple meanings, and so would comprise a subset of 'linguistic metaphors', since novel metaphors are excluded. To obtain any sort of comparison, we need first to assume that an utterance contains about 7 words. If 12 per cent of utterances contain one idiom, we get a figure of 17 idioms per 1000 words. It is impossible to know what to do with 'at least one', except to say that idiom density is 'at least' 17 per 1000 words, and metaphor density would be even higher, since we would have to add novel expressions.

Strässler's definition of 'idiom' is much tighter, excluding single words and phrasal verbs (Strässler 1982). In his spoken data (non-school), he reports production of 1 idiom per 1150 words. Johnson and Malgady (1980) report briefly a study by Johnson (1975) which estimates that five metaphors occur in every 100 words of general talk.

Metaphor in written texts

Written language, being linear and permanent, would seem to present a simpler empirical database with fewer problems in counting metaphors. This is not the case, and only a few relevant studies can be found. Pickens *et al.* (1985: 483) report a proportion of 'figurative language' in basic readers of 1 per cent, less in content-area texts (Arter 1976; Dixon *et al.* 1980) and 2.5 per cent in recognized literature excluding poetry (Smith *et al.* 1982). Hollingsed (1950), reported by Abkarian *et al.* (1990), calculated 100–300 idiomatic expressions occurred 'per book' in elementary readers, but without further information on the average length of a book, these data are of little use. Nippold (1991) examined books from three reading schemes aimed at 8- to 13-year-olds and found that 6.7 per cent of sentences contained an idiom. Evans and Gamble (1988) report Ortony (1979b) as giving a frequency of occurrence of figurative language of 10 instances per 1000 words in school textbooks for 10- and 11-year-olds. If we estimate 8 words per sentence, Nippold's figure converts to 8.4 per

1000 words. On this limited evidence, the number of idioms in children's readers is low, and lower than in other texts, but increases across the primary years. Subject textbooks appear to have even fewer instances of metaphor.

The results of studies of both talk and text directed at children are combined in Table 3.2, with figures made as comparable as possible using 1000 words as a sensible unit within which to average numbers of metaphors. Although the gaps in information provided in published papers put limitations on how the present study might expect to relate to previous studies, we can make several tentative points:

- Spoken discourse (the top half of the table) appears to use substantially more metaphors than written discourse.
- If figurative language includes, and approximates to, metaphor, and if idioms are often metaphorical, while at the same time metaphors are not always idiomatic, the table indicates that around 10 metaphors per 1000 words might be expected in classroom texts.
- Spoken discourse might be expected to have a metaphor density of between 20 and 60 per 1000 words, which is a huge range.

Table 3.2 Summary of previous studies and figures for metaphor density

Study	Discourse context	Unit counted	No. per 1000 words
Strässler (1982)	non-school talk	idioms (excluding single words and phrasal verbs)	0.87
Pollio et al. (1977)	teacher talk	figure of speech	57
Lazar et al. (1989)	teacher utterances	idioms	> 17
Corts and Pollio (1999)	college lectures	figures	21
Johnson (1975, reported in Johnson and Malgady 1980)	'ordinary discourse'	metaphors	50
Arter (1976, reported in Pickens et al. 1985)	basic readers	figurative language	10
Smith et al. (1982)	recognized literature (sic), excluding poetry	figurative language	25
Nippold (1991)	reading scheme books	idioms	8.4
Ortony (1979, reported by Evans and Gamble 1988)	school textbooks	figurative language	10

- Strässler's figure is excessively small due to his very tight definition of 'idiom', but, by taking a subset of the results of the first study reported here, it will be possible to use them in a comparison.

The difficulties in constructing comparable figures for Table 3.2 demonstrate the importance of careful operationalizing and defining of units of analysis. What is 'found' in the data depends on the researcher's decisions about what is categorized as 'metaphor'. If research is to be replicable or to build on previous studies, it is clearly essential to make explicit and precise statements about what is counted.

Data analysis: metaphor identification

The task of identifying linguistic metaphor

To answer the first research question, 'What is the nature of metaphor in educational discourse?' the first task was to quantify the amount of metaphorical language used in the discourse, before moving to describe it more qualitatively. As we saw in the literature reviewed in the previous section, quantifying the amount or density of metaphor requires very careful operationalization of the unit 'metaphor', and in this section I begin to explain how this was done.

We should note first that 'identification' here refers to identifying linguistic metaphors in discourse; recent work in the cognitive paradigm (Steen 1999a) uses the term 'identification' to refer to a wider activity that goes beyond linguistic expressions to infer the underlying conceptual metaphors and mappings. In Chapter 10, we will look at the possible conceptual mappings underlying some of the metaphors in the data, but I do not attempt to interpret all the linguistic metaphors in this way.

My initial readings in the metaphor literature (as reported in Chapter 1) did not lead me to expect the problems that were encountered in metaphor identification. In fact, writers on metaphor theory often avoid problems by constructing their own metaphors or by choosing examples that are indisputably figurative. Few studies require the identification of all metaphors in a piece of discourse. The standard procedure for a researcher undertaking a task of identifying instances of a phenomenon in data would be to construct a working definition of the unit, an operationalization, which is then used as a template against which possible instances can be judged. It is conventional to check on the identification procedure with intra-rater and inter-rater reliability measures, in which the researcher carries out the procedure again on some part of the data, or has another person carry out the procedure, and the outcomes are checked against each other.

Taking a prosaic approach and using spoken discourse data meant that, beyond the most obvious metaphors, there were many borderline instances where metaphor slid into non-figurative comparison or extension of use and meaning. Decisions needed to be made about each of these borderline cases. It seemed that the more closely the transcripts were examined, the greater the number of possible metaphors. The borderline cases far outnumbered the certain cases, to the extent that the existence of a real category began to seem questionable. Each time I carried out an inter-rater reliability check, further possible instances of metaphor arose and disagreements were sometimes difficult to resolve.

When such problems arise with the basic category under study, it is important to consider why this is happening. It might be that the operationalization was not adequate and needed tightening. I explain in the next sections how this possibility was addressed. However, there may be deeper reasons for the problems and this, I believe, is the case with metaphor. The difficulties indicate real theoretical issues that spring from assumptions about the nature of metaphor. To resolve them we need to revise our view of metaphor and how it works in language use. I return to this theme as the book progresses.

Establishing the category 'linguistic metaphor'

An operationalized construct that is to be identified and counted should ideally be described through statements of necessary and sufficient conditions that fully describe a category. The necessary conditions identify all possible cases, and the sufficient conditions exclude some of those possible cases. What is left, in this ideal world, is a set or category that includes all examples of the construct and no examples of anything else. Such a category is a 'classical category' of the type used in mathematics and logic (Lakoff 1987). In this section, we begin to confront the problems of describing language use in terms of such categories.

A necessary condition for linguistic metaphor is the presence in the discourse of a focus term or Vehicle, a word or phrase that is clearly anomalous or incongruous against the surrounding discourse. So when the teacher told the pupils in the dancing lesson *you are* <u>*spokes in a wheel*</u>, the phrase <u>*spokes in a wheel*</u> could be identified as marking the presence of linguistic metaphor. The first step in metaphor identification is then to identify possible Vehicle terms, that have the potential for incongruity, either semantically as in this example, or pragmatically, in the sense that the discourse context would disallow a non-figurative meaning. An example of pragmatic incongruity would be the teacher's declaration, in the same dancing practice, that *you deserve a medal*. This could have been a literal statement if medals were indeed being competed for. However, my knowledge of the dancing event that they were practising for included the fact that it was a celebration of May Day rather than a competition, and that no medals were to be given. The teacher's phrase was thus counted as metaphorical.

A further necessary condition is that the incongruity produced by the Vehicle term can be resolved by some 'transfer of meaning' from the Vehicle to the Topic, where 'transfer' is used in a loose sense that can be described theoretically as 'interaction' or 'conceptual blending'. In the first example, *spokes in a wheel* can be made sense of in the discourse context by finding a parallel between the abstract shape of a wheel and the shape made by the dancers on the dance floor.

Vehicle incongruity and possibility of meaning transfer are necessary conditions for the presence of linguistic metaphor, but they are not sufficient. However, the reality of language in use seems to rule out the possibility of producing a precise and finite set of sufficient conditions that will delineate a classical category 'linguistic metaphor'. Language in use is continually stretched and bent, words are used to do new things in slightly different ways, in processes that produce gradation and outlaw the possibility of bounded categories in language (Pawley and Syder 1983). People use incongruous terms by mistake or for fun. Language users create new words or new uses for existing words. At the time of writing this book, radio presenters can be heard using prepositions as nouns and adjectives as verbs in phrases such as *a big up to John* (= greetings to John) or *we were larging it* (= having a good time), while new social or technical developments require the invention of totally new words. We find meanings that were not intended and we interpret the same phrase in more than one way to enjoy 'double entendres' or puns.

This problem of finding necessary and sufficient conditions for metaphor identification was recognized by Black back in 1979. Ortony (1979) suggested that metaphors may be better seen as linked through family resemblances, with no common property but 'complicated network(s) of similarities, overlapping and criss-crossing' (Wittgenstein 1953: 1–56). As discussed in Cameron (1999b), it may be useful to use the working assumption that 'metaphor' is not a unitary phenomenon and to adopt a family-resemblance approach. To develop the implications of this proposal for the identification of metaphor in discourse requires a theoretical interlude in the middle of this empirical section.

A family-resemblance approach to metaphor identification

When we compare family-resemblance categories with classical categories, we find three important differences (Wittgenstein 1953; Lakoff 1987), each with implications for a family-resemblance categorization of 'linguistic metaphor'. First, the members of a family-resemblance category, or, in Lakoff's terminology, a 'cognitive' category (1987: 56), do not necessarily share common properties, but can resemble each other in a range of different ways. There will be types of language use that we label as different types of 'metaphor' and that relate to each other in different ways. A useful outcome of a study of prosaic discourse would be a description of different types of 'metaphor' and how they relate to each other.

A second distinction between family-resemblance and classical categories lies in the boundedness of the category. Classical categories are bounded and finite; family-resemblance categories are open because new variations can develop, or relations can be noticed or constructed that produce new links between types. We can note that, in being open and unbounded, family-resemblance categories are like complex systems. Limits can be placed on family-resemblance categories to produce bounded sets, as mathematicians might do for the concept 'number' (Wittgenstein 1953: 32). It is important to note that rigid boundaries to family-resemblance categories are imposed, and are generally imposed for specific purposes: mathematicians need to limit the category 'number' in order to develop theorems about 'number'. In the process of identifying metaphor, boundaries will need to be imposed on categories; in each case, it will be important that the boundaries, and the purposes that underpin them, are made explicit.

With this in mind, we can also re-assess theories of metaphor for the particular boundaries that were placed on the category 'metaphor' in developing the theory, explicitly or implicitly. A further implication is the need to be aware of the limits of theory that result from the imposition of category boundaries: we cannot automatically transfer theory about strong poetic metaphor to weaker, more prosaic metaphor.

The third distinction that may have an impact on the study of prosaic metaphor is the idea that family-resemblance categories often have prototypical or central members (Lakoff 1987). In metaphor studies, strong, active poetic metaphors have commonly been placed at the centre of the category as prototypes. In this book, too, poetic metaphors have been used as a starting point to think about other types of metaphor. The process of identifying metaphor can begin by identifying metaphors in talk that resemble poetic metaphors, as do the examples *spokes in a wheel* and *deserving a medal*. Instances in the data may, though, resemble the central type in various ways, and these different types of resemblance may lead to different subcategories of 'metaphor'. The process of identification also becomes a process of exploration of the data, as specific types of metaphor are labelled and included in the larger, more general category. In Chapter 1, the theoretical categories of substitution and comparison metaphors were identified as specific types of the more general category metaphor, and contrasted with metaphors that work through some kind of 'interaction'. The data-based work to be carried out should produce empirically grounded subcategories that form the family-resemblance category of 'linguistic metaphor'. Having identified such categories, we may wish to readjust what we see as prototypical.

The theoretical shift to thinking of metaphor as a family-resemblance category results in a shift in the aims of the empirical study. We are no longer counting instances of something cut-and-dried. Instead, we are exploring the category metaphor in spoken discourse with the hope that, by refining how the category can be described in terms of specific types related to the general construct in various ways, we add to the understanding of how people use metaphor in specific discourse contexts.

Strengthening analyst decisions in a family-resemblance approach

The adoption of a family-resemblance approach has an impact on research methods. Since there is no longer a pre-existing, watertight category to be 'found' in the data, the identification procedure is not unlike catching fish with a net. Our main methodological concerns are not with making sure the holes in the net are the right size (validity) or that the casting and pulling in of the net are done efficiently (reliability). In order to explore the data for possible subcategories and their relationships, the procedure becomes a recursive and convergent process of analysing parts of the data, considering and refining the categorization possibilities, and revisiting the data for further analysis.

The first step – establishing the necessary conditions of Vehicle incongruity and meaning transfer – can be strengthened by using converging sources of evidence and accuracy checks. The analyst's knowledge is one source, and includes both knowledge of the language and knowledge of the context. Further linguistic sources of evidence can be used to check out intuitions, and information now available from large corpora of English such as The Bank of English offers possibilities for metaphor researchers (Stubbs 1996; Kintsch 1998; Deignan 1999a). The Cobuild dictionary (Collins COBUILD 1995) was consulted to check out the relative frequency of various senses of Vehicle items. A more detailed check of frequencies of co-occurrence, measured as 't-scores' (Hunston and Francis 1998), was carried out for just a few Topic and Vehicle items, and proved useful in checking intuitions about conventionality of metaphors, for example that the Topic–Vehicle combination, *buying time*, is much less frequent than other expressions around the same Topic, *spend / waste time*.

Accuracy in identification was increased (intra-rater reliability) through repeated checking of the data over several years, and through the use of a computer concordancer (Longman Mini-Concordancer 1989). The transcribed data were stripped down to bare text by removing pause markings and other symbols, and could then be searched by the concordancer to find all instances of specific words or phrases. This proved particularly important for very common or indexical words.

A further important strengthening of the identification procedures was the use of several other raters. The inter-rater reliability procedures involve something much more than the cross-checking of accuracy. As explained in the next section, they can become an integral part of the recursive process of moving between data and categories to converge on a 'final' set of metaphors.

Inter-rater procedures

As we have seen, inter-rater reliability checks require the presence of classical categories that are assumed to exist in the 'scientific' research paradigm. When we move to work with family-resemblance categories, the nature of the procedure shifts, but the importance of having other researchers work on the data remains. Their independence from the research project helps ensure that the work is, as far as possible, free of bias or manipulation. It is all too easy for the committed researcher to view data over-optimistically and find things in it that may be less convincing to others.

Inter-rater reliability basically requires another researcher to go through the same procedures with a sample of the data. The identification outcomes of the two raters are then compared, usually quantitatively, to give a measure of reliability. If Rater 1 identifies 100 instances of a phenomenon, and Rater 2 agrees with 78, the inter-rater reliability is said to be 78 per cent. A rate of around 75 per cent or more is usually considered acceptable. Not surprisingly, given the discussions in previous sections, such quantitative checks proved less than helpful in this study; the major contribution of the procedures lay in increasingly refined descriptions of categories and category boundaries.

Samples of the data were checked at least four times by other metaphor researchers in what has become a process of gradual approximation towards agreement. At each stage, the same data sample was used – the transcription of the geology lesson, about 2.5K words or just under 10 per cent of the total data.

In the first round of checking, I identified 25 metaphors. Rater 2 agreed with 17 of these. However, in addition to the 8 that only I had identified, there were a further 12 that Rater 2 identified, making 20 possible metaphors that we disagreed about. Most of the disagreements were discussed and resolved; some had just been missed, and a large group of the disagreements were personifications, e.g. *the temperature acts upon the rock*. A decision was taken to include personifications as linguistic metaphors, on the basis that they may represent a child-like way of thinking and talking that has to be adjusted for the development of 'scientific concepts' (Vygotsky 1962). A further set of disagreements related to delexical verbs, e.g. *got*; their identification was tightened up. With the addition of metaphors from the first round of cross-checking, the total number of metaphors in the transcript was now 42.

In the second round of checking I used another metaphor researcher. In this exercise, Rater 3 identified 78 metaphors, with 27 that we both agreed on. The number of metaphors over which there was agreement between all three raters was just 17. These figures make a little more sense when some of the instances of language use are shown in their discourse context. The lesson that was analysed included a section in which the teacher explained to the children the meaning of the word 'classification'. In order to do this, she had a small number of children stand up and then grouped them according to their sex, hair colour and so on. The children were moved around to demonstrate different classifications. As the demonstration proceeded, the teacher spoke instructions aloud as a support to the children's understanding:

> let's <u>have</u> Mark and we'll <u>have</u> Cheryl here
>
> you can <u>put</u> them together because . . . they're humans

The children were grouped and regrouped five times altogether on different criteria. Rater 3 identified the verbs *have* and *put* as linguistic metaphors on the grounds that they are used here with people rather than with concrete objects as in their primary sense, and each was used between four and eight times. In the teacher's demonstration the children were actually moved around, and my final decision was to exclude the uses of the verb that referred to real and concrete *having* and *putting*.

The third inter-rater check involved me (Rater 1), Raters 2 and 3, and Rater 4, also a metaphor researcher. This time the group worked through a part of the transcript together, discussing each possible metaphor at some length, and trying to use the identification criteria set out in Steen (1999a), which are very similar to those of the study. When disagreements occurred, the group drew on evidence – from corpus data, from translation into other languages known to the group, and their extensive previous experience – in an effort to justify a potential mapping across incongruent domains. By this stage, with the addition of a further set of personification metaphors and delexicalized phrasal verbs, the set of linguistic metaphors in the lesson totalled 65.

In a fourth round of checking, Rater 4 examined the whole of the geology lesson transcript and identified 167 instances of linguistic metaphor. It might seem that things were getting worse rather than better at this point! However, 58 of my 65 were agreed on, and the disagreements were mostly about items I had excluded. Sixteen suggested inclusions did not for me satisfy the minimal necessary conditions of two different domains and transfer of meaning. The remaining problematic decisions were generated by large numbers of very frequent items such as *get, on, in, do*, including the uses of *put* and *have* that had been excluded at an earlier stage. Having made further decisions, I added 17 linguistic metaphors and excluded one. Concordance searches added a further 11, not spotted by any of the raters, mostly involving *in*. The 'final' total was 98. The set of metaphors identified in the sample of data is given in Appendix 1.

The disagreements between raters centred on the following issues, which each produced categories or category boundaries of importance for the study of metaphor in discourse (discussed in more detail later):

- technical language
- personification
- context-related decisions
- conventionalized senses of words
- delexicalized verbs
- prepositions
- comparisons

The disagreements and changes in the identification process were about the most prosaic metaphors – the indexical and delexicalized verbs, and prepositions. The most difficult decisions related to the most frequent items, and thus make the most difference to the total numbers. Quantification seems inherently unreliable, although the recursive process of decision-making, comparison with other raters, and concordance searching led eventually to a fairly stable figure across the whole data set.

The identification difficulties have illustrated the process of 'metaphorizing' that occurs when a word is used frequently in discourse. Small but continual metaphorical shifts take place in word sense as it is used in slightly different linguistic contexts. We notice metaphorical use either when a large, often deliberate shift is made, or, more prosaically, when many small shifts have moved the sense of a word away from its core sense and use.

Data analysis: category decisions

This section reports the range of decisions that needed to be made about what should count as 'metaphor' in the spoken discourse data. They are included so that future studies can replicate the analysis, or at least decide explicitly which decisions to follow and which to adjust.

Excluding errors

There were a few uses of language in the discourse that produced an incongruity that could have been a metaphor, but that most likely happened because of a slip of the tongue:

> a slither of rock [for sliver]

There were not many instances, and in each case there was no evidence that a metaphorical meaning could be made relevant in the discourse context, so the second necessary condition was not fulfilled.

Technical language

Kittay (1987), who pointed out the need to remove errors, also suggests removing uses of language that arise from the shared discourse world of speakers. Her (theoretical) argument is that, within the discourse world, such language is not metaphorical, although it may seem so from the outside. The data included school-level technical discourse, such as (from the maths lessons):

> 2 and 3 <u>make</u> 5
> the <u>difference</u> between 6 and 4 is 2

Because the studies were concerned with children in formal education, I decided not to follow Kittay and to include technical language as metaphor if it satisfied the necessary conditions of possible incongruity and meaning transfer. Children have to learn the discourse of the subjects they study as part of entering into the subject, and when they encounter new technical language, they may well try out metaphorical interpretations if it carries that possibility (recall the weather forecaster's spells in Chapter 1).

To avoid confusion, I should explain that this decision reverses that set out in Cameron (1999b), where technical language was excluded from the category 'metaphor'. One of the reasons that pushed me in the direction of this change of mind was the experience of presenting simple technical texts to second-language users of English (Cameron 2001b) and seeing how difficult it was for them to find the boundary between technical language created through metaphor and non-technical, but metaphorical, uses of language. Because the study has educational purposes as well as linguistic purposes, the exclusion of technical language was reversed. This is a good example of how the category depends on the purposes and boundary decisions of the analyst.

Animating metaphors

Some animating metaphors, including the subset of personification metaphors, were initially excluded and then included. Many of the explanations of natural processes in the geology lesson used verbs that characterized processes as deliberate action by an agent:

> minerals that <u>come out of</u> rocks
> where's my rubber [= eraser] <u>gone</u>?
> granites are <u>laid down</u>
> steps that <u>go down from</u> Binns [name of a shop]

Such animation or personification is a kind of 'grammatical metaphor' (Halliday 1985), although I have preferred not to deal with it in terms of deviation from some primary grammatical form, but to make a semantic case. We can see this as a type of metaphor in which the domain of the verb would, in a primary semantic sense, involve animate collocates. The Topic domains are not animate, and so we can argue that there exists an incongruity.

Again, an educational argument persuaded me that animating metaphors should be included. If we want to understand how metaphorical use of language affects thinking, then it may be important to explore how animation and personification are used, and how children are helped to move beyond animation to a technical or scientific understanding of a process.

Decisions affected by other metaphors

While pragmatic and discourse contextual frames influenced every decision about metaphor, some decisions were made on the basis of the presence of other metaphors.

As an example, we can consider the use of the word *way*. This was a frequently occurring item in the discourse, often in phrases such as

> *there's another way we could do it*

Rater 3 also categorized *way* as a metaphor, contrasting it with a non-metaphorical use referring to a physical direction. I had in my earlier identification first excluded this word, then included it and finally decided to include some uses of this word and exclude others. The difficulty lies in deciding whether the sense of *way* as *method of doing something* has become so conventionalized that it has lost possible transfer of meaning from a domain relating to the sense of *path*. The COBUILD dictionary presents 93 senses of *way*, the first ten of which relate to *method*, suggesting that this is the most common use.

However, in a stretch of maths talk about how to calculate the length of a field, *way* was used with several other metaphors that were much more strongly metaphorical and also related to the domain of *travelling* and *distance*:

> how might we <u>arrive at</u> a fairly accurate result?. . .
> you might do it that <u>way</u>
> you could do it that <u>way</u>
> you've <u>arrived at</u> a figure
> let's do it <u>the long way</u> [division]
> we'll <u>stop at</u> eight just for now

In such a linguistic context (which also linked to the physical context which took them outside to the field to measure it in strides), a *journey* schema may be activated by the co-occurrence of several words relating to the domain. As the 'semantic prosody' (Louw 1993) spreads across the discourse, a normally afigurative word like *way* seems to become more clearly metaphorical. I decided that when the discourse context strengthened the metaphoricity of *way*, it would be included, but other isolated uses would be excluded.

It might be argued that if one use of an item is included or excluded, then all further uses of the same word should be treated in the same way, but, as this example shows, each instance needs to be considered in its micro-level discourse context. Metaphoricity does not inhere in the word or even necessarily in the Topic–Vehicle contrast, but can increase and decrease through the nearby use of other words related to the Vehicle domain and also through non-linguistic or non-verbalized phenomena (see 'parapraxis' p. 138).

Metaphor and metonymy

> I want <u>all your eyes looking at</u> me

In this example, the possibility of metaphor arises because the teacher is demanding the pupils' attention and uses the Vehicle domain of *eyes/looking* to talk about the Topic domain of *attention*. However, at the same time, the utterance is literally true. The phrase *eyes looking at me* is a metonymy, in fact a synecdoche, because part of attention is used in order to refer to the whole. Such examples were included in the count of metaphors when, as here, the distinctiveness of Topic and Vehicle domain could be argued for.

In some cases, the boundary between metaphorical and non-metaphorical metonymy depended on linguistic and discourse context. For example, the verb *see* was used metaphorically to mean *understand* and *find out,* as in

> I <u>see</u> what you mean
> <u>see</u> if any bells ring [= find out if you remember]

It was also used metaphorically to mean *find out/understand,* but at the same time metonymically, in that vision was involved:

> <u>see</u> what you can do
> I've been able to <u>see</u> what their problem is

As the vision sense became slightly stronger, and the finding out sense weakened, some expressions seemed to be on the edge of metaphoricity, as when the teacher walked around the class looking at pupils' books and warning them about drawing lines neatly:

> I don't want to <u>see</u> any lines drawn [without a ruler]

In analysing the data, it was not possible therefore just to decide that all instances of the verb *see* would be included or excluded as metaphor; instead, each occurrence had to be checked and a case made for inclusion or exclusion.

Idiomaticity and metaphor

Over sociohistorical time, the dynamics of language change shift some words and phrases from being consciously metaphorical to merely conventional. Traditional metaphor theory would describe these as 'dead' metaphors, but research in cognitive metaphor suggests that so-called dead metaphors may draw on active conceptual mappings in processing (Gibbs 1994). In identifying linguistic metaphors in discourse, we must make decisions in the absence of processing information, and my general principle was to include words or phrases that included the possibility of a cross-domain mapping. However, here too boundary issues must be faced.

An interesting problem arose with the phrase *a bit*, and its antonym, *a lot*. The latter was not considered for inclusion as metaphor, although its etymology shows that *a lot* was originally *a portion* or *share*. *A bit* was identified by two of the three external raters as metaphorical. It was used in the following ways:

> to quantify abstract nouns:
> *a bit of time/thought*
> *a good little bit of memory*
> *a little bit of history/information*
> *a little bit more description*
>
> to premodify an adjective:
> *a bit tired/mean/dark/thick/depressing*
>
> as an adverb:
> *go back just a bit*
> *straighten up a bit*
> *pulled up a bit*

Each of these might be said to be metaphorical if the primary sense of *bit* is taken to be 'a small amount of something quantifiable or concrete'. However, the data contain only one instance of *a bit* used with something concrete: *a bit of air freshener*, and the (attested) examples in the COBUILD dictionary are overwhelmingly non-concrete. It appears that *a bit* is very seldom used with its concrete sense, as in the (constructed) example: *a bit of cake*. I suspect that in British English, as *bit* has moved into metaphorical use, the more or less synonymous word *piece* has become the way the idea is produced non-metaphorically.

Conventionalization has then at least two aspects: frequency of choice by, and familiarity to, language users, both of which may dull its metaphorical edge; and the possibility of using the word in other ways, which may disappear as metaphoricity aligns with a particular form in the evolution of a language (Deignan 1999b). In 10 or 20 years, *a bit* may be treated in the same way as *a lot*, and be classed as non-metaphorical because it has become so conventionalized in both ways. Meanwhile, it seems to be on the cusp in its evolution, and so the analyst may choose to include it, on the grounds described above, or to exclude it, on the grounds of its parallel with *a lot* and its limited non-metaphorical possibilities. My decision was again motivated by the educational purposes of the study and my observation that it was often softened to *a little bit*, as part of a general trend to minimize the cognitive demands placed on pupils. This seemed to make it worthy of further examination.

Verbs as metaphor Vehicles

A focus term that indicates a metaphor can, as we have seen, be a word or a phrase, and can contain nouns, verbs, or words from any other word class. The notion of Topic and Vehicle works most effectively, however, for nouns. A concept domain is most easily understood if labelled by a noun that refers to an entity and its underlying concept. So, in the type of linguistic metaphor most often selected by theorists, two nouns are connected metaphorically: *Juliet is the sun*. The tradition of adopting the noun as prototypical has been continued in the cognitive theory of metaphor, where conceptual metaphors, as an abstract mapping between domains, are denoted by nouns + copula, e.g. LOVE IS A JOURNEY.

Verbs, on the other hand, do not express reference, but prototypically in discourse express relations between entities (Gentner 1978; Hopper and Thompson 1984). As a result, when verbs are used metaphorically, something more complicated happens than a mapping from one concept domain to another, and the condition of incongruity needs some modification in order to be applied to verbs, and also to prepositions. Verbs in English are extended, metaphorically and non-metaphorically, by being used with collocates beyond the most basic and typical. The new collocates push the verb into a slightly different meaning. To illustrate this, we can take the verb *plough*, and consider two sentences

> the horse ploughs the field
> the tractor ploughs the field

The concept underlying the lexical verb would have a slightly different content in the two cases, for example, the speed of the process and the nature of the furrows. The collocated noun affects the meaning of the verb. A similar thing happens when the verb is used metaphorically:

> *the ship ploughs the waves* [from Brooke-Rose 1958]

The concept domain for *ploughs* that would contain *tractors* or *horses, fields* and *earth*, is distinct from the domain that contains *ships* and *waves*. In order to identify the metaphoricity of the verb, it is necessary to move away from the verb to the nouns which collocate as Subject and Object of the verb. The case for identifying a verb as a focus of a linguistic metaphor is made, not just from the lexical meaning of the verb but from the incongruity between the domain of the conventional or expected collocated nouns and the domain of the collocates that appear in the discourse.

A further example demonstrates the need to consider the collocating nouns when identifying metaphor. Consider the different senses of the verb *throw* that emerge when different nouns are collocated as Object (all examples from COBUILD dictionary, 1995):

> *The crowd began throwing stones*
> *He threw Brian a rope*
> *Economic recession had thrown millions out of work*
> *Why not throw a party for your friends?*

In the first two examples, slightly different movements are involved but the uses of the verb share the idea of physical movement using the arms and a concrete object. In the last two examples, the physical movement and the concrete O(o)bject have disappeared, and the verb is being used metaphorically.

The use of conventional or typical collocates to decide on the presence of metaphor also helps with the most common and most delexicalized verbs, such as *make, get, do, have, put*, which are said to have multiple uses but minimal meaning (Sinclair 1991). The frequency of these verbs in any discourse in English entails that decisions whether or not to count any of their uses as metaphorical will have a large impact on quantified data. For each of these most frequent verbs, one sense was selected to act as 'primary' or 'core', and uses that invoked distinct conceptual domains then counted as metaphor. With delexicalized verbs (and with prepositions, see p. 73), the sense most strongly physical and concrete was selected as primary, against which metaphoricity would be judged:

> *go*   physical movement towards concrete object
> *make* construct + concrete object
> *have* possess + concrete object/feature, or experience + event
> *get* receive + concrete object
> *put* place + concrete object

Uses of the verbs with abstract collocating nouns rather than concrete ones could then be considered as metaphorical. Full details of the process of identifying metaphorical uses of the verb *have* are given in Cameron (1999b).

A few of the most indexical or delexicalized verbs were excluded altogether: *do, have got* and *get* with the sense of *become*, on the grounds that they are so frequent and used with so many different collocates that any primary, non-metaphorical sense is extremely hard to pin down and distinguish from other uses.

Prepositions as metaphor Vehicles

A similar process of placing boundaries had to be carried out with prepositions. Most of the possible metaphorical uses of prepositions occurred as phrases, like *off her own bat*, or in combination with verbs, as in *get on with it*, rather than as single words. But there were instances where the use of a preposition could be considered as a linguistic metaphor, e.g. *how many 9s in 909?* and *getting through this book*. Again, justification for including these as metaphors lies in incongruity between the domain of the preposition's collocates and that of its collocates when used with its primary sense. The primary sense of a preposition was taken to be the physical/spatial, as in Quirk and Greenbaum (1975: 153) for *in* and Lakoff (1987) for *over*. Other prepositions for which physical/spatial senses can be identified were: *from, off, through, on, on to, up, down, behind, in front of, into, after, between*. Some prepositions have become so delexicalized that they cannot practically be attributed a primary sense – *of, for, with*.

To illustrate the process of identification of preposition metaphors, we can look at *through*. It was used 17 times in the data with a range of uses from literal to metaphorical as displayed in these examples:

(A)	the liquid	goes	through	the tube
(B)	we	got	through	passport control
(C)		turning	through	four right angles
(D)		to walk	through	[a dance]
(E)	could I just	go	through	what you managed to do [= written work]
(F)		getting	through	this book
(G)	I	'm halfway	through	[writing about] *day three*

Example (A) shows the primary sense of *through*: moving internally from one position to another position relative to a hollow or permeable object that forms an enclosed space (the Complement NP of the PP). (B) and (C) involve physical movement with noun phrases that verge on the abstract rather than, or as well as, the concrete. In (D), there is no concrete object, but *dance* metonymically refers to the stages or positions of a dance; there is an air of metaphor about *through a dance*.

In (E), (F) and (G), the preposition no longer collocates with a concrete enclosed space and the Topic is intellectual processes of reading and writing. (E), (F) and (G) were thus counted as metaphors.

Comparisons as metaphors

As we saw in Chapter 1, the theoretical view of metaphor as an implicit comparison or reduced simile has been criticized as being too narrow and because it downplays the creativity of interpreting metaphors by finding similarities where they did not previously exist. However, the data produced uses of language in which two unlike things or ideas were brought together in a statement of comparison, which satisfy the two necessary conditions of domain incongruity and meaning transfer:

> the rock . . . becomes . . . like sticky treacle

A possible reason for excluding this and similar examples from the category of linguistic metaphor is that the comparison is literal: *treacle* and *hot rocks* are alike in their consistency.

The presence of the word *like* is not sufficient to indicate that this is not a metaphor, in spite of the type of superficial definitions of 'metaphor' and 'simile' that are sometimes found, e.g. in school textbooks. Some similes may involve quite obviously metaphorical comparisons, as in Eliot's

> the evening . . . spread out against the sky / Like a patient etherized upon a table

(quoted by Kittay 1987: 18). However, comparisons can vary in the degree and type of similarity and comparability that can be found between the two entities referred to. Ortony (1979a) contrasts the literal comparison *a wolf is like a dog* with the figurative or metaphorical comparison *a man is like a wolf*.

My inclination is to include all but the most obviously non-metaphorical comparisons as linguistic metaphor. So, *the campsite was like a holiday village* is excluded but *the rock becomes like sticky treacle* is included. The subset of comparison metaphors that are found in the data can then be further studied.

Category decisions: conclusions

It will be clear that metaphor in language use is an extremely complicated and multi-faceted phenomenon. Identifying linguistic metaphor in discourse is not a trivial task, and each decision made by the analyst will have knock-on effects on totals and on other aspects of analysis. Decisions can be strengthened by seeking out a range of sources of information, by checking through the data several times, and by having others check samples of the data. It is essential that decisions are explicitly described, both for replication and so that findings can be properly understood.

In this study at least, identification was not a process that could be carried out quickly before engaging with the 'real business' of the research. It raised fundamental questions about the nature of metaphor and contributed to theory development. In the process of sifting categories for identification, the following sub-types of linguistic metaphor were identified:

- 'strong'/prototypical linguistic metaphors: identified by all raters, with fewest problems;
- technical metaphors: subject-specific language constructed through metaphorizing non-technical language;
- animating metaphors: non-human processes described as orchestrated by an agent;
- metaphors of different grammatical form, including verb and preposition metaphors;
- comparison metaphors: two incongruous domains are brought together to make an explicit comparison.

These subcategories have 'emerged' in the complex systems sense of not being intrinsic to the necessary conditions for linguistic metaphor that we started with. In this, they are early stage 'findings' and remind us that as soon as we begin to make decisions about analysis, we have begun to do analysis. These subcategories can be used to help answer Research Question 1 on the nature of metaphor in classroom talk, as we investigate their size, nature and role in more detail across the whole data set in the following chapter.

Data analysis: lexical content and grammatical form of linguistic metaphors

The set of linguistic metaphors identified in the data was further analysed for lexical content and grammatical form. These were 'product' analyses, treating the linguistic metaphors as static 'pieces' of discourse. However, some of the analyses relate one metaphor use to another, and in this linking of products we begin to develop a picture of the process of metaphor use. A fuller process perspective required a dynamic analysis, described in the next section.

Metaphor types and tokens

Each instance of a metaphor, i.e. of a particular Topic and Vehicle lexical combination, was counted as a 'metaphor token'. Alongside the very frequent metaphorical use of some delexical verbs already noted, more schematic metaphor Vehicles were also often repeated, partly reflecting the tendency for participants to re-use lexis in spoken discourse (McCarthy 1988; Tannen 1989). To gain a picture of repetition and re-use of specific linguistic metaphors, the number of 'metaphor types', i.e. distinct lexical pairs of Topic + Vehicle items, was also counted and the ratio of tokens to types calculated.

Lexical content of Vehicle terms

Cognitive metaphor theory predicts that the mappings of conceptual metaphors lead to the presence in discourse of sets of linguistic metaphors with systematically connected Vehicle lexical content. Vehicle lexis was analysed for patterns across the discourse, to look for evidence of systematic metaphor use in the classroom discourse.

Lexical content of Topic terms

Research Question 2 (how metaphor is used for mediating thinking, learning, affect and action) was partly addressed by analysis of the topics that were spoken of metaphorically. Certain topics, e.g. mental arithmetic processes and scientific concepts of literacy, were selected, and the Vehicle terms used to talk about them across the discourse events analysed.

The grammar of the Vehicle term

Single word Vehicle terms were described by their word class:

Noun	a <u>blanket</u> of gases
Verb	a circle that <u>says</u>
Adjective	any <u>wasted</u> time
Adverb	it won't take <u>long</u>
Preposition	getting <u>through</u> this book

Multi-word, phrase level Vehicle terms were classified by the word class of the head word in the phrase:

Noun phrase	you're <u>spokes in a wheel</u>
Verb phrase	you've <u>thrown my system</u>
Adjective phrase	you got <u>mixed up</u>
Prepositional phrase	your toes are . . . <u>at five to one</u>

Verb phrase Vehicle terms that comprised a verb and one or more prepositions were grouped together as 'phrasal verbs', e.g. *we're going back to possession*. No distinction was made between verbs with prepositions and verbs with 'particles' following. Further details of the grammatical analysis are presented in Chapter 4 with the findings.

Nominal and verb metaphors

To get a contrasting picture of how nouns and verbs work metaphorically, two further categories were constructed. The category nominal metaphors was formed by putting together metaphors with single word nouns or noun phrase Vehicle terms. The parallel verbal category was called verb metaphors.

Lexical and grammatical analysis of linguistic metaphors: conclusion

The product analyses of the set of linguistic metaphors can take the research only so far. In order to answer the questions of how metaphor is used and how it creates opportunities for thinking and learning, we need also to analyse the pedagogical function of the metaphors and to investigate discourse as dynamic. For example, when the grammatical form of the combined Topic and Vehicle in linguistic metaphors was analysed through the syntactic roles played by the lexical items, certain forms emerged as characteristic for particular types of mediated action in discourse. We now move to the dynamic analysis of the data.

Data analysis: the dynamics of discourse

The previous sections have described how the linguistic metaphors were analysed as 'product' of talk. In this section, we see how metaphor was studied as a process phenomenon in discourse (van Lier 1988). Research Question 2 requires that we attend to the ideational and affective aspects of metaphor use, and that we consider metaphor in the situated, social action of the classroom.

Timescales of metaphor use

A complex systems view of classroom discourse analyses the learning environment and learning opportunities as constructed through the dynamic co-adaptation of the talking and thinking of participants. To do this, we use inter-related timescales of activity to track how change on one scale produces qualitative change on another, for example how an encounter with metaphor might result in a shift in conceptual understanding. The choice of timescales depends on the nature of the phenomenon under investigation (Thelen and Smith 1994), so we need to identify for this study the timescales on which the inter-relation of language use, thinking, learning, affect and action will be analysed, and then the features of metaphor use that will be described on each timescale.

The smallest temporal and discourse unit is the linguistic metaphor, described in terms of the features of content and form as noted in the previous sections. The other unit that has already been established is the discourse event, which is basically a segment of the school day, but which often is labelled by participants as a pedagogical unit, e.g. a maths lesson or dancing practice. In between the metaphor and the event, we have established the timescale on which the unit of analysis is mediated action. Discourse events are in turn units within the larger timescale of the child's school day or school life. On the longer timescales we are interested in how students encounter the metaphors of particular discourse worlds and genres, how metaphors might emerge from interaction in the classroom, and how metaphor contributes to the emergence of new understandings and to the construction of institutional norms. The analysis proceeds by mapping these timescales against each other, and by tracing how action on one level leads to change on another, to try to find out how metaphor creates opportunities for learning in classroom talk. First though we see how the unit of analysis, 'mediated action', was operationalized in the data analysis.

Episodes of mediated action in discourse events

Mediated action is the theoretically derived unit of analysis that takes a pedagogical perspective on the discourse. Mediated action refers to episodes within discourse events in which one participant mediates perceived alterity between participants towards a state of greater shared understanding or 'pragmatic intersubjectivity' (Edwards 1997).

In the discourse that was recorded, all events were teacher-led and there was very little student–student talk. The unit of mediated action that was constructed for the analysis is thus called a 'teaching sequence'; if student–student talk was to be analysed, a similar operationalization process could be followed to construct 'peer talk sequences'.

In a teaching sequence, a particular type of pedagogic activity predominated, creating particular kinds of learning opportunities. The set of teaching sequence types was constructed for the particular data set through a recursive procedure that moved between theory and data, breaking up each discourse event in terms of what teacher and pupils said and did, and adapting descriptors from published work, with the empirically derived categories of Tharp and Gallimore proving most useful (van Lier 1988; Tharp and Gallimore 1988; Mercer 1994; Barnes and Todd 1995; Alexander 1997; Tharp 1993; Wells 1999). At each move between the data and the set of teaching sequences, categories were refined by adding, dividing or combining, until a final set emerged that would serve the whole data set. In interpreting classroom action in this way, I used evidence from the discourse data (e.g. what the teacher explicitly told pupils) and from my field notes (e.g. what pupils did as a result of teacher talk). I also drew on my experience as a teacher and teacher educator in similar classrooms to infer where necessary the goals of teachers' actions.

Each sequence type can be described by a clustering of features of:

- use of language
- action of teacher and pupils
- content, including level of generality of lexis relative to preceding talk

A sequence continues across the discourse until a change of activity, topic or goal.

Each sequence type is now described in turn, using examples from the data. The set of teaching sequences is summarized in Table 3.3.

1. Framing

The use of language for procedural purposes or 'framing' (Bateson 1972; Goffman 1974; van Lier 1988) is covered by two categories – organization and agenda management – that make a distinction between procedures about classroom objects and procedures around content.

1.1 Organization

Language is used to give pupils instructions or information about the logistics of the classroom or lesson 'hardware' (chairs, pencils, worksheets, etc.)

    so (.) looking at the first sheet   (geology lesson)

1.2 Agenda management

The teacher talks about what will happen in a discourse event. At the beginning of lessons, pupils and teacher might negotiate the content or process of a lesson or task; at the end of a lesson, the teacher might look forward to the next one. This type of talk includes 'task structuring' (Tharp, 1993), in which the teacher adjusts or modifies what students are to do. The topic is not realia, but ideas, concepts, mental activity, etc.

> *what I'm going to do this afternoon*   (geology lesson)
> *(1.0) . . . is give you (.) a little bit of*
> *information*

2. Explanation

In these sequences, the teacher uses language to explain the whole or part of a concept, idea, action, skill, activity, etc. to the pupils. Tharp (1993: 272) labels this 'cognitive structuring'. For example, in the geology lesson, the teacher, having used the word 'classification' on a worksheet, realized that she needed to explain this to pupils. Explanation was done in two main ways – explication and exemplification.

2.1 Explication

Direct, verbal explanation, often using declarative verbs. For concepts, this involved talking about attributes or relations of concepts:

> *you can be part of (.) one classification group (1.0) and then lo and behold you can be part (.) of another*

2.2 Exemplification

Use of an example, talk or realia to explain more about the concept or to give 'a remembered image' (Tharp 1993: 272). This often involves a move from abstract to concrete, or general to specific, and use of a linguistic marker such as *for example, say.*

> *for example (1.0) if I give you a dish (.)*   (geology lesson)
> *that's full of coloured marbles and plain*
> *marbles (.) and asked you to classify them*
> *. . .*

> *we're talking about the pencil belonging to*   (apostrophe lesson)
> *the boy*

3. Checking understanding

Teacher asks pupils a question about concepts, instructions, etc. in order to check their understanding of previous content. The teacher knows the answer to the question, and it is followed by pupil response, and often teacher feedback in an Initiation-Response-Feedback pattern (Sinclair and Coulthard 1975).

> *you can put them together because. . .?*   (geology lesson)
>
> *what's classification a big word for?*   (geology lesson)

4. Summarizing

Teacher recaps or (re)formulates (Heritage and Watson 1979) all or part of preceding discourse content at the end of a lesson or stage of a lesson. Often linguistically marked by a long pause and the use of *so*. Content lexis is at a higher level of generality than that which immediately precedes it (*things* in the example below). The discourse changes topic after a summarizing sequence.

> *(3.0) so classification (.) is really a way of*   (geology lesson)
> *grouping things together*
>
> *and then it would have a knock on effect*   (class work)

5. Feedback

The topic of this type of sequence is something the pupils have done or said that the teacher responds to. Two main sub-types were distinguished through the nature of the teacher's response – evaluative and strategic.

5.1 Evaluative feedback

Direct comments on the quality of work or performance, often relative to teacher expectations. Often using evaluative lexis:

> P: *does it mean grading?*
> T: *it can mean grading (.) that's that's a*   (geology lesson)
>   *good (.) a good reason*

5.2 Strategic feedback

Teacher suggests how pupils can improve their performance, often using imperatives or modals:

> T: *think before you speak*   (maths lesson)

6. Control

Teacher uses language to stop or pre-empt unwanted behaviour, or to reinforce preferred behaviour in 'contingency management' (Tharp 1993). Identified by preceding pupil behaviour and comment about it. Often uses imperatives.

> *can we not have the little rhyme yelled out*   (dancing practice)
> *loud this time please*

> *will you keep the kettle boiling?* [= keep the   (class work)
> queue for the toilet moving]

7. Problem setting

Teacher presents a problem or part of a problem to pupils through a series of questions that are not to check understanding. Pupil responses are not used to find out what they understand but to build up with the class a joint structuring and solving of a problem. This sequence occurred only in the maths lesson, but is given a separate category because it is not covered adequately by the other types and because it is educationally important. Tharp calls this 'questioning' (1993).

> *is there a way (.) without any apparatus at*   (maths lesson)
> *all (1.0) in which you could find out roughly*
> *(2.0) the length (.) of (.) the field (.) and*
> *back?*

8. Information search

Teacher asks pupils for genuinely unknown information. Content is often tangential to the ongoing lesson content, or there is reference to previous shared discourse.

> *we said that ones would go over first (.)*   (dancing practice)
> *did we?*

9. Other

This is the 'dustbin' category, containing teacher talk not categorizable in other ways. In line with the general aims of categorization of discourse data (Sinclair and Coulthard 1975), this was minimized, and contained mostly teacher asides and interruptions by visitors.

Embedding of teaching sequences

Each discourse event was analysed into teaching sequences. The lesson events could be broken down into stages. The less structured class work events contained bursts of discourse activity that could be analysed in this way, interspersed with independent writing work by

Table 3.3 *Types of teaching sequence*

---

1. FRAMING
   1.1 ORGANIZATION
   Teacher gives instructions or information about hardware and logistics of classroom activity.

   1.2 AGENDA MANAGEMENT
   Teacher talks about the content or process of an upcoming discourse event.

2. EXPLANATION
   2.1 EXPLICATION
   Teacher explains a concept, action, skill, etc. to pupils.

   2.2 EXEMPLIFICATION
   Teacher uses language, realia, or physical action to give an example of a concept, idea, etc.

3. CHECKING UNDERSTANDING
   Teacher asks question to check understanding of previous discourse content.

4. SUMMARIZING
   Teacher recaps or reformulates all or part of preceding discourse content at the end of a lesson or stage of a lesson.

5. FEEDBACK
   5.1 EVALUATIVE FEEDBACK
   Teacher comments on quality of pupils' work or performance.

   5.2 STRATEGIC FEEDBACK
   Teacher suggests how to improve performance.

6. CONTROL
   Teacher uses language to stop or pre-empt unwanted behaviour.

7. PROBLEM SETTING
   Teacher helps pupils to solve a problem through asking them a set of questions whose responses build up a structuring and solution to the problem.

8. INFORMATION SEARCH
   Teacher asks for genuinely unknown information.

9. OTHER
   Teacher talk not covered by the other categories.

---

students. However, teaching sequences do not occur in neat linear fashion in the discourse data and it is not possible to break down even the most coherent lesson in a reductionist way. The teacher might, for example, begin an explanation of one idea, then, realizing that students have a problem, she may give an example to clarify one aspect of the idea. That aspect is exemplified, the example explained,

Metaphor in educational discourse

and the information given in this side-sequence summarized, before the discussion moves back to the original larger idea to continue explanation. In the following extract from the geology lesson, the teacher side-tracks from the more general topic of *igneous rocks* to a specific example of a volcano familiar to the children:

Extract 3.1 *Embedding of teaching sequences*

Transcribed talk	Teaching sequences
T: right (.) let's go back (.) to these rocks (1.0) fire formed (2.0) I think you probably all know (.) how (.) igneous rocks comes to be formed (2.0) you should know this (1.0) you love watching this on the telly (.) and if one starts working again (.) it's very exciting (.) and it's on the news for days (.) in fact I have seen one working recently (1.0) and there's a village (.) in Italy (1.0) and they're dropping things to try and stop the village from being destroyed (3.0) yes (.) Ellen? E: volcano T: yes (.) it's a volcano (1.0) and (2.0) the rocks (.) that are formed by fire	framing: agenda management explanation explication exemplification explication

At other times, practical business intervenes in the middle of a teaching sequence, as when the teacher sends some students off to make more copies of a worksheet.

If we view this phenomenon of embedded sequences from a dynamic systems perspective, we can say that mediated action occurs on interacting timescales, with an embedded sequence following a similar pattern on its smaller scale to the larger sequences it is embedded in. There is a kind of 'fractal' pattern to the mediated action in the event. Something similar – 'insertion sequences' – is familiar to conversation analysts.

Embedding means that we cannot do linear counting, e.g. of how many summarizing sequences occur in the data. But we can look more qualitatively for patterns of metaphor use across these interacting timescales.

Use of metaphor in teaching sequences

An analysis in terms of teaching sequences produced a kind of pedagogical map of a discourse event, onto which the linguistic metaphors could be plotted. This helped me to see how metaphor was used in the construction and organization of the event. Moreover, by analysing metaphor use in each type of teaching sequence across the range of discourse events, it was also possible to investigate the role of metaphor in particular types of teaching action.

This chapter has described how the classroom discourse data were analysed for the use of metaphor within the various timescales, from the metaphorical expression up to discourse event and beyond. The different types of analysis, of form, of content, of pedagogic function and of discourse function produce rich, thick qualitative descriptions, together with some quantitative description, of metaphor in action that will help answer the first two research questions – the nature of metaphor and how metaphor is used to create learning opportunities. In the next chapter the results of the analyses are presented, and a picture of metaphor use in educational discourse will begin to take shape.

4 The linguistic form of metaphor in classroom discourse

Quantitative overview of linguistic metaphors in classroom discourse

This chapter presents the results of the formal product analyses of metaphor: numbers of metaphors and of various linguistic forms of metaphor found. The process analyses reported in the following chapters will give a much richer, qualitative description of metaphor in use.

Chapter 3 explained how linguistic metaphors were identified in the discourse data. This was found to be a problematic task with outcomes highly dependent on decisions taken by the analyst. Notwithstanding these difficulties, some quantitative descriptions will be useful to summarize the nature of the metaphors in the classroom discourse. As Silverman (1993: 163) says, 'simple counting techniques can offer a means to survey the whole corpus of data . . . to gain a sense of the flavour of the data as a whole'.

The products of the identification process formed a 'dataset of linguistic metaphors' that was analysed for frequency of use and for grammatical form. The results presented here should be interpreted in the light of the caveats and decisions described in Chapter 3.

Metaphor density

The 'final' dataset contained 711 instances of linguistic metaphor in the 26,613 words of transcribed discourse, giving a figure for metaphor density in the spoken discourse of 27 metaphors per 1000 words. In the various alternative analyses of the same data, the figures for metaphor density ranged between 14 and 27 per 1000 words.

The figures are at the lower end of the range suggested by the previous studies summarized in Table 3.2. As we saw in Chapter 3, published figures of metaphor density are often rendered useless for further studies because they do not state explicitly how metaphors were identified, what was counted and what was not counted. Although there were many problems in this study in arriving at a category of linguistic metaphor, the range (together with explicit information on identification decisions) offers an indication of metaphor density in spoken discourse that may be useful to other researchers.

Re-use of metaphor

The figure of 711 metaphors includes 346 different Topic–Vehicle combinations, giving a 'type-token ratio' of 0.5, or a re-use of metaphor figure of 2. This calculation smooths out huge variation, from 92 metaphorical uses of *in* to many one-off metaphorical uses of lexical items. The actual nature of repetition and re-use of metaphor is much more interesting when considered qualitatively (see next chapters).

Use by teachers and students

In the recorded and transcribed lessons, only 42 of the metaphors, or 6 per cent, were used by students, while the two teachers between them used 651, or 92 per cent. A small number, 16 or 2 per cent, were read aloud from books or used on the TV programme. The proportion of teacher and student metaphor use reflects the distribution of teacher and student talk in the classroom. There was also a difference between teachers and students in the form and function of metaphors that reflected their different status in the discourse. There was limited, but interesting, evidence of students' reaction to some of their teachers' metaphors (see Chapter 6).

Metaphor density by discourse event

The density of metaphor use in each of the discourse events is shown in Figure 4.1. The variation was due partly to the content of the events and partly to the nature of the events. For example, the lesson on apostrophes included many instances of the metaphor for 'contraction', *shortening the word*. The TV programme included three distinct types of discourse: the narrator's commentary, short stretches of discourse between people in the film clips that were talked about by the narrator, and the short class discussion that followed. The commentary had very few metaphors at all, reducing the overall density in comparison with other events.

The distribution of the linguistic metaphors by form

A first level of analysis of linguistic form asked about the length and word class of the Vehicle terms. The results of this analysis are shown, as a raw count of tokens, in Table 4.1.

Metaphor in educational discourse

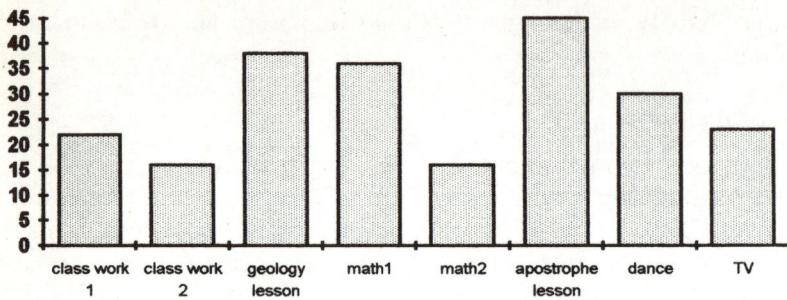

Figure 4.1 *Metaphor density of discourse events*

Table 4.1 *Numbers of metaphors of different linguistic form*

Linguistic form of Vehicle term	Number of metaphors using this form	% of total metaphors
single noun	33	5
noun phrase	70	8
single verb	171	24
verb phrase	26	4
relative pronoun + verb group	10	1
phrasal verb	126	18
single adjective	20	3
adjective phrase	2	0.3
single adverb	9	1
preposition	200	28
prepositional phrase	44	6
Total	**711**	

Key findings from this initial frequency count:

- Metaphors with prepositions as Vehicle terms are the most common form, closely followed by metaphors involving single verbs and phrasal verbs.
- Metaphors with single nouns as Vehicle terms, often the form used to exemplify metaphor theory, account for only 5 per cent of the total and rank sixth in terms of use of the various forms.
- 53 per cent of all metaphors involve prepositions, either with verbs, alone or in prepositional phrases.

The overwhelming use of prepositions and verbs as metaphors is further emphasized when the results are presented with metaphors grouped as 'nominal metaphors', those whose Vehicle terms centre around nouns and 'verb metaphors', those whose Vehicle terms centre around verbs, etc., as given in Table 4.2.

Table 4.2 Linguistic metaphors by word class of Vehicle terms

	Number of metaphors	%
nominal metaphors	103	15.0
verb metaphors	333	47.0
adjectival metaphors	22	3.1
adverb metaphors	9	1.3
prepositional metaphors	244	34.0

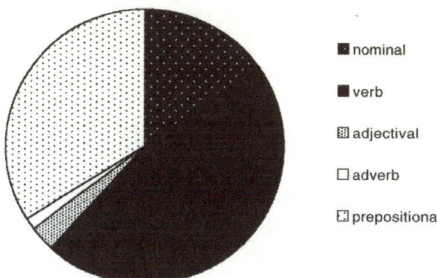

Figure 4.2 Grammatical forms of linguistic metaphors

Figure 4.2 displays these figures as a percentage of the total number of linguistic metaphors identified.

While these quantitative results are important because they show a clear pattern of how language is being used metaphorically, we have seen how decisions on what was to be included as metaphor were far from straightforward. We might justifiably ask how far the above picture of linguistic form in metaphor is merely an outcome of the identification decisions. A first response to this question is to note that decisions about borderline candidates for the category 'linguistic metaphor' concerned verb and prepositional metaphors rather than nominal metaphors, and that if a more generous identification procedure had been followed, these categories would have been even larger. However, a more detailed and descriptive account of the grammatical forms of metaphor will give a fuller picture of the dataset. I now take each grammatical category in turn, describing the types of metaphor found in each and the syntactic relation of Topic and Vehicle items.

Nominal metaphors

Four major syntactic patterns were found that combined nominal Vehicles with Topic domain terms:

Copular nominal metaphors

{T *is/is like/looks like* V}

Twenty-one metaphors linked a Vehicle noun or noun phrase to the Topic through some form of the verb *to be*, or as a comparison with *like*:

> she's my <u>bodyguard</u>
> he was <u>an intrepid explorer</u>
> it's like a <u>miracle</u>
> you're <u>spokes in a wheel</u> [describing a pattern made by dancers]

Vehicle pre-modification of Topic noun

{V + T = NP}

Six nominal metaphors were formed by collocation of a Vehicle noun acting as pre-modifier to a Topic head noun:

> <u>butterfly</u> clips
> <u>glue</u> ear
> <u>lollipop</u> trees

In discourse, this form can evolve from a copular form: for example, the *lollipop trees* metaphor emerged in the course of talk, shortly after being encoded in fuller forms such as *the trees looked like little lollipops* (see Chapter 5). We can note that the other {V + T = NP} metaphors can be expanded in a similar way: *butterfly clips – clips which look like butterflies*. The condensation of a comparison into a pre-modified noun phrase seems to be one way in which metaphors can develop dynamically, or emerge, in English in use.

Nominal group metaphors

{V *of* T}

Fifteen metaphors linked the Topic and Vehicle together in a 'nominal group' (Sinclair 1991). This particular form brings a Vehicle term as the first noun phrase in the form NP *of* NP:

> <u>a feast</u> of fun
> <u>the first rule</u> of good dancers
> <u>a little bit</u> of the history

Students produced two nominal group metaphors in which the first, Vehicle, NP arose from hyperbole:

<u>loads and loads</u> of us
I've done <u>millions of</u> [sums]

The 'nominal group metaphors' in the data can be split more or less equally into metaphors like the first two examples above, in which the Vehicle term has clear schematic content, and metaphors like the other examples, in which the first Vehicle term is some kind of quantifier.

The importance of nominal group metaphors is signalled in the few linguistic analyses of metaphors. An analysis of the linguistic form of metaphor in English poetry (Brooke-Rose 1958) referred to nominal group metaphors of the first type as 'the Genitive Link metaphor', and found it to occur more frequently than all other noun metaphors. Brooke-Rose describes the meaning and function of *of* in such phrases as 'extremely complex and often ambiguous' (1958: 147). A dictionary of poetic terms calls this form 'the preposition metaphor ... the quickest and easiest kind of metaphor to construct' (Myers and Simms 1982: 181). A more recent corpus linguistic analysis of the use of *of* in the Birmingham corpus of English (Sinclair 1991) found that 80 per cent of uses of the word occurred in nominal groups. Although Sinclair did not investigate metaphor in relation to nominal groups, many of the examples he takes from the corpus have a metaphorical first NP in the nominal group.

The less schematic type of nominal group metaphors appears to be characteristic of spoken rather than written language. The nature of the relation between first and second noun phrases seems to present difficulties to theoretical grammarians; Huddleston (1984: 304) labels them 'determinatives'. In the dataset, nominal groups were counted as metaphorical when the first term, e.g. *bit,* quantified a Topic noun which is non-quantifiable, e.g. *information, memory.* Lakoff and Johnson (1980) class these as linguistic expressions of one type of conceptual metaphor, labelled 'ontological metaphor'. This type of metaphor is here called 'determinative nominal group metaphor', contrasted with 'schematic nominal group metaphors'.

It would seem that the Nominal Group {V *of* T} form provides an important way of linking Vehicle and Topic terms syntactically in English. While research into written text has emphasized the frequency of schematic nominal group metaphors, with schematic lexis in both T and V positions, the data indicate that determinative nominal group metaphors are also quite frequent in spoken discourse.

Substitution nominal metaphors

{V stands for T}

In 17 nominal metaphors, a Vehicle term was used in the place of a Topic term:

> you've had <u>an awfully good innings</u>
> it will have a <u>knock-on effect</u>
> the <u>key</u> is to

A further 13 used the phrase *a bit*, or a variant of it such as *the next bit*, as a Vehicle noun phrase without any direct Topic referent. These might also be seen as elliptical determinatives, i.e. *a bit of (*Topic-term).

The decision to include *bit* as metaphorical when used with a Topic that is not quantifiable or concrete strongly affected the nominal metaphors: of the 103 nominal metaphor Vehicles, 50 included *bit*, including *a little bit, a wee bit, the next bit, a good little bit of*. In addition to those already mentioned in the four groups above, a further 30 uses occurred as pre-modifiers in adjective phrases or acting as adverbial:

> <u>a bit</u> depressing
> go back just <u>a bit</u>

Verb metaphors

Single verbs

One hundred and seventy-one single verbs were used as Vehicles linking to Topic terms in at least one other slot in the clause: Subject, Object, Complement or Adverbial:

> I might <u>cut</u> netball Verb Vehicle + Topic as Subject and Object
> the next little bit <u>says</u> Verb Vehicle + Topic as Subject

The decisions about what was to count as a metaphorical use of delexicalized verbs, described in Chapter 3, resulted in approximately equal numbers of delexicalized and schematic verbs being counted as metaphorical. Table 4.3 gives the number of uses of the major delexicalized verbs counted in the data. We can see from this table that the identification decisions did, on the whole, restrict the numbers of delexicalised verbs included as metaphors. Some individual verbs were used extensively, especially *put* with the meaning of *write*. The most frequently occurring schematic verb was *shorten* (5 uses), with the sense of grammatical contraction, as in *the apostrophe is shortening the word.*

Table 4.3 Delexicalized verb uses counted as metaphorical

Delexicalized verbs	Number of metaphorical uses
come	1
give	7
get – got	4
go – gone – went	11
have	6
keep	6
make	5
put	21
take – took	9
TOTAL	**70** (out of 171)

Multi-word verb metaphors

A similar number (162) of verb Vehicles involved more than one word. Distinctions were made in an attempt to organize what one analyst has described as the 'fragmented and blurred' categories characteristic of verb use in spoken discourse (Hopper 1997: 101). In common with Hopper, I found many metaphorically used verbs were extended, with exponents of the verb distributed across a clause, so that it was not always straightforward to say where a verb ended. Very often verbal expressions could be said to stretch across prepositions. In addition, it was necessary to identify which constituents of a clause referred to the Vehicle domain and which to the Topic domain. Two main types of multi-word verb metaphors emerged from this analysis:

- **verb phrase metaphors:** the verb and some other clause constituents are from the Vehicle domain;
- **phrasal verb metaphors:** the verb and its following prepositions are from the Vehicle domain.

VERB PHRASE METAPHORS

A small subset (11) of verb phrase metaphors had a relative pronoun, in addition to the verb group, referring to the Vehicle domain:

> I know where the time goes
> where does the crow fly?

In a further 26 verb phrase metaphors, Vehicle terms occupied the verb slot and at least one other constituent (or part), up to the whole clause:

I think you all <u>deserve a medal</u>   (verb + Object NP from Vehicle domain)
make a mental <u>note</u>   (verb + Head noun of Object NP from Vehicle domain)
we'll have to <u>bear</u> that <u>in mind</u>   (verb + Adverbial PP from Vehicle domain)
<u>take it step by step</u>   (whole clause from Vehicle domain)
<u>we've got to</u> twenty five to twelve   (Subject pronoun + verb from Vehicle domain)

PHRASAL VERB METAPHORS

A large number (126) of metaphors involved a Vehicle verb followed by one or more prepositions:

I'm <u>with</u> you now   (= I understand you)
we were <u>talking about</u> apostrophes   (= we were studying apostrophes)

Again, analyst decisions about which verbs to include clearly affected the numbers identified. As Table 4.4 shows, delexicalized verbs counted for about half of the number, but with a different distribution from that of Table 4.3.

Table 4.4 *Frequency of delexicalized phrasal verb metaphors*

Delexicalized verb + preposition(s)	**Number of occurrences**
come + back to / in / out in / out of / up with	6
do + with	1
get + down to / into / on to / through	5
give	–
go + away from / back / back to / by / in / into / off / on / on from / over / up in / through	31
have	–
keep	–
make	–
put + down / in	3
take + away	10
Total	56 (out of 126)

Several schematic phrasal verbs were also heavily used (Table 4.5).

Table 4.5 *Most frequently occurring schematic phrasal verb metaphors*

Schematic verb + preposition(s)	**Number of occurrences**
talk about	12
look at / out	6
laid down	5
sort out	5

The delexicalized nature of many verb metaphors revealed here is somewhat counter-intuitive, as it might be expected that metaphors would make use of more schematic lexis in order to have rich and striking domain transfer. What we are seeing here, though, is not the use of rich poetic metaphors, but prosaic metaphors in discourse. In spoken interaction, items with high indexical valency can also be made rich and productive carriers of metaphorical meaning.

The nature of prosaic verb metaphor is perhaps best exemplified by the verb *go*, which is the verb most frequently used metaphorically; 12.6 per cent of all verb metaphors involve a form of this verb, with or without prepositions. In one sense this is a trivial finding: the verb *go* is used to refer to many types of dynamic actions, and, as human beings, many of the things we do and talk about are dynamic actions. However, the range of prepositions used with *go* in Table 4.4 emphasizes how in everyday, prosaic discourse we do not just make heavy use of the verb, but do so by exploiting the prepositions to create shades of metaphorical meaning. We return to consider *go* as a linguistic expression of a conceptual metaphor in Chapter 10.

Adjective and adverb metaphors

A small number of adjectives and adverbs were used metaphorically. The most frequent adjective was *big*, with four occurrences:

> <u>big</u> numbers
> <u>big</u> word

Other adjectives included:

> brilliant, clear, convenient, long, lazy, settled

Most were borderline metaphors for which it was possible to make a marginal case for incongruity and transfer of meaning. For example, when the teacher asked about classification: *what's it a <u>big</u> word for?* the intended answer was *sorting*. The relative size of the two words was presumably not the teacher's real concern, but rather something to do with their degree of abstraction, formality or technicality. *Classification* is the formal 'scientific concept', whereas *sorting* refers to the children's 'spontaneous concept'. Since the two ideas – <u>size</u> and <u>more advanced, specific, technical</u> – are distinct, the use of *big* was included as metaphorical.

Long, used metaphorically, accounted for 4 of the 9 adverbs in the data, as in:

> how <u>long</u> are you having on it?
> it won't take <u>long</u>

Here the Topic domain is 'time', and the Vehicle domain is 'physical length'.

The two examples of *big* and *long*, while both using Vehicle domains relating to physical size, differ pragmatically. *Long* is conventional English usage in talking about time, whereas *big* is commonly used when adults talk to children, but not more generally.

Prepositional metaphors

Preposition metaphors

The prepositions included as metaphorical (see discussion in Chapter 3, p. 73) on how these were selected) are set out in Table 4.6.

Table 4.6 *Prepositions used metaphorically*

Preposition	Number of occurrences
after	1
between	2
from	32
in	89
in between	3
into	3
off	1
on	48
on about	1
on to	1
out of	1
over	1
through	5
under	1
up to	2
up until	1

As the most frequently used metaphorical preposition, *in* also showed most topic variation. It was used to talk about time, feelings, writing and maths:

> <u>in</u> about two minutes
> <u>in</u> a bad mood
> <u>in</u> twos
> <u>in</u> your best writing
> ends <u>in</u> an S

Most uses of *on* referred to current work being done by a student, and 13 of these were said by students:

> which page are you <u>on</u>?
> you're always <u>on</u> areas
> I'm <u>on</u> eighty six now

Other uses occurred in conventional phrases such as

> <u>on</u> tv
> <u>on</u> the computer
> <u>on</u> Friday

From these examples, the reader will notice that the distinction between 'verb + preposition' and 'phrasal verb' is not always straightforward. Where the verb was being used non-metaphorically, as with *end* in the example *the word ends in*, only the preposition was counted as the metaphor Focus or Vehicle term. However, while conventionally the verb *to be* is not counted as a phrasal or prepositional verb, the verb *to be on* with the meaning of *to be working on* seems to act as a phrasal verb and should perhaps have been put in that category. This is a further example of how categories blur into each other. Sometimes verbs and prepositions seem to work interdependently in spoken discourse, with prepositions serving to extend verbal expressions onwards into adverbials.

Prepositional phrase metaphors

To be counted as metaphorical, all components, i.e. both the preposition and the noun phrase, had to be justified as acting metaphorically:

> <u>at that point</u>
> <u>for a long time</u>
> <u>in fact</u>
> <u>on the right track</u>

A borderline example was

> *in your head*

which was used four times in maths by one of the teachers to describe the process of mental arithmetic or doing a calculation without writing it down. A justification for metaphoricity rests on a kind of mind/body dualism: that the Topic domain of *thinking* and the Vehicle domain of *the physical location inside the head* are distinct, or could be seen as distinct, particularly when children were instructed to *put the one in your head*. Because of its relevance to education and learning processes, it was included. The same teacher also used the phrase *in your mind* in similar discourse contexts, but with slightly different cotexts. Each use of *in your mind* referred to a process of recall or imagination, as in

> so <u>in your mind</u> then you know that that's 84

The *head* was talked about as the place for doing calculations, whereas the *mind* was the place for storage, recall, or representation.

The linguistic form of metaphors in classroom discourse: summary

The first research question concerned the nature of metaphor in classroom discourse, and this chapter has answered the question in terms of metaphor density and grammatical form. Key findings are:

- The density of linguistic metaphors across the classroom discourse was 27 per 1000 words. To reach this figure, the data were analysed several times with gradually refined identification criteria and increasing accuracy, stabilizing around the final figure. This is towards the lower end of the range expected from the studies summarized in Table 3.2.
- Verb and preposition metaphors were found to be much more common than nominal metaphors, and a large number of linguistic metaphors involve both verbs and prepositions in extended verbal expressions.
- The set of nominal metaphors included two interesting dynamic phenomena of language in use: nominal group metaphors that use *of* to bring together Topic and Vehicle items, and the link between copular metaphors and pre-modification metaphors.

The findings support the claim that we need to attend to the language of metaphor if we are to understand the phenomenon of metaphor, since the picture of metaphor in spoken discourse revealed here differs in many ways from the assumptions of metaphor theorists – that typical metaphor is nominal, vivid and active. When metaphor theory is developed in relation to this type of linguistic metaphor, it may not be immediately applicable to more prosaic metaphor. Conversely, an adequate theory of metaphor must take account of prosaic use of metaphor, and of the link between prosaic and poetic metaphor in language use. From a prosaic perspective, portraying prosaic metaphor as a diluted form of creativity with metaphor would seem to explain the link from the wrong direction. The use of metaphor in classroom discourse shows speakers exploiting the possibilities or affordances of their language resources, with a large part of this adaptation using the most minimal lexicogrammatical units such as *of* and *go*. The underlying processes of our capacity to create metaphor appear in these most prosaic discourse moments, but there is no evidence of the capacity to produce more poetic metaphors. It seems more acceptable to explain this poetic capacity as a deliberate acquired skill, in the best cases built on some particularly strong individual affordance that we might call 'talent', similar to the relation between basic human capacities to notice and draw shapes, and highly valued artistic skills.

5 Deliberate and conventionalized metaphor in classroom discourse

Introduction

As we saw in Chapter 1, cognitive metaphor theory has moved away from the traditional concern with active and novel linguistic metaphors to study metaphor as conceptual mappings underlying linguistic expressions. The applied linguistic approach to metaphor developed here returns to language, but as part of on-line thinking and talking processes in social interaction. The numerical and grammatical analyses of the previous chapter take us a little way in understanding how the teachers in the study used metaphor. To go further, it is necessary to see metaphorical uses of language from a discourse perspective, taking into account the participants in the discourse, and their motivations and purposes.

Qualitative analysis of the dataset of linguistic metaphors included examining the lexical choices of metaphor Vehicles, the Topics that were talked about metaphorically, and how metaphorical uses of language occurred within ongoing discourse. As the analysis proceeded, a key distinction became evident between metaphors that seemed to be used deliberately and metaphors that occurred because that was 'just the way to say it', which I term 'conventionalized' in order to give a process emphasis. Deliberate and conventionalized metaphors can only be so described relative to their specific discourse context.

The two types of metaphor are illustrated in Extract 5.1, taken from class work. Here the teacher explains the origin of a character's name using conventionalized metaphors *come from/after/drop* (lines 2, 3, 4) and (probably) deliberate metaphors *nickname/corruption* (lines 5 and 6).

Deliberate and conventionalized metaphor

Extract 5.1 *Deliberate and conventionalized metaphors*

```
1  T: for people who are writing about Skidda ( . ) um ( . )
2     remember it actually comes from the word Skiddaw which is a hill ( . ) but ( . )
3     he's been named after it ( . ) but ( . ) it's been ?????
4     you drop the W and it's Skidda ( . )
5     and it's a sort of nickname ( . )
6     a sort of corruption of Skiddaw
```

This short extract exemplifies several of the contrasting discourse and linguistic features that typically cluster around the two types of metaphor:

- conventionalized metaphors tend to be verbs; the deliberate metaphors are nominal;
- the deliberate Vehicle items are less frequently used words in English than the conventional Vehicle items;
- the concept domains referred to by the deliberate Vehicle items are likely to be less familiar to students than the conventional Vehicle domains;
- the deliberate metaphors are marked by hedging (*sort of*);
- the deliberate metaphors are used later in the episode, after non-metaphorical and conventionalized metaphors develop the Topic.

It is important to re-iterate that the distinction between deliberate and conventionalized linguistic metaphors is discourse-derived and discourse-relative. Deliberate metaphors are not necessarily novel or creative metaphors as in traditional metaphor theory, identified at sentence level and independent of discourse context. The deliberateness lies in the use of the linguistic metaphor in its discourse context, for a particular purpose on a particular occasion. Conventionalized metaphors, on the other hand, are part of the participants' shared language resources for talking about the particular topic.

As a minimal indication of deliberate use, a metaphor had to occur on only one occasion in the discourse data. The deliberateness of use was then further estimated by using my native speaker knowledge of English and my experience of how teachers talk in classrooms to decide whether, beyond the single occasion of use in the data, a particular Vehicle term was likely to be conventionally used with that metaphor Topic. Ideally, further triangulating evidence of the deliberate use of metaphors would be gathered through retrospective interviews with the users, but it was not possible to do so in this study. As mentioned in Chapter 3, concordancing and other corpus software is also beginning to offer measures of probability of frequency of co-occurrence which may help to rate the novelty/conventionality of a metaphor (Hunston and Francis 1998; Kintsch 1998). These tools are not yet well enough developed, and the relativity of decisions to the discourse context will also mean that the corpus on which the tools operate must be selected with care, as well as being large enough to give reliable figures.

At the end of the recursive processes of qualitative analysis of the data, 72 linguistic metaphors (around 10 per cent of the metaphor dataset) were classed as 'deliberate'. Interestingly, seven of these were from students, either in response to teachers' use of metaphor or in peer talk. These seven comprised 17 per cent of their total production, a much greater proportion than the teachers'. While teachers used deliberate metaphor mainly to explain concepts, students used deliberate metaphors in more playful discourse, mostly between themselves. Their subordinate role in the classroom and in the discourse seemed to allow them greater freedom to play with metaphor (see Chapter 6).

The inevitably approximate figure is of less interest than the features of deliberate and conventionalized metaphors that became apparent as the analysis proceeded (see Chapter 3), and that are reported in this chapter.

Deliberate metaphors in discourse

In this section, I use a longer extract from the classroom discourse to describe discourse features of deliberate use of metaphor. These features are discussed in terms of the dynamic creation of learning opportunities for students through the management of alterity. The extract occurred in the geology lesson, when the teacher explained the formation of igneous rocks by volcanic action. It is chosen because it shares key features with discourse around other deliberate metaphors in the data, but, since it is slightly longer, it also allows us to see most of the features at work in one contextualized episode.

Linguistic metaphors in the volcanic lava episode

Extract 5.2 comes from about half way through the lesson at a point when the teacher is explaining to the students how igneous rock is formed. In the first 15 lines (Extract 3.1) she reminds the students that they have seen volcanoes on television. The teacher then proceeds to explain how rock can get so hot that it melts and changes into igneous rock. The linguistic metaphors identified in the extract are underlined. Our main concern here is with the deliberate metaphors that occur in lines 20 to 32 and are double underlined.

Deliberate and conventionalized metaphor

Extract 5.2 *Deliberate metaphors in discourse: the volcanic lava episode*

```
 1  T:   right ( . ) let's go back ( . ) to these rocks (1.0)
 2       fire formed (2.0)
 3       I think you probably all know ( . ) how ( . )
 4       igneous rocks comes to be formed (2.0)
 5       you should know this (1.0)
 6       you love watching this on the telly ( . )
 7       and if one starts working again ( . )
 8       it's very exciting ( . )
 9       and it's on the news for days ( . )
10       in fact I have seen one working recently (1.0)
11       and there's a village ( . ) in Italy (1.0)
12       and they're dropping things to try and stop the village from being destroyed (3.0)
13       yes ( . ) Ellen?
14  E:   volcano
15  T:   yes ( . ) it's a volcano (1.0) and (2.0)
16       the rocks that are formed by fire ( . )
17       the rocks that are ( . ) are molten ( . ) molten rocks (1.0)
18       just imagine rock (1.0) getting so hot (2.0)
19       that it actually melts (1.0)
20       so that it becomes like ( . ) sticky treacle
21  Ps:  ugh
22  L:   (whisper) treacle
23  T:   or even ( . ) like ( . ) runny butter
24  Ps:  ugh
25  T:   have you ever put ( . ) a little dish ( . ) with butter in ( . ) into the microwave?
26  Ps:  yes
27  T:   and left it for too long?
28  Ps:  yes
29  T:   do you know what happens? ( . )
30       I did it at the weekend ( . ) so I know what happens
31  P:   is molten lava like wax?
32  T:   yes (1.0) it can be a bit like wax (1.0)
33       but do you know what happens to butter? ( . )
34       it does ( . ) there are two things it does ( . )
35       which are like ( . ) volcanic ( . ) rocks ( . ) when they're being ?????
36  P:   it bubbles
37  T:   it bubbles ( . ) well done ( . ) yes ( . )
38       and it sort of keeps doing this ????? ( . )
39       so that's where these rocks come from (1.0)
```

Extract 5.2 is a complete episode in the discourse around a single subtopic, with clear opening and closing statements. The opening utterance (lines 1 and 2) begins with the boundary marker *right*, and presents the topic of the upcoming talk, using the metaphor *go back to*. The extract, and the talk about volcanoes and igneous rocks, closes with a summarizing metaphor *where these rocks come from*, and the discourse then moves to another topic.

In explaining the process of the formation of igneous rocks, the teacher makes a deliberate comparison of volcanic lava with *sticky treacle* and *runny butter*, while a student suggests a third comparison with *wax*. In identifying linguistic metaphors, a decision was made to include all but the most literal comparisons as metaphor. Reading Extract 5.2, we can see that, although the comparisons are probably familiar to participants, they are also quite vivid and not literal. The domains of *volcanoes* and *kitchens* are very far apart. The students' responses of *ugh* in lines 21 and 24, suggest that, in imagining *lava* as *treacle* or *butter*, they may indeed be making links between incongruent domains.

In using more than one metaphorical comparison, the teacher is carrying out the exhortations of Spiro *et al.* (1989, reported on p. 39) for effective use of analogy. However, only the comparison with *butter* is really an analogy, mapping not just properties of the Topic and Vehicle concept, but also explanatory theories or 'relations' within the conceptual domains: heating butter causes it to change in parallel ways to heated rock (lines 34–8). *Treacle* and *wax* are not analogies in this sense, since *treacle* does not need heat to change it to a liquid, and *wax*, once melted, does not further change its form as it gets hotter.

Having seen the linguistic metaphors in the extract, we now zoom out a little and examine the discourse in which they are embedded. Using the sociocultural constructs of Chapter 2, the extract is seen as an episode of pedagogical action in which the teacher's goals are to increase students' understanding of how igneous rocks come to be formed (lines 4 and 39). The initial state of understanding is established as shared knowledge or intersubjectivity in lines 1–15, and is a kind of spontaneous or experiential conceptual knowledge derived from watching volcanoes on television. It appears that the teacher believes students know from this experience how igneous rocks are formed but have not explicitly made the link with volcanic activity (line 3). The gap between initial knowledge and explicit knowledge is the alterity that needs to be managed and reduced through the discourse.

The dynamics of the discourse are led by the teacher who plays a dominant role in initiating and guiding the talk, as she does throughout the lesson and all the events recorded. However, the teacher is engaged in dialogic interaction rather than monologic presentational talk, and the opportunities for learning emerge from the co-adaptation during the discourse of the thinking-and-talking of both teacher and students.

The episode between the opening and closing has two parts; the first establishes *volcano* as a key concept, and the second (major) part makes explicit the link between *volcanoes* and *igneous rocks* via the three metaphors. In the first part (lines 5–15) the teacher seems to be encouraging the students to guess the topic, as she gives a succession of increasingly specific clues to the idea of *volcanoes*. This sub-section of the discourse has its own sub-goal – to activate the word and concept of *volcano* – and its own alterity in the gap between what the teacher has in mind and what the students are thinking about. In lines 14 and 15, the discourse stabilizes around the word *volcano* and (assumed) shared understanding between teacher and students of the sense of the word. From this point, the interaction around the three metaphors creates a series of stabilities in the developing discourse that gradually bring the teacher's and students' understanding of the formation of igneous rocks closer together.

As in Extract 5.1 (p. 100), the metaphorical comparison of *molten rock* (the Topic) with *sticky treacle* (the Vehicle) is produced after specific details about the Topic: *getting so hot it actually melts*. In other words, before the metaphor is used, the students have been given clues as to how to interpret it. It is interesting to see in lines 18 and 19 how the teacher signals that a non-metaphorical interpretation of *melts* is appropriate by pre-modifying it with *actually*. This suggests that, at some level, she is aware that the collocation of *rock* and *melt* is incongruous and takes action to prevent metaphorical interpretation, in turn suggesting that the possibility of metaphor is always present in people's minds as they engage in discourse. While theorists claim that the use of metaphor carries a risk (e.g. Goatly 1997), participants seem to be equally aware of the risk that a non-metaphorical use of language may be metaphorically interpreted.

The students respond to the metaphor in line 21, and a whispered repetition of *treacle* from Louise is picked up by the microphone. A similar response (line 24) follows the introduction of the second metaphorical comparison: *like runny butter*. The use of a second Vehicle term to refer to the same Topic is called 'Vehicle relexicalization'. The use of two Vehicles may help interpretation by restricting features that might be mapped across to the Topic to those that apply to both Vehicles.

The immediate linguistic context of the Vehicle terms provides support for understanding by limiting or constraining possible interpretations of the relation between Vehicle and Topic in two further ways. First, both Vehicle noun phrases include a pre-modifying adjective from the Vehicle domain that serves to narrow the possible mappings between Topic and Vehicles. This prevents the activation and use in interpretation of irrelevant features of the Vehicles, such as colour or taste. Second, each Vehicle noun phrase is preceded by *like* and a pause. *Like* performs a 'hedging' function (Glucksberg and Keysar 1993) and indicates that the mapping to be made between the Vehicle noun phrase and the Topic *rock* is some kind of comparison.

The pause serves to isolate the metaphorically used words and they are given further emphasis by their positioning at the end of the clause and of the turn. Strässler's analysis of idioms in spoken discourse found that they were often framed with micropauses and with inhalation, phenomena which he labelled 'idiomatic markers' (Strässler 1982: 98). Intuitively, such markers would seem to indicate the pronouncement of something anomalous that a listener might find hard to believe.

The teacher then proceeds to develop the mapping with *runny butter* by giving more specific information. This 'Vehicle development' is interrupted at line 31 by a student, who offers *wax* as a further Vehicle relexicalization and comparison to *molten rock*. The teacher responds only briefly to this possibility and returns to her exposition of what happens to butter when it gets very hot. Negotiating analogies or metaphors offered by students is suggested as important for learning (Spiro *et al.* 1989) and it perhaps is a missed opportunity for reducing alterity further. We can only guess why the teacher did not pursue the possibilities of the *wax* comparison, but as noted above, *runny butter* makes a better analogy with *molten rock*. The interruption does indicate something of the student's thinking during the discourse. Across the data there are multiple instances where use of one metaphor is followed by further metaphorizing. This is an intriguing characteristic of metaphor in discourse that might merit further study. Corts and Pollio (1999) found a similar phenomenon in their study of undergraduate lectures, where metaphors about content tended to occur in bursts. In educational discourse, these bursts or clusters of deliberate metaphors occur in explanations of difficult concepts. If deliberate metaphor clusters occur in other types of spoken discourse, this may suggest that the topic at that point is in some way difficult ideationally as here, or perhaps interpersonally.

The discourse around the changing nature of *heated butter* (lines 25–38, excluding the exchange in 31 and 32) makes specific details about the properties and relations in the Vehicle domain explicit.

Table 5.1 Summary of the dynamics of metaphor development in volcanoes episode

Line	Topic/Vehicle	Key words	
1	T	rocks	Topic stated
4		igneous rocks	Topic development
6		this, working	Topic contextualization
15		volcano	Topic development
16		molten rocks	Topic specification
19		hot, melts	Topic development
20	V_1	sticky treacle	Vehicle statement
23	V_2	runny butter	Vehicle relexicalization
25		dish, microwave	Vehicle contextualization
27		too long	Vehicle contextualization
31–32	V_3	wax	Vehicle relexicalization
33	V_2	butter	Vehicle repetition
34		two things it does	Vehicle development
35	T	volcanic rocks	Topic linked to Vehicle
36	$V_2(+T)$	it bubbles	Vehicle development
38		keeps ?????	Vehicle development
39	T	rocks	Topic development – summary

Interactionally, this is done with a series of questions from the teacher around the various stages (lines 25, 27, 29, 33). The questions not only help ensure the students' continued attention but also carry content about the Vehicle. This type of talk, which links the concept to the everyday experience of the students, is labelled 'Vehicle contextualization'.

In line 35 the explicit mention of *volcanic rocks* reminds participants that, although the talk is about *butter*, it is being developed as an analogy for the over-arching Topic of *rocks*. The restating of the metaphor increases the probability that when the two properties of *heated butter* are stated in lines 37 and 38 (although 38 is indecipherable on the tape), they will also be seen as relevant to *rocks*. The Topic becomes the topic again in the final line, as *rocks* is the Subject of the final clause.

Table 5.1 summarizes the movement between Topic and Vehicle(s) in this episode, and the instances of Vehicle relexicalization, development and contextualization. Although longer than many other episodes in the data, the pattern of movement between Topic and Vehicle is quite representative – from Topic information to introduction of Vehicle, through the development of the Vehicle to the re-entry of the Topic into the discourse, linked to the now-developed Vehicle.

If we relate the pattern summarized in Table 5.1 to the mediation of alterity, we can see how the development of the Vehicle concept and its re-application in developed form back to the Topic offers an opportunity for students to activate, build up and make more explicit their understanding of how igneous rocks are formed. The premodification and relexicalization of the Vehicle emphasize aspects of the Topic and, at the same time, constrain the features of the Vehicles that can be applied to the Topic, reducing the degree of implicative elaboration required of the discourse participants. The vividness and appropriacy of the chosen Vehicle terms, shown through the students' reactions and responses, suggest that the new knowledge may be more memorable because of its association with the metaphor.

The learning and thinking opportunities are not created just by the mere fact of including metaphorical comparisons, but also through their embedding in intricate and supportive patterns of talk. The discourse appears to be finely tuned to the students' needs through the teacher's lexical and grammatical choices, intonation and pausing, questioning, topic movement between Topic and Vehicle domains, and the gradual building and development of ideational content.

Hedging or tuning?

The marking of metaphors through hedging deserves some discussion and comment, because it signals something of a conflict between metaphor theory and the reality of metaphors in spoken discourse. From a theoretical perspective, Glucksberg and Keysar (1993) propose that hedging reduces metaphoricity. They present a set of increasingly hedged examples, including:

> *cigarettes are time bombs*
> *cigarettes are like time bombs*
> *cigarettes are deadly like time bombs*

They suggest that the first example is more metaphorical than the other two because of the extra information provided by the hedges. By including explicit references to the salient predicates of the Vehicle, the degree of implicative elaboration or resonance (Black 1979) of the metaphor is reduced.

From a discourse perspective, hedging seems to perform a similar role to metaphor development in supporting participants to access appropriate interpretations during talk. The mediation of ideational content is a delicate and skilled business, and speakers are likely to draw on many discourse resources to reduce alterity in talk. As we saw in the explication of igneous rocks (Extract 5.2), *imagine rock getting so hot it actually melts*, non-metaphorical language may also be hedged to warn participants away from a metaphorical interpretation.

While, theoretically, hedging may be said to reduce metaphoricity, it has an important role in discourse that can be described less negatively. In discourse, hedging around metaphorical uses of words is designed to increase the probability of reaching shared understanding. I have suggested (Cameron and Deignan 2001) that it be recast with the more dialogic label 'tuning', and extended to include other discourse support mechanisms that help participants target appropriate interpretations.

The tuning mechanisms that offer students information about relevant properties and relations in the Topic and Vehicle domains, and about mapping between them, then include:

1. Topic development
2. Repetition of the Vehicle term
3. Relexicalization of the Vehicle
4. Modification of the Vehicle term
5. Hedging of the Vehicle term
6. Contextualization of the Vehicle
7. Development of the Vehicle
8. Re-linking of developed Vehicle and Topic

It may be thought that the fine-tuning of the discourse to support metaphor understanding is due to its educational context. However, there is some evidence from studies of non-classroom talk, including general conversation and counselling talk among adults (Strässler 1982; Drew and Holt 1998; McCarthy 1988; Tannen 1989; Quinn 1991; Carter and McCarthy 1995), to suggest that these supportive features of metaphor in use do occur in other types of discourse. My colleague Alice Deignan and I have investigated whether the use of these tuning devices extrapolates to a much larger corpus. In the COBUILD spoken corpus, we find parallel pragmatic uses of tuning devices in casual conversation (Cameron and Deignan 2001).

It seems to me that we should expect to find tuning of deliberate metaphor in its discourse context, although the precise nature of the support would vary with participants and content. Furthermore, in written text, writers might be expected to provide equivalent forms of tuning to support readers' understanding, although again these may take different forms.

The converse of this hypothesis is that when discourse does not provide such support for the understanding of deliberate metaphor, the absence of tuning may be significant. Typical poetic metaphors often come without tuning. The extreme metaphors of poetry can be deliberately constructed to defamiliarize the reader and provoke extra interpretive work.

Tuning of content by discourse participants for each other is an important feature of metaphor in talking-and-thinking.

A complex systems view of the volcanic lava episode

A complex systems view of the discourse in Extract 5.2 would identify the dynamic process of talking-and-thinking as a co-adaptation between the cognitive and linguistic resources of participants. The talking-and-thinking trajectory is drawn into the attractors of the metaphors and talk around the metaphors, pushing the discourse in a new direction. The attractor trajectories can be minimally disruptive, as in the brief exchange around *wax*, with the discourse returning to its previous path, or, as with the development around *butter*, the attractor may severely perturb the overall trajectory so that it moves to a new part of the state space. The driving force of the system is the teacher's perception of alterity between what the students already know and what she wants to teach them.

If learning occurs as a result of the talk around the metaphor, then the initial state of participants' resources will have been shifted to a new state. This conceptual development dynamic operates on a different timescale from the episode of classroom discourse. On this longer timescale, a student's understanding of a particular concept is a complex system in continual flux with a trajectory that shifts from one attractor to the next. As discussed in Chapter 2, these attractors of understanding may also involve metaphorical models.

Taking a complex systems view is itself a process of understanding metaphorically: the complex systems view is a Vehicle for the Topic of learning through discourse. It offers an alternative to other metaphors for learning, such as knowledge as the contents of a container (mind) that is added to incrementally. The application of complex systems theory to metaphor and discourse begins with this fitting of a new description to empirical data. More such work will be done as we proceed.

Conventionalized metaphors

Conventionalized metaphors are expressions that have become part of people's language resources, run-of-the-mill ways of talking about things. They remain metaphorical because they retain the possibility of acting as a Vehicle, activating an incongruent domain from which some meaning can be mapped to the Topic of the ongoing discourse. They may even be used as deliberate metaphors but, if so, they would probably need to be marked by some supra-segmental feature(s) in talk or orthographic feature(s) in writing.

Conventionalization of metaphor occurs through use in a discourse community in which, as with other features of discourse, co-adaptive processes of accommodation lead to shared ways of talking among members (Coupland and Giles 1988). Cooper (1986) developed the idea that the use of metaphor is 'sustained by intimacy', in that metaphor presupposes a shared background. It also contributes to the construction of intimacy by requiring receivers of metaphor to enter the perspective of the producer in order to understand it. In this way, metaphor contributes to 'membershipping' people into a group and developing the shared discourse of a group.

The metaphors used by teachers and students can be analysed from this group membership perspective; this helps us to classify and understand the non-deliberate metaphors in the dataset. Students and teacher are members of a range of overlapping sociocultural groups; conventionalized metaphors are used within each of these groups as they develop as discourse communities. In addition, school students often engage in discourse as novice members of particular groups, e.g. they talk about mathematics as novice mathematicians. Their discourse may reveal something of the process of learning the metaphors of the group.

In this section, examples are given of the use of metaphors that are conventionalized within different groups that teachers and students belong to.

Idioms

Teacher 1 used a range of metaphorical idioms, by which I mean phrases that are used as wholes with little, if any, syntactic flexibility and varying degrees of semantic transparency:

> I'm hoping Mr C will come up trumps and (.) bring me some of those to show you
> keep your fingers crossed
> we'll have to bear that in mind
> put your thinking caps on
> you've had an awfully good innings
> you have to stick to your guns

Teacher 2 used fewer idioms, and these seem less sociohistorically marked:

> make a mental note
> see if any bells ring in your mind

Idioms such as these are conventionalized across speakers of English, although the repertoire of individuals may be influenced by socio-economic class or age.

Students produced metaphorical idioms that marked out their own peer group membership:

> this rash is <u>driving me insane</u>
> <u>bog off</u>
> it's <u>brilliant</u>

In one exchange between students, a metaphorical idiom was questioned, revealing a lack of understanding of an expression already conventionalized within the discourse community but still to be fully mastered by the child. A maths question had asked them to calculate a distance *as the crow flies*. This idiom is used to mean the shortest distance between two points, and only occurs in this exact phrasal form. When Louise's friend asked her, *where does the crow fly?* she was activating the fixed phrase. This is what is often done in play with metaphors, but in this case, the intonation and reactions of those present ruled out the possibility of this being play.

Delexicalized verbs and prepositions

At the other end of the scale in terms of lexical content, we saw in Chapter 4, Tables 4.5 and 4.7 that many of the metaphors in the data used delexicalized verbs like *come, go, get,* and prepositions, particularly *in* and *on*. These are again conventionalized across all speakers and registers of English.

Technical language

The language of specialist groups often makes use of metaphor to create technical discourse, and learning the technical language is part of becoming a member of the specialism. Part of the role of school education is to induct students into the specialist discourses of different subject areas and, in doing so, metaphors may also be used to simplify ideas, generating a kind of sub-technical language that is used for long periods of time within what we might call an apprentice–specialist discourse. Extract 5.3 shows how the technical language of geology uses personification (or animation) metaphors to describe natural processes of rock formation.

Extract 5.3 *Conventionalized technical metaphor*

T:	there are sedimentary rocks (.) which were <u>laid down</u> in shallow seas (.)
	. . . it depends what the river (.) was <u>bringing down</u> (.) that flowed into this part of the sea (2.0) and <u>deposited</u> the mud

Much more common than metaphorical technical language was the use of sub-technical metaphor. The language of mathematics illustrates this phenomenon of conventionalized sub-technical metaphor in talk about the basic operations of arithmetic (all examples are from the data):

addition	*gives/makes/carry the one*
subtraction	*take away/bring down/from*
multiplication	*gives*
division	*get into/goes into/shared by/split into/in*

Walkerdine (1982, 1984) makes the important point that these uses of language are verbalizations of earlier concrete operations, e.g. when children carry out 'division' by splitting up 12 wooden bricks into groups of 3. The sub-technical metaphors are an important step in disembedding thinking from the concrete on the way to using the more abstract technical language. There are episodes in the discourse where the teacher moves between the technical language and the sub-technical metaphor, thus giving the students meaningful opportunities to hear the less familiar technical language in use. An example is given in Extract 5.4 which begins with the technical term 'divide' but continues with sub-technical metaphor.

Extract 5.4 *Moving from technical to sub-technical metaphor*

> then you have to **divide** that (.) by 16 (2.0)
> and that is quite a tricky one to do
> so let's do it <u>the long way</u> . . .
> <u>the long way</u> to do it (.) is to say 16 <u>into</u> 2 (.) well (1.0)
> that won't <u>go</u> (.) we know that (.) so <u>16</u> <u>into</u> 20 (1.0)
> <u>goes</u> once (1.0) 16 (.)
> <u>and</u> 16 <u>from</u> 20 <u>leaves</u> 4 (1.0)
> and then you <u>bring down</u> (1.0) the next (.) that number

In Extract 5.5 the teacher uses sub-technical metaphor in explaining the technical idea of *classification* to the students. After a verbal example, she further exemplified the idea by moving the students physically around the classroom into different groups. In talking about putting students into groups, the teacher referred metaphorically to *groups* as *circles*, and to *labelling* as *saying*. These metaphors might sound quite novel or vivid to an outsider to education, but are familiar to group members through previous shared discourse.

Extract 5.5 *Conventionalized sub-technical metaphor*

> T: then we've got another classification (1.0)
> they're still human (.)
> so we can put them in <u>a big circle</u> that <u>says</u> human (.)
> but we can also put them into two <u>smaller circles</u> (.) that <u>says</u> (1.0)
> male female (1.0)
> is there another way we could classify them?

The word *circles* in Extract 5.5 is probably another reference to shared concrete experience, in this case of sorting into sets, which is part of the early maths curriculum. Sorting is introduced to children with objects, such as counters or beads, that are very often placed inside wooden or plastic hoops to represent a set. When sorting into sets is to be done in a written form, children are often given circles to draw in. The term is likely to hold, for teacher and students, memories of school sorting experiences. Earlier in the same episode, the teacher used the word *groups* and the accurate technical term *classification*, as she does in the first line of the extract. The use of *circles* appears to be a slip back to earlier language use that is probably no longer conceptually needed by the students.

The verb *says* used metaphorically is another example of language deriving from concrete experiences in the shared discourse world; in school classrooms, objects are often labelled with written cards, and (as we will see in Chapter 10) written text in school talk is often held to *say* or *tell*.

There is very little evidence of students talking that might indicate their ability to use technical language or to move between sub-technical metaphor and technical language. However, Extract 5.6 (the mathematics lesson) shows two examples of a student making errors in using subtechnical metaphorical language (in **bold**):

Extract 5.6 *Student errors in use of sub-technical metaphor*

> In talk about the series 36, 49, 64, 81:
>
> P: I thought there was (.) it was only **going in** threes
> T: you thought it was going up in threes
>
> In talk about reducing a fraction to the lowest common denominator:
>
> T: remember how you get it down (.) to the lowest fraction it can be (1.0) what do you have to do to the top and the bottom?
> . . . when you want to get it down to the (1.0) smallest possible numbers (2.0) what do you do Catherine?
> P: do you (.) **higher** the (.) ?

In the apostrophe lesson, the sub-technical metaphor *shortening*, meaning 'showing contraction', first occurred in a student's response (Extract 5.7). It was picked up by the teacher and used throughout the episode and the rest of the lesson. The physical idea of reducing length is used as a Vehicle for the more abstract idea of reducing morphemes.

Deliberate and conventionalized metaphor

Extract 5.7 *Sub-technical metaphor in the apostrophe lesson*

1	T:	what's the apostrophe there (.) instead of? Dougal?
2	D:	um (.) it's just (.) um <u>shortening</u> the word
3	T:	it's <u>shortening</u> the word (.) it's (.)
4		what (.) what letter would be <u>in</u> there then (.) instead of the apostrophe (.)
5		if you wrote it out <u>in its long form</u>?
6	D:	it (.) <u>put</u> an I
7	T:	you would <u>put</u> an I (.) good lad (.)
8		you would (.) you'd <u>put</u> an I (.) it is (.)
9		and they've <u>shortened</u> it to (.) it's (1.0)

We can see how the metaphor is explicated through Vehicle development in lines 4–8 when the teacher checks further to find out if the student can identify the letter that has been replaced by an apostrophe. It is not possible to tell from the data whether *shortening* emerged in the discourse of this class just at this point, or whether it had become common currency at an earlier point.

The prevalence of sub-technical metaphor in the data suggests that it is an important feature of classroom discourse at this level. It offers access to scientific concepts and may provide a stepping stone to technical language. However, sub-technical metaphor may also prevent or delay students moving on to the technical language of the specialist group if it remains in use when students are conceptually able to progress to use of the full technical forms.

School talk

In Extract 5.7 above, the verb *put* is used to mean *write,* as it is throughout the data. A further example of a metaphor conventionalized within 'school talk' is the use of the preposition *on* to mean something like *occupied with*, as in the following extract of student–student talk:

Extract 5.8 *School talk conventionalized metaphor*

	L:	Ellen are you already <u>on</u> this page?
	H:	I'm <u>on</u> (.) I'm <u>on</u> that as well
	L:	I'm only <u>on</u> the circle part
	P:	I've finished that (.) I'm <u>on</u> eighty-six now

Further, systematic, examples of metaphors conventionalized within the school context will be discussed in Chapter 10.

Personal conventionalized metaphors

The two teachers differed in their discourse style, as well as in their dialect and accent. Teacher 1 was English, spoke with 'Received Pronunciation' (a non-regional accent) and, as we saw above, used more metaphorical idioms. Teacher 2 was Scottish and her discourse style was most obviously different when she was giving feedback to the students. Her feedback was marked by the use of the lexeme *think*, as students were encouraged to *think hard* and those who succeeded were described as those who *used their heads and thought,* in contrast with students who *didn't think too much at all.* These uses of *think* were borderline metaphors, stretching the meaning of the item a long way, but in the final analysis most were not included. The uses of the lexeme in Extract 5.9 were counted as metaphorical because of the preposition *through*, and appear to be conventionalized in the teacher's personal style, since this use is slightly different from the more generally used sense of 'considering something thoroughly, together with all its possible effects or consequences' (COBUILD English Dictionary 1995: 1737).

Extract 5.9 *Conventionalized metaphors in personal discourse style*

> some people had thought this through but didn't finish it
>
> quite a few who had thought (.) very hard (.) through the hard bits (.) the difficult bits (.) and then got the easy bit wrong

Conventionalization then is a process affecting a speaker's language resources that takes place over time. Individuals' use of metaphor is highly determined by the discourse communities in which they operate, but always in interaction with personal style.

A complex systems view of conventionalized metaphors

To say that a metaphor is conventionalized is to take a dynamic socio-historic perspective on individuals' use of group language resources. The complex system metaphor is applied in this case to the language resources of the sociocultural group or discourse community. This system is continually changing as it is used by members of the group, and conventionalized metaphors can be seen as stable attractors in the trajectory of the system. One of the goals of formal education is to stimulate the development of the systems of students. We have seen in this section that a key pedagogic issue may lie in moving systems of discourse from the conventionalized sub-technical metaphor that suits younger children.

The conventionalization of deliberate metaphor

In the final section of this chapter I present a piece of discourse data

Deliberate and conventionalized metaphor

that captures the moment of emergence of a shared metaphor. The talking-and-thinking in Extract 5.10 occurred during the class work as the teacher talked to an individual student about a picture she had drawn. Louise, wearing the microphone, was sitting nearby. The alterity driving the discourse was the gap between the student's simplistic drawing of trees that *look like lollipops*, and capturing something more like the shape of the trees she had actually seen. The teacher first helps the student to notice the gap and then suggests how the drawing might be improved. She also explicitly gives permission for the student to ignore her suggestion if the comments are inappropriate, relating an anecdote about a child who was familiar with trees that really did look like *lollipops*.

Two exciting things happen in the episode: the evolution of the metaphor *lollipop trees*, and its use by Louise in the final line, as she picks up the phrase and uses it in her private extension of the dialogue

Extract 5.10 *The emergence of the 'lollipop trees' metaphor*

```
 1 T:  as long as you don't start day two until ???? I think that ( . ) what is that bit? (1.0)
 2     now I think that's the trees (1.0)
 3     you've got ( . ) you've got a visual memory of what you saw at Humphrey Head ( . )
 4     now to actually get your trees right ( . ) ???? what do you have to do? (1.0)
 5     look out of the window at THESE trees (1.0)
 6     let's look at THESE trees to see ( . ) how the branches and the twigs grow out of the tree
        (1.0)
 7     and then go back to your MEMory (1.0)
 8     of the tree that you're trying to draw ( . ) because that's tended to (2.0)
 9     to look like a lollipop hasn't it (3.0)
10     now if it was that shape ( . ) then say so ( . ) because I remember ( . )
11     when I ( . ) when I was a very young teacher and I kept on saying to a little girl ( . )
12     will you PLEASE stop doing lollipop trees (2.0)
13     and then I went to visit her home (2.0)
14     and all along the street where she lived ( . ) they had pollarded ( . ) the trees ( . )
15     chopped all the branches off ( . )
16     and the trees all looked like ( . ) little lollipops (1.0)
17     so she was actually quite right to draw them like that ( . )
18     so if it WAS actually like that ( . )
19     then you have to stick to your guns and say that's how it was (1.0 )
20     I don't remember seeing one quite like that (1.0) not quite ( . )
21     and I think you need to look ( . )
22     and see ( . ) how the branches are attached on to the trees ( . )
23     DON'T rub it out (2.0)
24     (to S2) ???? why was that? ???? was that going down on to the beach ( . )
25     yes that's super (2.0) and (1.0) you've only got one tree so far ( . )
26     I think there was more than one ( . )
27     see how you can do ( . ) it's lovely that one ( . ) don't spoil it ( . )
28     the only thing that I'm going to criticise ( . ) is (1.0)
29 L:  (to herself)                                        [ lollipop trees
```

between the teacher and another student. In the space of a few minutes, a metaphorical comparison takes shape as a deliberate linguistic metaphor and begins a process of conventionalization. Of course, we don't know from this data whether the metaphor *lollipop trees* does become established in the discourse community of the class as a conventional way of referring to simplistic drawings of trees, but this does not seem unlikely.

Looking more closely at the discourse around the metaphor, we can see how the alterity is explained non-metaphorically in lines 4–9, which develop the domain of the Topic *the trees seen at Humphrey Head*. The suggestion in line 5 *to look out of the window* at the trees near the school is a kind of contextualization of the Topic for the student, relating the distant memory to what is present and visible. The Topic is made more specific in line 6 when the student's attention is directed to the branches and how they grow from the trunk. The first use of the metaphor Vehicle occurs in line 9 at the end of this sequence. As in previous examples, the metaphor comes after explication and serves as summary, comment and marker of change in a subtopic. Because of the preceding explication, there is little risk that the comparison will be misunderstood. The form of the metaphor is an explicit comparison, *that's tended to look like a lollipop*, that we might hesitate to include as a metaphor if it were not for its link to the later condensed form *lollipop trees*. The hedging of the metaphor begins with the main verb *tended* and continues with the *look like* which dictates a visual comparison.

The past tense anecdote in lines 11–17 is opened (line 10) and closed (lines 12 and 13) with links to the present situation. The key feature that links Topic and Vehicle *shape* is named in line 10, and the detail of how a tree could actually be made to look like a lollipop in lines 14 and 15 provides more Vehicle development. The metaphorical idiom *stick to your guns*, which closes the telling of the anecdote, again functions as summary, as comment and as marker of a subtopic shift. Lines 20–23 appear to be further justifying the teacher's perception of alterity and intervention, after which she moves on to talk with another student.

The *lollipop trees* is used as a deliberate metaphor, embedded in patterns of talk developing Topic and Vehicle that we saw earlier. It functions as an attractor in the trajectory of the thinking-and-talking of this discourse, and when the talk moves into this attractor it stays there for some time.

Louise's silent participation as an eavesdropper in this discourse is evidenced by her verbalized comment that works as a response to the teacher's incomplete utterance and long pause (line 28). The teacher is talking to another student about her drawing, and the transcript shows that she is actually commenting on the colour of the border around the drawing, not the shape of the trees. Louise predicts wrongly but she is monitoring the talk closely enough to predict and to fill the gap with a syntactically and semantically possible phrase. What we also see is that she has been listening to the lollipop trees episode, and that the metaphor *lollipop trees* has been sufficiently vivid to be internalized, recalled and savoured (judging from the expression in her voice on the tape). The use of metaphors in this episode of discourse provided a learning opportunity not only for the addressee but for other students like Louise who could overhear. The phrase has already become a memorable condensation of an idea for her, and if used on future occasions would be likely to work as an efficient reminder of the teacher's point.

In this episode, the linguistic metaphor is dynamic, changing form as the talk progresses from the explicit comparison to the condensed noun phrase metaphor used by Louise. The use of the metaphor is dynamic, from its initial deliberate use (which is developed at some length in supporting talk), to its final conventionalized use, now loaded with shared implicit meaning. Not only has the use of metaphor affected the mediation of alterity, but the mediation has co-adaptively affected the metaphor.

To summarize, this chapter has introduced and discussed several categories that were developed to account for the use of metaphor in discourse, and that will be used in further analyses. First, deliberate metaphors and conventionalized metaphors in the discourse were described. We then saw characteristic features of discourse around the use of deliberate metaphors and how they support understanding. Ways in which the teacher elaborated the Vehicle and Topic domains of a metaphor were classified, including relexicalization, development and contextualization. Complex systems theory was used to describe, metaphorically, the processes of reducing alterity in discourse, and the emergence and conventionalization of metaphor in the discourse of sociocultural groups.

6 Metaphor in classroom activity

In this chapter we look at the role of metaphor in classroom activity. The eight discourse events (listed in Table 3.1) each involved a range of types of pedagogic action. This chapter presents the results of analysing metaphor use in pedagogic action. We will see how metaphor contributes to the construction of opportunities for learning and participation, as well as finding out more about the nature of metaphor used for different purposes.

The recorded and transcribed discourse events were analysed in terms of mediated action by labelling the teaching sequences (listed in Table 3.3) that occurred within them. When the identified linguistic metaphors were mapped on to these pedagogic descriptions, two clear findings emerged:

- Different types of teaching action make differential use of metaphor.
- Metaphors frequently occur in clusters, rather than being distributed randomly throughout the discourse.

The geology lesson is taken first and metaphor use is described in some detail to illustrate the processes of analysis and the nature of the results. A brief presentation of the results for the other discourse events follows. We then look at typical uses of metaphor in different types of teaching sequences. The nature of the clustering of metaphors and the affective role of metaphor are discussed. Finally, the few instances of students' use of metaphor are reported.

Metaphor use in the geology lesson

The geology lesson took place at the end of a school day, after dancing practice and a break. It was teacher-led and structured through the use of a worksheet that the students completed as the lesson proceeded. The topic was the three major rock types – igneous, sedimentary and metamorphic. The teacher's overall goal (as stated at the beginning and as evidenced from the action) was to introduce these labels and explain each of them, then to relate them to the students' recent school trip to Cumbria where they had seen examples of the rock types. In Vygotskyan terms, the students' spontaneous, experientially based concepts about rocks were to be developed towards the scientific concepts around the classification of rocks according to their formation.

The lesson began with Framing sequences: Organization of the worksheets, followed by Agenda Management, in which the teacher set out what the lesson would contain and how it related to future lessons. When the students began to read the worksheet, the term *classification* was encountered, and this led to an episode in which Explanation sequences explicated and exemplified the idea of classifying. In this episode, the teacher first used a verbal example, of sorting marbles by colour, and then a concrete example, in which the students were moved around into groups by sex, size, and hair colour. The idea of classifying was then related to the work of geologists who classify rocks and the explanation of each type began. Although *igneous rocks* came first on the worksheet, discussion of them was delayed a little, and *sedimentary rocks* were talked about first. The teacher introduced the subtopic of *crinoids*, small organisms that are found fossilized in sedimentary rocks. To explain *metamorphic rocks*, the teacher took a plastic cup and squashed it to exemplify how pressure can change the form of rocks. *Igneous rocks* were then explained, by reference to volcanoes and volcanic lava as the source of igneous rocks (as described in Chapter 5).

At the end of the volcanic lava episode, the topic of the talk shifted to Cumbria and examples of the types of rock that the students had seen there. The worksheet was filled in as the discourse progressed. After a final Summarizing sequence about rocks in Cumbria, the teacher concluded the lesson with Framing sequences in which she set out the agenda for the next lesson and organized clearing away of materials.

Mapping metaphors onto teaching action

Mapping metaphors onto the teaching sequences is shown in Appendix 2. The event as mediated action is also portrayed visually in Figure 6.1, which shows the cumulative frequency of metaphors over the time of the lesson. In the study of complex dynamic systems, visual display is a central tool of analysis. In the study of discourse, however, visual display is underused as a support for understanding dynamics by presenting both product and process of discourse in one image (but see Nelson's visualization of the talk of her child subject in a first language acquisition study, Nelson 1996). To capture the dynamics of metaphor production, I followed Corts and Pollio (1999) but with one major difference. Their (spoken) lecture data were divided into blocks of five 'sentences', but such a unit makes no sense for spoken data. Some other unit was needed. I decided to work with blocks of ten transcribed words, using the assumption made in Chapter 3 that a spoken 'sentence' in a prepared lecture is likely to average around ten words. The number of metaphors was counted, cumulatively, over each 10-word unit from the start of the lesson to the end (258 blocks of 10 words), to produce the graph of cumulative frequency (Figure 6.1). The steepness of the line on the graph indicates the rate of production of linguistic metaphors as the lesson proceeds.

The boxes were placed at points where the gradient of the line was particularly steep, indicating the places where metaphors occurred in a cluster, or burst. The clusters represent the following teaching sequences in the event:

Cluster 1   Agenda Management: opening sequence
Cluster 2   Explication of *classification*
Cluster 3   Explication of putting into groups as *circles*
Cluster 4   Explication of *crinoids*
Cluster 5   Explication of *volcanic lava*
Cluster 6   Explication of *slate roofs in Wales*
Cluster 7   Agenda Management: summarizing and closing sequence

The position of the boxes across the lesson also shows the symmetry of metaphor use in the event, with metaphorically charged Agenda Management sequences opening and closing the lesson, and framing a series of explanation sequences using ideational metaphor. The volcanic lava episode acts as a centrepiece to the lesson.

The preponderance of metaphors in Agenda Management, Summarizing and Explication sequences in the geology lesson is striking, but needs to be checked across a wider range of types of classroom activity. This event did not, for example, include Feedback or Control sequences. The next section describes briefly the structure and dynamics of each of the other events, and the use of metaphor in their teaching sequences.

Metaphor use in the other discourse events

Class work

Class work was quite different in nature from the teacher-fronted, whole-class lessons like geology, and constituted a large part, around 50 per cent, of the children's daily school experience. In the class work

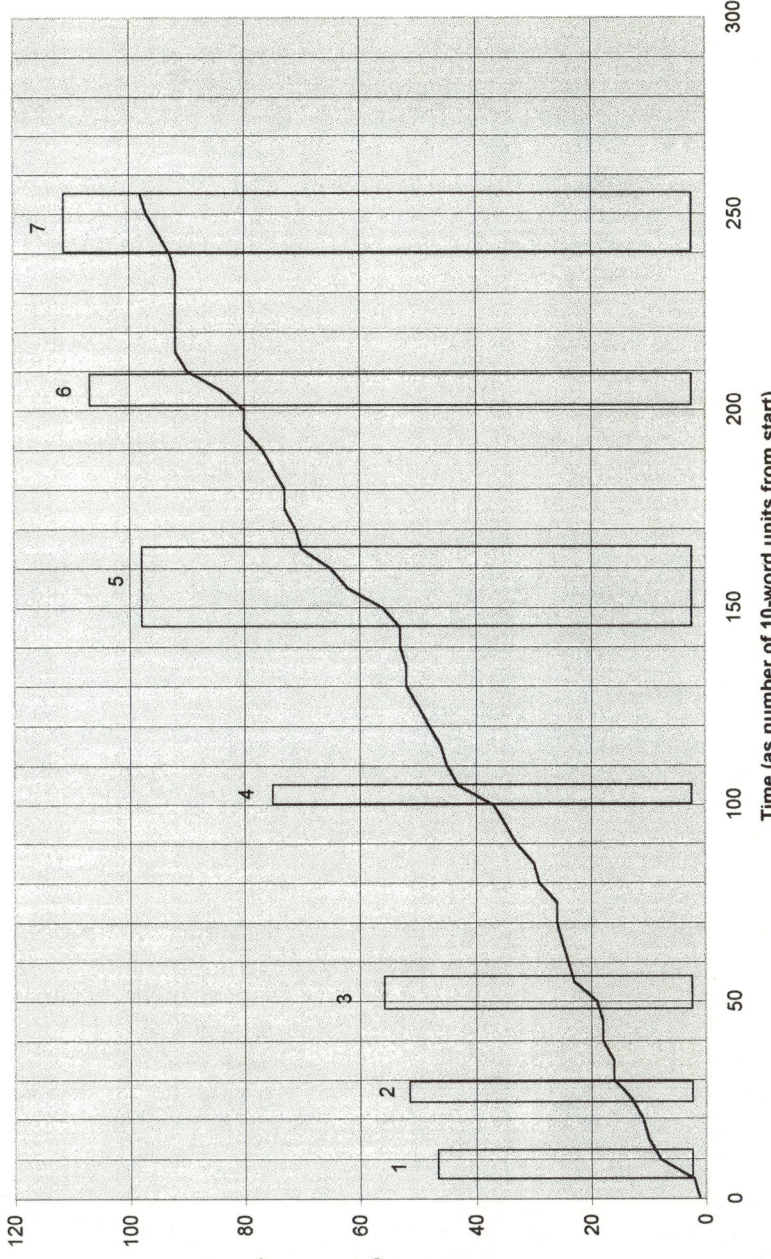

Figure 6.1 Cumulative frequency of metaphors

events, the teacher typically sat at her desk while the students worked more or less independently. Although they sat in small groups, the work I observed was individual, and student–student talk was mostly off-task. Students would go to the teacher at intervals to have work corrected or to read aloud from their reading books. At times the teacher would walk around the class, checking on students' progress. She might also address the whole class to ask for information, or to explain a point that had arisen with one student but was of relevance to the whole class. The discourse that could be analysed into teaching sequences were episodes when the teacher addressed the whole class, a group or an individual student. Each episode had its own alterities and pedagogic goals, many of which arose contingently, as happened in the lollipop trees episode (pp. 117–18).

Metaphors were heavily used in the Framing (Agenda Management) sequences that began Class work 1, when the students had to report on what they had achieved the day before and the teacher set them their own agendas of work to be done. The two class work events also included metaphor in Control sequences, mainly when groups got too talkative, and in Feedback sequences, when the teachers worked with individual students. Class work 1 also included some Explanation sequences that used metaphor.

Dancing practice

Again, this was a very different type of event, since physical rather than intellectual activity was central as the teacher led the students through several maypole dances in preparation for a public performance. (Maypole dancing is an ancient English tradition in which dancers each hold a ribbon attached to a central pole and move so that the ribbons overlap and interweave into intricate patterns.) Music was played on a cassette recorder, and the event was structured through the series of dances that were practised. Not surprisingly, Organization and Control sequences featured strongly, with Explanation sequences occurring when the teacher explained or demonstrated the moves of the dances. The teacher also gave Feedback, both evaluative and strategic, to improve performance and to keep students motivated. The affective use of metaphor in Control and Feedback was particularly striking.

Maths 1

This event took up most of a morning, interrupted by a school assembly. The teacher's goals, stated at the end, were to help students with the concept and process of 'finding an average'. To achieve this she presented them with a problem – *how many times would a brontosaurus fit into the school field?* – and led them through solving it by having each child pace out the school field and then, back in the classroom, adding and dividing the results to calculate an average length of the field. The length of the field was then divided by the length of a brontosaurus.

Metaphor again occurred in the Agenda Management sequences that framed each part of the event. The problem-setting and problem-solving nature of the event meant that alterity was managed contingently through questions and answers. Explanations of ideas were constructed interactionally, built up through answers and feedback, rather than being offered to the students through presentation talk (Chang-Wells and Wells 1993) as in the geology lesson. The teacher used metaphor in summarizing ideas at the end of a stretch of interaction. Metaphor was used affectively, most obviously in Feedback sequences, but also in metatalk around stages of the problem. Sub-technical language around division and averaging also involved metaphor (as in Extract 5.4).

Apostrophe lesson

This and the Maths 2 event were taken by the second teacher, whose different personal style also affected the use of metaphor. The lesson was on how to use the apostrophe to indicate possession, building on previous work on apostrophes to show contraction. It started experientially with students asked to find examples of apostrophes in their reading, and was structured by the use of a book that gave rules for use (that the teacher explained and exemplified) and practice exercises (copied on to the board for students to complete). As the voice of authority in the lesson, the 'holder' of scientific concepts, the textbook was like an additional discourse player, with the teacher mediating the textbook content for the students. She sometimes aligned herself with the students rather than with the book, as when she commented on an exercise item:

> this is a funny one (.) I wonder who thought this one up

In the by now familiar pattern, metaphor was used in the Framing (Agenda Management) sequences that opened the lesson and that were needed procedurally at other points. The other main use of metaphor was in Explanation sequences around the apostrophe and in Checking Understanding, in both of which the technical language of apostrophe use was 'softened' (see Extract 5.7).

Maths 2

This event was structured by a test that the students had completed in a previous lesson. The overall goal of the lesson was to *go over* the test, to take each item in turn and discuss it. It began and ended with Agenda Management and with Evaluative Feedback on the overall results of the maths test. As each item was talked about, metaphor was heavily used in Feedback about students' success or otherwise in getting the right answers. Some of the Feedback sequences evolved into Explanations of mathematical concepts or processes. The subtechnical language and mediation of these ideas made use of metaphor. Alterity was often affective as well as conceptual, with comments made on the correctness, the effort and the success of individual students and the class as a whole. Metaphor played an important role in these comments, and in thereby (re)constructing the expected norms of the classroom.

TV programme

The TV event had two separate stages: watching the programme and teacher-led discussion of the content. In the actual programme, the narrator's commentary included very little metaphor, whereas the short film clips of school activity included the types of metaphors similar to those used in the study school. In the discussion that followed, metaphors occurred in some of the anecdotes, particularly in Summarizing sequences.

Summary

While the aims and nature of the particular discourse events led to each one showing a different balance of action types, there was consistency across events in the use of metaphor in each type of teaching sequence and in the tendency for certain types of teaching sequence to use more metaphor than others.

The analysis of metaphor in teaching action across the discourse events showed that:

- The teaching sequences most likely to involve metaphor were Summarizing, Agenda Management and Evaluative Feedback. More than half of these sequences contained at least one metaphor.
- Metaphors occurred in about one-third of Control, Strategic Feedback and Explication sequences.
- Very few metaphors were used in Exemplification, Checking Understanding, Organizing and Information Search sequences.

The clustering of metaphors apparent in the geology lesson was also observed in the other events, not just in Agenda Management and Explanation sequences but in other types of teaching action too. An explanation of metaphor clustering is multidimensional, in that it arises from several interacting factors relating both to metaphor use and to discourse processes. It is further described on pp. 137–9. Meanwhile we take a closer look at metaphor in the teaching sequences.

The use of metaphor in teaching sequences

This section focuses on the teaching sequences which featured significant use of metaphor. Typical and telling examples are taken from the discourse data to discuss the nature of the metaphors used (Research Question 1) and the opportunities offered by the metaphors for the mediation of thinking, learning, affect and action (Research Question 2).

Metaphors in framing: Agenda Management

Agenda Management sequences were, across all the events, the most likely places to find metaphor in use. Metaphors occurred at the beginning and end of every event, and throughout every event, as sub-topics and sub-goals shifted in the dynamics of the activity. The combination of frequency of occurrence of the sequence type and a high probability of metaphor use in any one sequence showed that Agenda Management metaphors were the most common type of metaphor.

Extract 6.1 from the geology lesson shows how, after the students were organized with worksheets and pencils, the teacher set out the agenda of the forthcoming lesson(s). Agenda Management starts at the first line; an Explication of the verb *weather* (line 6) occurs inside the Agenda Management sequence at lines 7–9; and the agenda is restated in lines 10–12.

Extract 6.1 *Metaphors in Agenda Management: opening the geology lesson*

```
1   now what I'm going to do ( . ) this afternoon (1.0)
2   because I can't think of any other way to do it (1.0)
3   is to give you a little bit of information (2.0)
4   on which we can build ( . ) our understanding (1.0) of ( . ) rocks (4.0)
5   and the minerals that come out of rocks (1.0)
6   and also ( . ) how rocks weather (2.0)
7   in other words ( . ) what happens to rocks (1.0)
8   when ( . ) the snow ( . ) and the wind and the ice and the rain and the temperature (1.0)
9   acts upon them ( . )
10  so there are really two things we're going to look at (2.0) this half term (1.0)
11  one is ( . ) how the rocks weather (1.0)
12  and the other is ( . ) about the minerals ( . ) that are in them ( . ) that we can use
```

As in most Agenda Management sequences, metaphor is used to talk about two aspects of the lesson activity: procedure and content. The procedures and processes of teaching and learning are described in terms of *looking at, giving information,* and *building understanding.* The content of the lessons ahead involves conventionalized metaphor to describe inanimate geological processes as animate action: *come out of, acts upon.* In giving a forward-looking summary of lesson content, the teacher offers the students what has been called an 'advance organiser' (Ausubel 1960). Advance organizers are held to help learning by providing 'hooks to hang ideas on', i.e. ways to organize and recall new content as it is presented.

At the end of the lesson, the teacher looks forward to the next lesson in a closing Agenda Management sequence (Extract 6.2). Again, metaphors are used to talk about both procedure, with a further use of the verb metaphor *look at,* and the content.

Extract 6.2 *Metaphors in Agenda Management: closing the geology lesson*

1	now tomorrow again (.) we'll (.) <u>have a look</u> (.) <u>at</u> (.)
	why are all three rock types present (.)
	and how do the local rocks of Cumbria <u>fit into the overall picture</u> of the age of the earth (2.0)
	and I've got a very interesting diagram (1.0) to show you (.)
5	that shows how old we are (.)
	<u>in comparison with</u> the rocks we were walking over (3.0)

All the events had a similar pattern of metaphor rich Agenda Management sequences at their start, and at points during an event where procedures were renegotiated or restated. Extract 6.3 shows the teacher in the dancing practice doing some procedural talk between episodes of action to explain to students which dance they will do next (a dance called *Spider's Web*) while also motivating them to keep working at the dance steps.

Extract 6.3 *Metaphors in Agenda Management: during the dancing practice*

1	T:	now (.) I'm really <u>pushing</u> you this afternoon (.)
		because the more we can get practised and <u>worked out</u> (2.0)
		the more time we <u>have</u> (.) to really (.) <u>polish</u> it <u>up</u> (.)
		and make it look professional (2.0)
5		so (.) if you all feel <u>up to it</u> (.)
		I thought we'd <u>have a go</u> at Spider's Web

We can also see in Extract 6.3 how these framing metaphors often mediated affective as well as ideational content. In the first line, the use of a vivid metaphor *pushing* emphasizes the toughness of the task that the teacher is setting, but she shifts to the inclusive first person plural *we* (lines 3 and 6) to align herself with the students. Alongside grammatical choices, lexical choices may also act in an affective way to mitigate possible threats. Verbs like *give* or *look at*, as used in Extracts 6.2 and 6.3, are uncomplicated and, with additional use of metaphorical determinatives like *a little bit* (Extract 6.2, line 3), seem to try to reassure students by downplaying the effort that might be required in participating in the lesson and the shared discourse, and in mastering the content. We return to the affective role of metaphor later in the chapter (pp. 139–40).

Lexical choices in Agenda Management metaphors were seldom vivid or striking. Rather they showed evidence of systematic use of verbs of movement to describe lesson procedures and shifts of topic. The verbs *go* and *come*, often followed by one or more prepositions, were consistently used to refer to working, writing, thinking or talking about:

> let's <u>go</u> quickly <u>through</u> them (= exercise items) (apostrophe lesson)
> we'll <u>come back in a moment to</u> ..   (geology lesson)
> do you want to <u>go on</u> and do day three?   (class work)
> right (.) let's <u>go back</u> (.) <u>to</u> these rocks (1.0)
> fire formed (2.0)   (geology lesson)
> let's just <u>go into</u> that <u>a little bit more</u>   (geology lesson)

The systematicity of this group of metaphors is examined further in Chapter 10.

To summarize thus far, in Agenda Management the teacher often verbalizes her perception of the alterity that she will deal with in the forthcoming discourse. Agenda Management metaphors play a metacognitive role, often helping to construct students' experience of events at three levels: at an overall level in opening and closing sequences, at the level of episodes of action within an event, and at the utterance level through lexical choice of the Vehicle terms of the metaphors. The pattern of heavy and quite systematic metaphor use in Framing discourse means that learning and participation opportunities were frequently presented and described in metaphorical ways.

By sharing her perception of the alterity that will drive the event, the teacher offers the students shared access to goals and intentions. Through the discourse construction of advance organizers of content, and of the teaching and learning processes in these sequences, metaphor plays a key role in students' access to learning opportunities.

Metaphors in Explication sequences

Metaphor theory emphasizes the cognitive role of metaphor in understanding new or difficult concepts (e.g. Kittay 1987), and so it might be expected that metaphor might figure highly in Explication sequences. This was not the case in this study, where other types of teaching action seemed to make greater use of metaphor and where devices other than metaphor were used to reduce alterity around concepts, including:

- Practical demonstration: squashing a plastic cup to show the effect of pressure on rocks.
- Practical activity: having the students pace out the field and count paces to calculate an average.
- Writing about their experience: the diary of their school trip.
- Exemplification and non-metaphorical analogy: reminding students of the type of stone used in the entrance to a local shop.

It will be recalled that Explanation sequences were of two types: Explication, in which more information about a topic was presented, and Exemplification, in which the teacher gave an example, verbally, with realia, or by demonstration. Metaphors were used in very few Exemplification sequences but are found clustering in Explication sequences. However, even there, many of the metaphors were not deliberately used to explain, but were conventionalized ways of referring to the concepts being talked about (Chapter 5).

Metaphor was used in approximately half of the Explication sequences to help students understand concepts and processes including:

the shape of trees in a drawing (Extract 5.10)	(class work)
the fertilization of human ova	
the derivation of a name (Extract 5.1)	
the meaning of 'to feel persecuted'	
crinoids	(geology)
the formation of igneous rocks (Extract 5.2)	
the pattern of a dance	(dancing practice)
arithmetic series	(maths)
converting fractions to decimals	
the use of apostrophes	(apostrophe lesson)

The patterns of talk around deliberate metaphors described in Chapter 5 showed that it is not the metaphors alone that explicate, but the use of metaphors in the discourse, and the interplay of metaphorical and non-metaphorical language, to reduce alterity.

If we look at the lexis and syntax of the deliberate linguistic metaphors used in Explication, we find two main ways in which the mapping between Topic and Vehicle domains was encoded –

comparison and approximation. Metaphors in comparisons directly related the Topic concept to the Vehicle using a verb and the particle *like*. Both Topic and Vehicle are explicitly mentioned. The Vehicle was usually more familiar, more concrete, or less complex than the Topic.

> the trees looked like <u>little lollipops</u>
> [rock] becomes like <u>sticky treacle</u>

Some comparisons are also analogies, in that they map not only properties from Vehicle to Topic, but also the relations that hold within the domains. In the other type of deliberate metaphor, the lexicogrammar introduces a Vehicle concept that approximates to the Topic concept. The approximation is signalled by markers like *a sort of/kind of*:

> [the fertilization of an egg by a sperm is] *a sort of* <u>chemical reaction</u>

In both approximation and comparison, the teacher has tuned the talk to the students, probably increasing their chances of understanding.

Conventionalized metaphors linked Topic and Vehicle domains less explicitly, but again using Vehicle lexis that was likely to be more familiar, more concrete, or simpler than Topic lexis would have been. For example, instead of using the word *contraction*, the more familiar and more concrete term *shortening* was used to talk about the function of apostrophes. In the same lesson, the word *singular* was replaced by the more concrete *a noun which is <u>talking about</u> more than one thing*. Many of these metaphors involved animation or personification of the Topic. Since this was the case across the data (not just in Explication) the phenomenon will be discussed as an example of systematicity in Chapter 10.

To summarize, metaphors in Explication adjust conceptual alterity along three dimensions:

- the degree of abstraction   how abstract or concrete an idea is
- the degree of familiarity   how far an idea concerns content familiar to students
- the degree of complexity   how complicated an idea is in terms of other linked ideas that must also be understood

In most conventionalized metaphors, the adjustment in conceptual alterity was downwards: Vehicle concepts were less abstract, more familiar, simpler than the Topic concepts. In addition, if we consider the conceptual content of lexical items on a general to specific continuum, metaphor Vehicles were often less specific/more general than the Topic:

> the _key_ is to keep these shoulders together
> [a number pattern] was _going up_ in threes
> what's classification a _big_ word for?
> _do it in your head_ (= carry out the (mathematical) process without writing it down)

There appears to be a problem here. If classroom discourse (particularly explication of concepts) aims to push students' thinking to higher levels of abstraction and complexity, how can metaphor possibly help in this process if it tends to reduce abstraction and complexity? To resolve this we need to recall the complex systems idea of action on several interacting timescales and the nature of metaphor in discourse described in Chapter 5.

On the micro timescale of interaction in Explication sequences, the teacher's immediate goal is to reduce conceptual alterity from state a_1 to state a_2, where a_1 is her perception of students' initial understanding and a_2 is her perception of what they need to understand. To get from a_1 to a_2, the teacher may use conventionalized metaphors, or she may present, unpack and re-assemble deliberate metaphors. At each interim step, the Vehicle of the conventionalized metaphor may be less abstract or complex than its Topic, but the overall gradient, across the various Vehicles, is upwards. We can describe the process of reducing alterity in Extract 5.1 in this way:

> a_1 = students do not understand the derivation of the name _Skidda_
> a_2 = students understand derivation as a corruption of the name of the hill _Skiddaw_
> Conventionalized metaphors: _comes from, after, drop_
>   are used to build up understanding of
> Deliberate metaphors: _nickname, corruption_

The discourse about igneous rocks in Extract 5.2 uses both conventionalized and deliberate metaphors with less abstract, more familiar and simpler Vehicles, but the relexicalization and development of the Vehicle help to increase the complexity of the less familiar Topic as the talking-and-thinking proceeds.

The mediation of conceptual alterity can be visualized as the teacher reaching across the gap, offering stepping stones, and helping students move across the stepping stones to the new understanding. The skill of the teacher lies in estimating the gap, the number and positioning of the stones, and the help needed. Metaphors can act as stepping stones and as a description of the end point, and can occur in the discourse assistance the teacher provides.

Metaphors in Summarizing sequences

Summarizing occurred throughout the data in all events and at all levels. Summarizing sequences were one of the most likely places to encounter metaphor. Ends of events typically involved summaries but so did the end of shorter sequences of all types. For example, at the end of the volcanoes episode (Extract 5.2, line 39) the teacher summarizes the discussion of the formation of igneous rocks with a Summarizing statement that describes formation metaphorically as movement from a place:

> so that's <u>where</u> these rocks <u>come from</u>

At the end of explaining the lesson agenda (Extract 6.1) the teacher summarizes the content agenda:

> so there are really two things we're going to <u>look at</u> this half term

Summaries, in pulling together ideas, tend to use lexis of a less specific nature than that used in the talk being summarized. Metaphor is well suited to this level of talk, as Drew and Holt (1988) found in their study of idioms in talk (p.24). In addition, because summaries tend to come at the end of a topic or subtopic, this results in frequent metaphor use at topic change points.

It is typical of summaries of both content and process that the metaphor Vehicle is abstract and general. In Extract 6.4 (dancing practice) the teacher uses the shared metaphor of the pattern of a dance as *spokes in a wheel* to summarize her Feedback sequence. The *wheel* is not further specified.

Extract 6.4 Content metaphors in Summarizing sequences: spokes in a wheel

> Melanie (.) you're <u>a little bit</u> (.) turned towards the centre (.) can you turn (.) out (2.0) that's right (.) people <u>on</u> the outsides (.) should be right back (.) remember these **spokes in a wheel**

At the end of the maths lesson on averaging, the teacher summarized the process with:

> and all of this (.) <u>arose out of</u> me (.) wanting you (1.0) to know (.) how to <u>work out</u> (5.0) an average

Summarizing metaphors also sometimes carried affective value, again in parallel with Drew and Holt's findings for adult–adult telephone conversations. In Extract 6.5, the teacher brings to a close an anecdote about teaching deaf children in the discussion after the TV programme. The Summarizing sequence begins with the *so* at line 3, and closes with a metaphorical idiom that emphasizes values about judging other people.

Extract 6.5 *Evaluative metaphors in Summarizing sequences*

```
1   T:   and it was amazing ( . )
         just just watching how those teachers got them to speak ( . )
         so ( . ) you know ( . ) we've got to be very careful haven't we?
         it's what I say to you all the time ( . )
5        don't go by what you see ( . )
         because what you see might not actually tell you the true story
```

Metaphors were used to summarize content and process, often employing general or abstract lexis. At the end of episodes of teaching action, summaries offer students a final opportunity to consolidate the ideas in the preceding discourse. They also signal an upcoming change of topic in the talking-and-thinking, and so may be important in prompting students to close down the current topic in their minds and to get ready for the next.

The evaluative content of Summarizing sequences may play a role in constructing values and attitudes between teachers and the class as a whole.

Metaphors in Feedback sequences

Two main types of feedback were found in the discourse: evaluative and strategic. Evaluative Feedback rates performance or product, and may be addressed to individuals or to the whole class. Public evaluative statements contribute to constructing and reinforcing group norms of expected performance:

> you have to have <u>a good little bit of</u> memory here   (maths 2)
> I think you all <u>deserve a medal</u>   (dancing practice)

Strategic Feedback includes advice on how to improve performance. In this type of feedback, metaphor often encodes the content of the strategy, not just at a general level but also at a more specific level of lexis. In Extract 6.6 (dancing practice), the teacher introduces the Strategic sequence with the general and abstract metaphor Vehicle, *secret*, and then goes on to explain more specifically what the *secret* is, using the verb metaphor *pulled up* (*keep yourselves sort of tall* was a borderline candidate for metaphor):

Extract 6.6 *Metaphor in Strategic Feedback: the secret of skipping*

```
now ( . ) the secret ( . ) the secret to this skipping thing ( . )
even if you're not terribly good at skipping (2.0) ?????
the secret of this skipping ( . ) is to ( . ) is to try and keep your ( . )
keep yourselves sort of ( . ) tall ( . ) and pulled up a bit in your middles (2.0)
```

Extract 6.7, in which the teacher advises a pupil on strategies for answering mental arithmetic questions, shows the use of extended metaphors around *time*. She describes the strategy in general in line 3, suggests how the child can do this more precisely in line 5, and then models and summarizes one way of gaining time in lines 6 and 7. Investigation of the COBUILD corpus confirmed that the verb *buy* is a much less frequent metaphorical collocate of *time* than *spend*, *waste*, *give* (S. Hunston, p.c.).

Extract 6.7 *Metaphor in Strategic Feedback: buying time*

1	T:	how many pence in ten pounds? (3.0)
		think before you speak (2.0)
		give yourself a little time (2.0)
		you should watch the others (.)
5		to find out all the strategies they have (.) for buying time (.)
		they sort of go (.) umm (.) and that's that's to tell me (.)
		I'm still thinking but I need a bit of time

Metaphors occur more frequently in Evaluative Feedback, and it is striking how often the choice of Vehicle appears to have an affective function in mitigating threats to face, as in Extract 6.8 (dancing practice) where the teacher corrects the position of the boys' feet. This is a typical Feedback sequence in that the teacher avoids giving direct negative feedback by suggesting an alternative. It merges into Explication in lines 2–5, and the nearest we get to a negative comment is in line 6, where the teacher imitates the boys' feet. This visual hyperbole together with the metaphorical comparison makes the pupils laugh, and defuses any threat to face from the critical feedback.

Extract 6.8 *Metaphors in Evaluative Feedback: like Charlie Chaplin*

1	T:	boys (.) can you try and have your feet in what's called (.) first position (.)
		where your heels are just touching (1.0)
		and your knees are straight (3.0)
		and your toes are a little bit out (.) but not that much (2.0)
5		about at five to one (.)
		not like this (.) it looks funny (.) like Charlie Chaplin
	Ps:	*laugh*

Metaphorical idioms are also used to mitigate the force of negative feedback to a pupil:

> *you're on the right track*   (maths 1)

Analysis of the data relating to Evaluative Feedback reveals further distinctive features of the personal styles of the two teachers. Teacher 1, who is both the class teacher and headteacher, appears to have a child-oriented approach to classroom organization, discipline and feedback (Galton and Williamson 1992) which is manifested in the use of metaphor that aligns rather than distances her, through acknowledgement of her own problems and the use of an inclusive pronoun:

> my brain can't manage that... (maths 1)
> when we say got or get ...we're actually being
> a little bit lazy (class work 1)

Teacher 2 on the other hand appears to have a more direct approach to Evaluative Feedback. In the maths lesson, she urged children to *think hard* and *use their heads* to find the answers. At the beginning of the lesson she gave an overall Evaluation of their performance on the test (Extract 6.9) that shows her more direct, non-mitigating style. A cluster of metaphors refers to the processes of thinking and learning.

Extract 6.9 *Metaphor in Evaluative Feedback: the maths test*

---

1 I said I was going to give you (.) a set (.) which were (.) quite difficult (1.0)
but just to see who could really (.) use their head (2.0)
and think hard (2.0)
and work things out (2.0)
5 with a bit of thought you would do (.) not too badly (2.0)
well (.) it worked (.) because I saw the people (.) who used their heads (.) and thought (1.0)
and I found out the people who just looked at the question and (.) didn't think too much at all

---

The use of metaphor in Feedback sequences often seems designed to avoid direct negative feedback that might be de-motivating. There is evidence of personal style in how feedback was given to students.

Metaphors in Control sequences

Neither teacher needed to use many Control sequences because the class was small and mostly well behaved. However, the Control sequences that were used, mostly in the dancing practice, often contained metaphor. As in Evaluative Feedback, metaphor seemed to help avoid threats to loss of face as in the following examples where we see how Teacher 1's child-oriented style made use of metaphor with lightweight, sometimes idiomatic or humorous, Vehicle lexis that avoided giving direct orders to students:

> try and pick your feet up
> you sort yourself out
> you can't just let it rip

Metaphors in teaching sequences: summary

The analysis of metaphors in mediated action, using the teaching sequence as a unit of analysis, revealed that certain types of sequences – Agenda Management, Explication, Summarizing, Feedback and Control – made greater use of metaphor than did the other types. An unexpected finding was the relatively low frequency of metaphors used in explaining new or difficult concepts to students. The mediation of conceptual content occurred in some Summarizing and Feedback sequences, as well as in Explication. The reduction of conceptual alterity in discourse often combined the use of conventionalized and deliberate metaphors.

Metaphor played an important role in mediating the procedures and processes of discourse events, mostly in Agenda Management sequences, but also in some Summarizing and Control sequences. In addition, metaphor potentially mediated values and attitudes through affective content, in particular the use of highly evaluative metaphor in Feedback and Control sequences.

Metaphor clustering

Throughout the data, metaphors had a tendency to occur in clusters in sequential talk around a topic with a particular speaker/addressee combination. Analysis suggests that several different factors may contribute to the observed phenomenon: discourse factors, content factors and psycholinguistic factors. Evidence on each is reported below.

Discourse factors in metaphor clustering

Widespread repetition of Vehicle terms was found across the data. Once introduced into the discourse, a Vehicle term might be repeated, by the same speaker or by another speaker. Much of the repetition of metaphorically used lexis seems to be consistent with repetition and reformulation reported in studies of adult conversation lexis (McCarthy 1988; Tannen 1989). In addition, the three-part exchange characteristic of teacher–student talk, and used in some of the events, might increase the incidence of repetition, since teachers often repeat a student's answer before commenting on it.

There were very few examples of a metaphor repeated in reduced form (contra Goatly's findings for written text (1997: 256)) but there were many more instances of repetition with slight changes in morphology, change of word class or addition of an adjective:

> *in my head*
> *ring a bell in your mind*
> *make a mental note*
>
> *in your head*
> *if any bells ring in your mind*
> *make a little mental note*

Some of metaphor clustering may result from the general tendency in discourse to repeat and reformulate lexis.

Content factors in metaphor clustering

The topic being talked about may generate multiple use of metaphor. This may happen because conventionalized metaphor is needed to talk about the topic, or, as we saw with deliberate metaphors mediating conceptual content (p. 103), a topic that involves deliberate metaphor may require several metaphorical expressions to develop and then summarize the ideas.

Psycholinguistic factors in metaphor clustering

A shift to metaphorical ways of talking may perhaps have a knock-on effect through activated mental connections after the initial use of a metaphor. This remains a tentative suggestion, since the only evidence available is on the surface of the discourse. There is no access to the psycholinguistic processes of participants.

Once a shift to metaphorical thinking has taken place, further use of metaphor may become more likely. Extract 6.8 showed the teacher using a second, contrasting, metaphor *not like Charlie Chaplin* very soon after the first, *your toes are . . . at five to one*.

The data also contain some examples of parallelism in the lexico-grammar of metaphors that occur close to each other in the discourse:

> *off her own bat . . . . off you go*
> *[writing] goes on . . . . time's gone on*

Finally, there is just one example in the data of the phenomenon I have called, after Freud, 'parapraxis', which seems to arise from sub-conscious mental connections, or 'serendipitous Freudian slips' (Dennett 1991: 243). In Extract 6.10, two terms with semantic connections, *lock* and *key,* occur close to each other in the talk but are used as Vehicles for two quite different Topics.

Extract 6.10 *Parapraxis in the dance lesson*

right now (.) double plaiting (2.0)
Ellen and Rebecca (1.0) you must hold hands ?????
if you want to **lock** your arms inside each other (.) that's fine (.) but hold hands (4.0) that's it (.) right (.) because (.) the **key** is (.) to keep those shoulders (.) together (.) if you can

The humorous possibilities of exploiting links between metaphors were noticed by the students in their subversive discourse, reported in a later section (pp. 140–2).

Metaphor and the mediation of affect

In this section, the affective impact of metaphor, noted earlier in passing, is explored further. We have seen how metaphors in Feedback and Control sequences were used to mitigate potential threats to students' self-esteem from explicit expressions of disapproval. As many of the examples in this and the previous chapters suggest, the choice of Vehicle lexis often simplified and concretized Topic concepts in a child-friendly way. Indeed, the Vehicle often seemed to over-simplify well below the capacities of the students. But when we look at the discourse around the Vehicle terms, we find many other ways in which the language could be seen as offering opportunities to mediate attitudes and values. These are summarized in Table 6.1.

Table 6.1 Features of metaphor use that mediate affect

Feature of metaphor use	Data example
'childish' or simple lexis	lollipop trees
'diminishing' determinatives	a little bit of information
direct expressions of solidarity	my brain won't manage that
inclusive 'we' pronouns	we got as far as we've so far practised
humour	not like Charlie Chaplin
hyperbole	I thought someone was at least dead
'diminishing' adverbs	go back just a whisper
'diminishing' adjectives	we have a little problem

Graumann (1990), in a study of interactive spoken discourse, identified three dimensions of affect or 'perspective': evaluation, alignment/distancing, and emphasis.

The discourse use of metaphor was particularly noticeable for its aligning and emphasizing impact. Mechanisms of alignment include the direct expressions of solidarity and humour, and the use of inclusive first person plural pronouns and possessive adjectives. The informality of much of the metaphorically used lexis might also signal alignment from teacher to students.

Both emphasis and de-emphasis occurred around and with metaphor. Hyperbole emphasized, with the humour acting to defuse the risk of distancing. One of the most noticeable affective features of the use of metaphor was the de-emphasizing of the effort demanded of the students through the use of 'diminishing' determinatives, adverbs and adjectives, and by the choice of Vehicle lexis. For example, in explaining the learning agenda of the geology lesson (Extract 6.1), the teacher both de-emphasized the processes and aligned herself through her choice of pronouns:

> [I'm going to] <u>give</u> you <u>a little bit</u> of information
> on which we can <u>build</u> our understanding

The process for students is turned into one of receiving (*give*); the content is diminished into something non-threatening (*a little bit*); and longer term conceptual development is a reassuringly simple process of construction (*build our understanding*), which the teacher will be doing alongside them. Across the data, subject knowledge came in *little bits*, writing was *saying* or *putting*, studying was *looking at*, understanding was *seeing*, remembering was *bells ringing*, calculating was *finding out*. These metaphors seem to be designed to pre-empt any probability that students might be demotivated by the size of the learning task, i.e. their perceptions of alterity.

Metaphor was used systematically to mediate affect, particularly where alignment or motivation was potentially threatened, as in Feedback and Control, and to a lesser extent Agenda Management and Explication sequences. This accords with findings from adult–adult interaction (Strässler 1982; Drew and Holt 1998) but differs importantly in being one-way, from teacher to student. The status of the participants in classroom discourse is asymmetric. Teachers' status is given by virtue of their position in the institution, and is thus non-negotiable, and teachers are freed to attend to students' self-esteem. The systematicity of this practice suggests that the teachers are working with an underlying belief that students should share with them a common sense of endeavour and engagement with content, something that may be threatened if alterity seems too great. The use of metaphor, and talk around metaphor, plays a key role in mediating and managing affect and perceptions of alterity.

Student use of and response to linguistic metaphors

This section summarizes students' use of metaphor. Of the few uses of metaphor that occurred, most were produced in some type of response to a teacher's metaphor. The only instance of a student initiating the use of a metaphor in talk with the teacher was in the volcanic lava episode (Extract 5.2), *is volcanic lava like melted wax?* Student-initiated metaphors in peer talk were mostly humorous.

Student repetition of teacher's metaphor

The most frequent type of response to a teacher's use of metaphor was repetition of the Vehicle word or phrase. Often, as in Extract 6.11, the lexical item seemed to make some phonological or semantic impact that led to its repetition. Here, the teacher's use of the idiomatic form *earwig* to mean 'eavesdrop' or 'listen in' seems to be relished by Ellen, who repeated the word in a whisper as she carried on with her own work.

Extract 6.11   *Student repetition of teacher's metaphor*

T	I hope all the conversation (.) is (.) all about your friend helping you with something to do with your Humphrey Head work (.) having <u>earwigged</u> a little bit (.) =
E	whispers [<u>earwigged</u>
T	= to what is being said (.) I don't think (.) that's what's happening (.) I think some people are having a good old gossip (.) am I right? (.)

Louise repeated the teacher's use of *treacle* in a similar way in Extract 5.2, line 22, and *lollipop trees* in Extract 5.10, line 29. This 'private repetition' became apparent because Louise, who was wearing the microphone, was part of a larger ongoing 'commentary' on classroom events that took place between her and her friends.

Student extension of teacher's metaphor

There were several instances where students played with a metaphor by re-using the Vehicle term literally. This was done both publicly and privately. Extract 6.12 shows a student noticing the teacher's conventionalized metaphor about time, uttered in passing as she went to help Louise, and extending it in a response several minutes later.

Extract 6.12   *Student extension of teacher metaphor*

T:	(*to the class*) <u>where does the time go</u>? (2.0) (*to Louise*) finished?
L:	(*to T*) I'm having trouble with this
T:	you stuck? (.) right (.) . . .
	. . . yes Paul?
P:	I know <u>where the time goes</u> (1.0) <u>into the past</u>
T:	<u>into the past</u> (.) you're right ????? quickly <u>into the past</u>

In the next extract, a student does something similar but the extension is addressed only to other students sitting at the same table, possibly because the extension is rather subversive. The class has to choose a hymn to sing in the whole school assembly on the theme of God as the good shepherd, and the teacher discusses the possibility of singing the psalm 'The Lord is my shepherd'. The student playfully links the religious metaphor to a nursery rhyme.

Extract 6.13 *Pupil extension of conventionalized metaphor*

> T: we've got to think of a hymn (.) about (2.0) <u>the good shepherd</u> (2.0)
> the Lord's <u>my shepherd</u> (.) do you ? (.)
> I don't know whether you could manage the Lord's <u>my shepherd</u> (.) could you ? (.)
> it's quite difficult (.) for the breathing
> . . .
> P: *(to friends)* baa baa black sheep

These examples show that students are alert to the potential incongruity and creativity of even conventionalized and prosaic metaphors. As Gibbs (1994) argues, this kind of subconscious awareness of metaphors renders inappropriate the traditional label 'dead metaphor'.

Metaphorical hyperbole

Metaphors that were produced by students tended to involve exaggeration:

> I've done <u>millions</u> of sums
> <u>loads and loads</u> of us
> whoever did this is going to be <u>squashed meat with pepper all over it and mustard</u>
> this rash is <u>driving me insane</u>

Such metaphors could reflect the hyperbolic nature of peer talk among 10-year-olds, but may also reflect the relatively powerless participatory role allocated to students in classroom discourse. While teacher–class talk is officially sanctioned, their own talk is off stage and hence both freer and a contributor to the construction of sub-group identity and membership. Hyperbole is one discourse device that contrasts with the typical discourse of the teacher–class group.

Other voices and mini-dramas

The data included further types of talk that characterize peer interaction freed from the constraints of teacher control, and that have a link to metaphor. On several occasions, students switch into other voices, literally as well as in the Bakhtinian sense (Maybin 1996). The situations were away from the hearing of adults, e.g. over lunch or in a queue at the teacher's desk. The voices and roles adopted were usually those of adults, as when one girl said to another in the voice of a teacher:

> you ought to be proud of yourself my girl

Sometimes an adult voice was adopted for a single utterance, sometimes over several turns of talk to produce a kind of mini-drama, as when two students, while eating their sandwiches, acted out a scenario of a policeman stopping a driver who had been drinking.

This kind of discourse resembles metaphor in that it imports an incongruous semantic content into talk. It differs from metaphor in that the content is not used as a Vehicle domain to be linked to something in the ongoing discourse context.

Student use of metaphor: discussion

The use of other voices and the playing out of mini-dramas reminds us of the extent of students' discourse resources and their capacity to draw on them contingently in on-line discourse. Together with the private repetition and extension of metaphor, this provides some evidence of the thinking that occurs in conjunction with talking. Discourse data show us only what is actually said, but, beneath this exterior talk, minds are teeming with possibilities for the alternative content that Dennett (1991: 237) calls 'a pandemonium of word demons'. From this nonlinear, dynamical co-adapting of multiple ideas and words, talk emerges. Metaphor, because of incongruous Vehicle content, may play a somewhat special role in this talking-and-thinking process, of which the intriguing phenomenon of parapraxis may be only the most obvious manifestation.

Conclusion

The possibilities of metaphor create a range of opportunities or affordances (van Lier 2000). Analysis at the level of teaching sequences helps us to see how participants avail themselves of the opportunities and how they stretch them to meet their interactional needs. In the discourse examined here, metaphor contributed most markedly to the mediation of the agenda and procedures of events, to the description of upcoming content and processes, to give feedback on performance, and to summarize content and processes. In mediating conceptual alterity, deliberate and conventionalized metaphors helped bridge the gap with concepts and discourse. Metaphor was also used to prevent problematic discourse encounters when teachers might need to correct or control students. Various features of metaphor were exploited for affective purposes, often to mediate students' perceptions of alterity and the cognitive effort being required of them. Finally, we have seen how metaphor offers students a way to comment on teacher talk, publicly or privately, and to construct their own sub-group discourse.

7 Researching metaphor interpretation

Introduction

The empirical investigation reported in Chapters 3–6 in revealed something of how the teachers used metaphor to create opportunities or affordances in the environment of classroom discourse. In the following chapters, an account of the second study, investigating how students make sense of the metaphors they encounter, helps us to understand more about how such opportunities may contribute to learning.

We are again concerned with processes of understanding in interactive talking-and-thinking, but also with how immediate on-line processing might have an effect on the longer timescale of conceptual development. Before explaining how the study was designed, here is a review of the key aspects of teachers' use of metaphor in classroom discourse:

- Metaphor in classroom discourse is used with both affective and ideational goals. These goals interact in the choice of Vehicle lexis and the use of language in the immediate linguistic context of the Vehicle.
- Metaphor plays a gate-keeping role around learning opportunities through its frequent use in the creation, negotiation and control of the agenda of lessons.
- Metaphor is used in the explanation of key concepts and learning strategies, and may sometimes become a shared referent for teacher and pupils in future discourse, e.g. *spokes in a wheel, lollipop trees*. This function can be seen as an attractor in interactional talking-and-thinking.
- Concepts that are new or difficult are sometimes explicated with the use of deliberate metaphors, usually nominal.
- The talk around deliberate metaphors offers a range of supports for understanding and the reduction of alterity. This support seems to be tuned to the perceived needs of participants.
- Long-term systematic metaphor use occurs around particular topics, e.g. using lexis from the domain of speaking and listening in connection with literacy processes. The linguistic

expressions and the conceptual mappings of these systematic metaphors may function as shared attractors.
- The discourse sometimes mediates the metaphors from beyond school, e.g. the technical language of geology and maths is rendered less threatening through animation.
- Metaphor in the immediacy of talking-and-thinking was used primarily to simplify concepts or to make them more concrete and thus more accessible. These metaphors may act as an intermediary, or as stepping stones, in the longer-term reduction of alterity, which requires students to reduce the simplicity and concreteness of the concepts.

The first investigation produced no evidence as to the short- or long-term impact of such experiences with metaphor. It could be observed only that students are offered certain opportunities through the use of metaphor. The processes of understanding and learning from metaphor that had remained invisible now become the subject of investigation. The evidence of metaphor use from the first study suggested areas to be addressed in the second study:

- How students construct, in the process of interactional talking-and-thinking, understandings of deliberate metaphors.
- How mediation helps in reaching shared understanding of metaphors.
- How immediate processing of metaphors affects longer-term changes in understanding.

To investigate these concerns, students were presented with metaphors in texts. They then carried out a research task to explore how they made sense of the metaphors and the text content. In this chapter, I first set out the theoretical framework for 'understanding' metaphor that will be used and review relevant literature on children's metaphor understanding. I then show how understanding is operationalized in the design of the study: the research task is described, its validity discussed, and the procedures for data collection and analysis are set out.

Understanding metaphor in discourse: a complex systems perspective

A theoretical framework was required to underpin the empirical investigation. Theory and investigation are reported here in a linear fashion which suggests that the theoretical work was carried out prior to starting the empirical work. In fact, this was not how it happened, and in qualitative applied linguistic research is seldom how it happens. The move between theory and investigation is recursive: theory may be a starting point for formulating the questions that require empirical investigation, but empirical work reveals more fully what needs to be taken account of. This in turn requires further theoretical development. This section presents the theoretical framework that was developed to serve the study, acknowledging the dynamic 'unfinalizability' (Bakhtin 1981) of the process. It builds on the ideas in Chapters 1 and 2.

Understanding as reduction of alterity

When metaphor occurs in discourse, readers or speakers construct a meaning, or make sense of the metaphor in its discourse context. The metaphor is not made sense of in isolation, but in its discourse context. Interpretations will be constrained by the drive to maintain and develop the coherence of the ongoing interpretations of the discourse event so far (Meadows 1993: 72; Rumelhart 1979).

The interpretation processes are carried out in social interaction. In successful interaction, participants construct shared intersubjectivity by reducing the alterity in their joint talking-and-thinking, called 'discourse alterity'. On a longer timescale, we want to find out whether the shared understandings contribute to conceptual development; this can be seen as a reduction of 'conceptual alterity' between the individual's understanding, and the accepted and formalized 'scientific' concept.

Understanding as 'the reduction of alterity' is now further formalized for each of the two timescales, immediate and ontogenetic.

REDUCTION OF DISCOURSE ALTERITY

At this timescale, students engage in joint talking-and-thinking around text sentences, some of which include metaphors. Understanding a metaphor requires the construction of a coherent interpretation of the Vehicle in relation to the Topic domain. Mental processes must somehow combine aspects of the underlying semantic or conceptual domains of the Topic and Vehicle to reach an interpretation that is coherent with the understanding of the ongoing discourse built up so far, or which re-organizes that understanding into a new coherence. The activation and mappings of Vehicle and Topic domains is not a linear sequence of events; they are likely to proceed backwards and forwards between the sense of the lexis in the text and existing knowledge. Since this happens in interaction, the activation and mappings may also be co-adaptive between participants.

From a complexity perspective, we can see the shared talking-

and-thinking as a complex system that moves on a trajectory through a succession of jointly constructed intersubjectivities. When the system is in a phase of reduced or little alterity between participants, it can be seen as an attractor of shared language and understanding. We are interested in how the occurrence of a metaphor affects this trajectory. Does the use of a metaphor throw it off course, out of the stable attractor, or is the shared understanding sufficient to withstand the threat to its stability and remain in the attractor? If the metaphor does perturb the system of talking-and-thinking, does it move to a new attractor, perhaps of increased understanding or perhaps of uncertainty?

Understanding a metaphor is not a finite bounded process; a minimal interpretation of a metaphor may be reached, or an interpretation may be elaborated to various degrees (Siltanen 1990). In addition, the understandings constructed may align to varying degrees with those intended by the producer.

REDUCTION OF CONCEPTUAL ALTERITY

On the longer ontogenetic timescale, conceptual alterity refers to a gap between an individual's understanding and some other, more developed understanding. In formal educational contexts, these 'other' understandings are likely to be formalized and conventionalized 'scientific concepts'. In the study, the scientific concepts explicated in and mediated by the texts were the ozone layer and the working of the heart.

At this timescale, the complex system is the individual's conceptual understanding and their language resources to talk about it, seen as a dynamic system moving from one stable attractor to the next. Talking-and-thinking around metaphors may perturb the trajectory of the individual conceptual system and push it into a new attractor, or it may fail to destabilize the existing trajectory.

THE RELATION OF ACTION ON THE TWO TIMESCALES

We need also to theorize the connection between the immediate and the ontogenetic timescales, i.e. how involvement in discourse leads to conceptual development. Sociocultural theory does this through the idea of 'internalization', in which the shared talking-and-thinking is reconstructed in the mind of an individual to become part of his or her own mental resources.

In complex systems terms, shared attractors of understanding reached in discourse may be internalized by the individual in a 'phase shift' to become new attractors in conceptual development. It is unlikely that metaphor alone pushes the conceptual system to a new area of its phase space. As we saw in earlier analyses, metaphor is only one among several strategies for explicating ideas; the talk in which metaphors are embedded offers important support for understanding. By analysing what happens around phase shifts, and around perturbations that do not lead to phase shifts, we may find out more about how metaphor contributes to learning through interaction.

Previous research on children's understanding of metaphor

Children's understanding of metaphor will obviously be affected by their knowledge of the conceptual and lexical domains of Topic and Vehicle. Both the extent of domain knowledge and its relative salience affect the probability of successful understanding. Keil (1979, 1983) shows that, once a degree of domain knowledge is removed as a variable, the type of knowledge (abstract/concrete; general/specific) becomes a less important factor. Metaphor comprehension follows and can be predicted by the acquisition of domain distinctions. Basic level categories are among the first distinctions made, and should therefore offer easily comprehended metaphors.

When domain knowledge is controlled for, understanding may still be affected by the nature of the mappings that need to be made. For example, interpretation of the metaphor *dancing dinghies* (referring to boats moving up and down on the sea) may map perceptual similarities (shapes of dancers and dinghies), relational correspondences (moving up and down relative to some surface) or psychological links established as connotations in the sociocultural group (happiness in sunshine reflected on moving water). Winner (1988) suggests that relational links are understood later than perceptual links, although it may not be possible to make such general claims since, as Vosniadou (1987b) points out, properties and relations of an entity are often interdependent. Children are likely to employ the relations that are known and salient to them in interpreting metaphors. The empirical evidence of their increasing competence with relational metaphors reflects their increasingly sophisticated understanding of the relations between and within concepts, and increasing familiarity with a wider range of domains.

Gentner's (1982a) work on the nature of scientific metaphors produces some clues as to other possible developmental aspects of metaphor understanding. Precise mappings between clearly defined 'object nodes' are proposed as key features of the explanatory analogies that lie at the base of scientific metaphors, in contrast to the richness of potential mappings in more expressive analogies such as those in poetic literary metaphors. Furthermore, the precise mappings of scientific metaphors tend to be higher order in the sense that they are both more abstract and more general than the richer and less predictable mappings of poetic metaphors. So when *melted butter* is linked in such an analogy with *volcanic lava*, the relational mappings are at the general and abstract level of *melted by heat/bubbling/moving in a certain way* rather than the more specific or concrete relations, such as *colour/smell/use/origins*. Gentner suggests that individual development in the use of scientific metaphors may proceed from the concrete to the abstract.

It appears that sometimes children (and no doubt adults, too) fail to realize that a metaphorical understanding is appropriate. Wales and Coffey (1986), for example, found some evidence that children could identify salient attributes of the Vehicle terms in cross-domain metaphors and were 'capable of apprehending the domain correspondences which these expressions establish', but yet still frequently failed to interpret such metaphors and similes metaphorically (Wales and Coffey 1986: 91; Gibbs 1987).

Not only are children sometimes not aware of the need for a metaphoric interpretation of the language that they encounter, but they may well produce a meaning that is not wholly appropriate in terms of the level and number of mappings made between Vehicle and Topic. Children encounter a range of types of metaphor, and they need to develop the skills to reach appropriate understandings of the different types. Knowing which aspects of Vehicle are relevant to the Topic is centrally affected by existing knowledge. A study by Evans and Gamble (1988) provides an apt demonstration. They asked children aged between 8 and 13 to produce attributes of Topic and Vehicle terms, first in isolation and later combined into metaphors. Basing their scoring of 'correct' meanings on adults' interpretations, the study showed an increase in appropriate interpretations across the age range. The most frequent 'errors' in interpretation were of a type in which children picked on attributes salient to themselves, but not to adults, to use in metaphor interpretation. For example, when asked to interpret *her skirt was a balloon as she walked*, the property *bright red* was given as an attribute for *balloons* and then transferred to the *skirt* in interpretation. It is easy to imagine how the child's previous experience had led to *bright red* becoming an important property of *balloons*, and also how the attributes that were salient – being filled with air, floating or blowing about in the wind – might not have featured in their experience with *balloons*. This particular example also suggests that knowledge and experience of the Topic *skirts* might have helped interpret the metaphor; the child might never have noticed what happens to skirts on windy days. In fact, since the metaphors were not presented in any discourse context beyond the sentence, reaching an adult interpretation of the metaphor would require inferring the windy day schema from the juxtaposition of *skirt – balloon – walked* and their activated properties and relations. If a discourse context had explicitly activated that schema, the child might have reached the adult interpretation.

In summary, the major causes of comprehension and interpretation problems for children encountering metaphor stem from both discourse and conceptual factors:

- not realizing that metaphorical processing is appropriate at all;
- lack of concept knowledge, especially Vehicle knowledge and relational knowledge;
- inappropriate selection of attributes and relations to transfer from Vehicle to Topic concept domains.

The results suggested that classroom talk addresses the first problem to some extent, by providing various clues that a metaphorical understanding is required in the surrounding discourse. Supporting information that seems to be included around metaphorical use of language (Chapter 5) may help further by identifying which attributes or relations are salient. Gaps or inaccuracies in conceptual knowledge remain a potential problem for understanding metaphor.

Research questions

The aims of the study of interaction around metaphors in the texts set out at the beginning of the chapter can be made more precise as research questions:

RQ2-1 How do the students make sense of the linguistic metaphors they encounter in a text?

RQ2-2 How do encounters with metaphor affect conceptual alterity?
Do the metaphors prompt processes that lead to new understandings?
Do the metaphors assist recall of new information?

RQ2-3 What is the role of mediation in interpreting metaphors by the text/writer? peers in interaction?

Research design

The study was designed to explore the processes of making sense of metaphor in discourse, and the impact of metaphor comprehension and interpretation on conceptual knowledge. The method is more qualitative than the experimental formats of much of the research reviewed above and uses students' voices. To access thinking-and-talking about metaphors, Louise (aged 10;8), the data-collector in the classroom study, and her friend Ellen (9;11) were presented with information texts that contained metaphors, and, in a variant of Think-Aloud methodology, asked to talk about the texts. Informal assessments of their conceptual knowledge about the text topics were carried out before and after reading. At some points in the pre- and post-reading stages, Louise and Ellen worked as members of a group with three other students: Heather (10;7), Marie (11;5), Duncan (10;1).

Before going into further detail about the Think-Aloud methodology, I first consider how setting up a research task that involves thinking-and-talking about metaphors in a text constructs a realistic discourse context for investigating understanding and learning from metaphors.

The discourse context of metaphors in written text

The metaphors in this investigation originate in written text rather than in talk. The texts were selected as representative of the types of information books that children of 10 or 11 use to provide supplementary knowledge on topics such as the environment. Although the metaphors originate in written text, it would be unusual for a child to encounter them only in writing; such texts are usually discussed with other students, read with the teacher, or brought into classroom discourse when the topics are raised in the course of lessons. The text is thus typically encountered within a discourse context that includes social interaction. The relationship of metaphor to its discourse context, first set out in Chapter 1, can be adapted for metaphor in written text by seeing the discourse context of text metaphors as several nested contexts. The text forms the immediate material and linguistic context – metaphors embedded in phrases and sentences – which are in turn organized into chunks of text. These chunks are presented in particular layouts, combined on single pages and double-page spreads with graphics. The next contextual layer can be seen as 'the use of the text', or the text within the context of a task. Key factors in this layer are the goals of the task (both the goals as planned and goals adopted by participants in action) and the

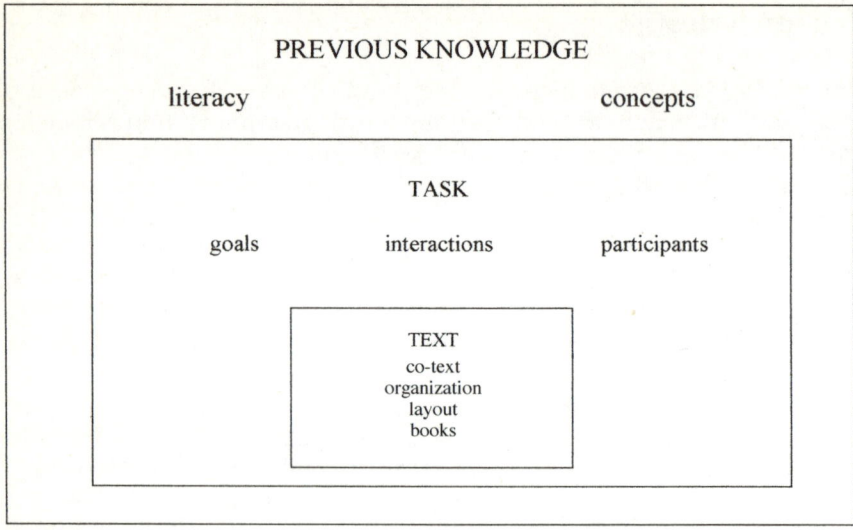

Figure 7.1 *Metaphor in text: layers of discourse context*

interactions of participants. Power relations and previous interactional experiences may be relevant. The task and text layers can be further embedded within 'previous knowledge', as the broadest discourse context in which the metaphors are processed. Previous knowledge here refers to concepts and experiences that the participants bring to the task and the text. It includes literacy knowledge linked to working with texts in various ways and, more importantly for the research purposes, conceptual knowledge relating to Topics and Vehicles of metaphors. The contextual layers are illustrated in Figure 7.1.

To investigate the interpretation of metaphor, a research task was designed that created a discourse context representative of the everyday classroom interactions. The research tool Think-Aloud (TA) was adapted to make it goal-directed and interactive, requiring students to make sense of the text and its metaphors through collaborative talking-and-thinking.

Adapting Think-Aloud techniques

The research design is based on work done by Steen (1992), who made use of concurrent sentence-by-sentence Think-Aloud tasks with individual adults to explore their understanding of metaphor in literary discourse. His method was used as a starting point, and was adapted to a social interactionist framework and to take account of the age of the subjects.

The first major adaptation was to turn the Think-Aloud from an individual to an interactive task. In a trial TA exercise with an individual 11-year-old, it was immediately obvious that solo verbalized introspection does not come easily at this age. Coté et al. (1998) suggest that children of this age can be trained to do individual Think-Aloud, although their own study with fourth and sixth graders showed that the performance of the younger children (close in age to that of my participants) was more strongly affected by the demands of the protocol task. The notion of 'training' participants also goes against the principles of research in a Vygotskyan tradition, since, it is argued, it is precisely when participants are struggling with a new or difficult task that their mental and interactional resources are most clearly revealed (Vygotsky 1962).

The classroom recordings had captured Louise and her best friend Ellen talking to each other throughout the day in a kind of unofficial commentary on the content of lessons and organizational matters, so I decided that the two girls should work together on the TA tasks. This 'Interactive Thinking Aloud', building from their everyday discourse, proved much more productive. It also changed the nature of the research task, and thus the requirements for construct validity, which will be discussed shortly.

The second adaptation to bring traditional Think-Aloud procedure more in line with everyday discourse practices was to construct an explicit, participant-oriented (non-research) goal for the reading task. In most TA studies, the goal given to participants is to report their 'thoughts' as they read a text (Stratman and Hamp-Lyons 1994: 89). Since this task is unfamiliar to most participants, it raises important issues of task validity. The girls in this investigation were asked, in a child-friendly manner, to read the text and evaluate its suitability for a child slightly younger than themselves. This goal drew their attention to the comprehensibility of the text, while allowing them to distance themselves from any problems they themselves might encounter. This research tool is, from this point on, labelled 'Goal-directed Interactive Think-Aloud' (GITA).

GITA allows students' voices to have a place in research into understanding of metaphor, but without asking them for direct explication of linguistic metaphor. The use of explication of metaphor has been shown to underestimate comprehension skills, since explication through paraphrase is not fully developed until around 11 years (Pollio and Pickens 1980).

VALIDITY IN GOAL-DIRECTED INTERACTIVE THINK-ALOUD TASKS

The TA method has been widely used to investigate text processing by adults, and considerable work has been done to establish its validity (e.g. Ericsson 1988; Ericsson and Simon 1984). Validation has had to address the key issue that thinking aloud alters the very cognitive processes it sets out to investigate, for example, by slowing down the reading process, and by imposing tasks on readers through the experimenter's instructions. Ericsson and Simon (1984) produce convincing evidence to show that cognitive processes are not substantially altered, and that TA can provide valid evidence of text comprehension processes. However, Ericsson and Simon's work is embedded in an Information-Processing (I-P) framework, which, for this study, and perhaps for the study of metaphor and language in use generally, has two key limitations. First, in an I-P framework, cognitive processes are seen as individual processes, with no allowance made for interaction or mediation by others; second, the content of such processes is seen as information when, as Rose (1993) points out, human brains work with meaning. I argue that GITA as a research method replicates aspects of children's normal classroom action fairly closely, and through this has construct validity. In GITA, human cognition is seen as centred around 'an innate drive for "coherence" and a high level cognitive mechanism for producing it' (Meadows 1993: 72). The concern is not so much with revealing and investigating individual text comprehension processes, as with processes of interactive and dynamic searching for meaning, and emergent interpretations of a text from the interplay of previous and new understandings. The cognitive processes involved in this 'making sense' include the coherent integration of new information from the text, some of which is encoded in metaphorical language, with previous knowledge (Kintsch 1988). GITA thus involves talking-and-thinking between peers, with some adult mediation by the researcher.

GITA produces processes that more closely resemble students' everyday reading practices than is the case with the TA used with older subjects. Students at the end of primary school have learnt to read through reading aloud, and still read aloud regularly in class, so that there is no need to deal with the issue of whether reading aloud slows down the normal silent reading processes of fluent adults; reading aloud to another person is a normal reading process for the students. Ericsson and Simon (1984) stress that fluent reading of easy texts produces very little in the way of TA protocols; texts that present some difficulties are likely to be more informative. Again, texts that present difficulties are probably the norm for students, rather than an exception contrived for the purposes of research; students daily encounter texts that present difficulties in decoding or in content complexity. The present study attempted to avoid decoding problems, but to incorporate potentially difficult (but not too difficult) content matter.

Two process aspects of GITA remain of concern for construct validity, both relate to the units of processing normally adopted as compared with that imposed by the research method. The first relates to how students attack a page of information in a book; the second to how they attack a chunk of text. In the first case, it became clear after the first GITA session that sentence-by-sentence reading was not the way the students would normally attack a page of information. The information books made frequent use of a double-page spread with a large print heading, and chunks of text integrated with graphics (pictures or diagrams), and their labels. When presented with this format, the students first scanned it for easily accessed information, then settled on a particular chunk to read, usually the labels on the diagram. With that information on board, they might then attack the larger chunk of text. The GITA task of sentence-by-sentence reading of a large chunk of text replicates a later stage of reading the text, and validity may be reduced by depriving participants of the same opportunity to derive meaning from visual information. As school textbooks follow commercial texts in using more visual formats, so the demands on readers are changed. While the sense-making processes revealed in GITA are relevant and reflect what a child might do when faced with a difficult text, the method could be further validated by comparing outcomes using texts with and without pictures.

The second issue concerns the GITA-generated effect of distancing sentences from each other in the reading process through requiring talk about one sentence before moving on to the next. The resultant splitting-up of the reading and thinking might affect the understanding of cohesive links, such as anaphoric reference, or recall of links between concepts. The method attempted to mitigate this effect by presenting each new sentence in the context of all previously read sentences. An examination of the protocols shows that problems with reference did occur, but were more likely to be caused by ambiguity created by the text structure.

The concurrent sentence-by-sentence verbal interaction was used to shed light on the role of metaphor in the social and cognitive processes of reaching shared understandings through talking-and-thinking. Analysis of the students' strategies and comparisons with those of adults in Steen's (1992) study and in studies reported by Ericsson and Simon (1984) allow some cross-checking of validity, in addition to the above arguments for construct validity. Preliminary task analysis, in terms of the role of the metaphorical language in the information content and discourse organization of the text, also contributes to establishing the validity of the categorization of utterances in the protocols (Ericsson and Simon 1984: 321).

The role of the researcher in GITA

In setting up the research task with the child participants, it was clear that some intervention from the researcher would be inevitable, but that, if the discourse context of the research task resembled a regular adult–children context, the validity of the study might be increased rather than reduced. As researcher, I thus attempted to intervene only to keep the task going and, where the threat to the task was due to lack of conceptual knowledge, to participate in the discourse in a 'teacherly' way, using my previous classroom experience. Analysis shows the nature of the researcher contributions to the talk.

<u>Number of turns</u>: The students had twice as many turns as the researcher on Text 1, and more than three times as many on Text 2. The difference was largely due to initial unfamiliarity with the GITA task and the need for prompting.

<u>Types of turn</u>: Four major functional types of intervention could be identified in the researcher's talk, with most of the researcher turns having function (4), Task Management.

> (1) Evaluation Prompt
>
> *any words that you think would be difficult for someone? say an eight-year-old was reading it?*
>
> (2) Understanding Check
>
> *what's the link between the gases and the liquid?*
>
> (3) Support for Understanding
>
> *have they mentioned something already that's harmful to life?*
>
> (4) Task Management
>
> *okay let's see what else he has to say*

The occurrences of each type of intervention for each text are given in Table 7.1. The figures represent the number of each type of intervention as a percentage of the total number of adult turns in the protocols for that text. (Note: The sum of column 1 totals 101 because of rounding up/down carried out for each type.)

Table 7.1 Occurrences of different types of intervention by researcher in GITA

Type of intervention	The Ozone Layer	The Heart
1. Evaluation Prompt	16 %	7 %
2. Understanding Check	31 %	42 %
3. Support for Understanding	9 %	15 %
4. Task Management	45 %	36 %
Total	101 %	100 %

Type 1 intervention (reminding the participants about the goal of the task to evaluate the clarity of the writer's language) dropped for Text 2, when the students were much more tuned in to the task. It in fact fell fairly quickly after the first few sentences of Text 1. The majority of Task Management turns were minimal supportive responses, usually *mmhm*. In assessing the validity of researcher intervention, it must again be recalled that GITA data are not claimed to be evidence of students' unaided reading comprehension processes, but of their interactive searching for meaning processes. Checking understanding is well established as an aspect of negotiation of meaning (Long 1983), and in educational expert–novice discourse is likely to play a key role in targeting additional explanation accurately. In addition, the GITA data are not used for quantitative analysis across subjects and texts, but for in-depth qualitative analysis of the development of understanding. The information provided by the Understanding Checks was very important. Sometimes a single checking understanding incident took several turns, and sometimes it was disguised, for example by asking one girl to explain to the other. The comprehension problems presented by the second text required some direct intervention through mediation of understanding, with resulting higher totals for Types 2 and 3.

This analysis of my role in the GITA interaction supports my claim that researcher intervention enhanced validity rather than reducing it.

The texts

The texts used for the Think-Aloud tasks were taken from the books *The Ozone Layer* (Bright 1991) and *The Body and How It Works* (Parker 1987). They were chosen because they were intended for students of this age range, and were on general science topics that the children were likely to have encountered, but since they included complex concepts they had potential for further learning. The readability levels were measured by the Gunning-Fog Index and Flesch Grade Level, computed automatically by Microsoft Word Grammar Check.

The text selected from *The Ozone Layer* comprised the first three pages of the book, a single page followed by a double-page spread; each page was illustrated. From the second book, a text on 'The Heart' was selected; it was one part of a double-page spread that included a diagram and labels. The two texts were of similar length, and both used nominal and verb metaphors.

The texts were prepared for sentence-by-sentence processing by photocopying and blanking out sentences, so that the subjects were presented with a succession of separate pages on each of which they found the text they had already read, together with one new sentence, which was highlighted. The ozone text covered 18 pages, and the heart text 17 pages.

While similar in many respects, the texts also provided contrasts in the demands they presented to the students. The use of the two texts provided a range of problems for the students to deal with in reaching an understanding of linguistic metaphors in their discourse context. The heart text proved problematic to make sense of because of its reliance on knowledge of the complicated underlying metaphor of the heart as a pump, whereas the text structure of the ozone layer presented particular problems of reference at the surface level.

Identification of linguistic metaphors in the texts

The linguistic metaphors in the texts were identified through finding metaphor Vehicle terms with a potential incongruity between the conventional meaning of the lexical items and the meaning of other items in the surrounding text referring to the same idea, i.e. the Topic domain (see Cameron, 1999a; Chapter 1). Inter-rater reliability was checked by presenting the texts to adults on UK master's degree courses (Text 1, N=25; Text 2, N=17) who knew about the researcher's criteria for metaphor. They were asked to underline metaphors. Any disagreements were carefully examined to reach a final decision on what was to count as the set of linguistic metaphors in each text. Metaphors were categorized as nominal or verb by the word class of their Vehicle term.

Analysis of metaphors in their text structure

The conceptual content of the text was analysed through the identification of the entities (people, objects, events, etc.), their properties, and the relations between them. A distinction was made between content explicitly included in the text, and content implied by the text and needed to reach an accurate interpretation. The combination of explicit and implied information is a kind of idealized 'text base' (Kintsch 1988), in which world knowledge and textual information interact to produce a coherent and stable interpretation (van Dijk and Kintsch 1983). It represents what an idealized skilled reader might be expected to understand from reading the texts, as well as the work required to access that understanding from the information presented. This serves as a basis against which to compare the students' reading. It is assumed that, in writing scientific information texts, the authors intend stable interpretations to be reached, rather than polyvalent, open-ended readings that might be expected of a more literary text (Steen 1994).

To see the informational and rhetorical roles played by the linguistic metaphors, the texts were analysed for their information structure through the identification of given-new information units, and for their thematic structure through the identification of theme and rheme in clauses (Halliday 1985).

The classroom investigation produced a set of mediational devices through which metaphor interpretation may be signalled or supported in discourse (Chapter 5). In the light of these findings, the metaphors in the texts were examined for evidence of the following features:

1. High degree of incongruity of the Vehicle terms of metaphors relative to surrounding discourse.
2. Signalling of metaphorical status through tuning devices, such as *like* or *kind of*.
3. Pre- and post-modification of Vehicle term by Vehicle-related adjectives or adverbs.
4. Clustering of metaphors: repetition and relexicalization of Vehicle terms and of the Topic–Vehicle combination.
5. Development of the metaphor.

GITA procedures

The investigation began on the sixth visit to the school, by which time the participants were used to the researcher and to being recorded. Data were collected on three further visits. The data collection procedures with the two texts differed slightly as a result of various constraints imposed by working in the real-life context of the school. The first visit included the first GITA text and task, with assessment of immediate recall. A discussion with peers about the content of the text to assess longer-term recall took place a week later. Three weeks after that, a second GITA task was carried out with a different text. Since this was the final visit, only immediate recall could be assessed.

Pre- and post-task knowledge activation and analysis

Discussions between researcher and participants were used to activate and elicit existing knowledge of the science topics before reading, and to check on changes to understanding after reading. For pre-reading knowledge of the ozone layer, the researcher asked Ellen and Louise where they had heard about the topic and what they knew. Initial statements were followed up with questions requesting clarification, until information seemed to be exhausted. The pre-GITA discussion for the heart text, carried out with the larger group, started from the topic of *pumps*, which the students in discussion themselves linked to the heart. The protocols show that these pre-GITA discussions activated ideas that were used in the processing of the texts and, as such, they function in a similar way to a teacher-led 'warm-up' introduction to a topic before presenting new information (contrast the geology lesson in classroom investigation, pp. 120–2).

It is not assumed that these discussions activated all relevant information the students might have had, but that the content of the discussions was the knowledge that would be most accessible and most likely to be drawn on in the GITA text reading that followed.

Post-reading recalled knowledge was checked immediately after reading, when Louise and Ellen discussed the content of the text with the researcher. The ozone layer text was further reviewed a week later, when the two students were asked to tell their peers what they had found out. The heart text was only reviewed immediately after reading because the data collection period had then finished. While exactly parallel methodology for the two texts would have been preferable, the in-depth qualitative nature of the analysis means that useful information was obtained from all sessions. In analysis, contrasts are only made across data obtained within each session, i.e. between individual students, or between metaphor types. If made across sessions, they are only made between parallel parts of those sessions, i.e. the two TA sessions carried out by the same students.

The discussions that took place before and after the GITA tasks were recorded and transcribed. Investigation of activated knowledge was carried out through analysis of the transcriptions, in which the contributions of individuals were placed in separate columns, with the interactional sequence retained left to right and vertically. An extract from the pre-GITA discussion for the ozone layer text is given in Extract 7.1. In order to follow the interaction, the reader should read across columns from left to right, and then move down to the next horizontal line. Turns are numbered to help the reader follow the sequence. Since the focus in this analysis is on content, pauses and other non-fluency features are mostly omitted. Analysis of conceptual content was carried out by working vertically through the columns of individual students. Sources of information mentioned by the students were collected. The effects of interaction on ideas and concept activation, e.g. how mention of one idea might prompt a further contribution, were examined by considering the data across columns. By comparing pupils' existing knowledge as displayed in the discussion with the information contained in the text, it was possible to estimate the potential of a text for contributing to learning, i.e. to add to or change existing knowledge.

Extract 7.1 *From the pre-GITA discussion on 'The Ozone Layer'*

Researcher's question	Louise's response	Ellen's response
(1) what do you know about the ozone layer ? have you heard about it?	(2) I've heard about it cos I sometimes watch the news	(3) heard about it a lot on the news and green programmes but we haven't learnt
	(4) BBC1... Newsround	(5) Blue Peter
	(6) ... might be some books	(7) Blue Peter
(8) so what have you picked up from listening to all those? where is it? what is it?	(9) it's a big hole ..erm	(10) a big protective thing protecting the earth from the sun

A similar analysis was carried out on the transcript of the discussion which took place one week after reading the first text to identify evidence of recall, and of positive or negative contribution to longer term cognitive change. The analysis looked for evidence of recall of ideas in the text and the linguistic metaphors used to carry them, and for evidence of weak or strong restructuring of concepts. Examples of recall and restructuring were checked against the original text content for accuracy and completeness.

This method of data collection and analysis can clearly not support claims to produce a full picture of a child's conceptual knowledge. It is claimed, however, that information that 'comes to mind' and is articulated for others in this type of informal but directed discussion is likely to overlap significantly with the information that is used in interpreting written text.

Procedure for GITA tasks

Before the reading of the first text, the instructions in Extract 7.2 were given.

Extract 7.2 *GITA instructions given by researcher to participants*

> R: what we're going to do today is is look at some (.) language on paper (.) some writing (.) right (.) um (2.0) and it's about the ozone layer (1.0)
> I don't know what you know about the ozone layer but I've got a little boy (.) who's (.) eight (.) well he's just nine but he's eight and he's not terribly good at reading you see (.) but he wants to know about the ozone layer (.) so I found a book (.) and I want you to help me to decide if you think (.) it will work for him (1.0)
> right (.) so he's just a bit younger than you (1.0)

The contextualization of the task as 'reading to check the suitability of the text for a younger child' appeared to be convincing, and was used by Ellen in her evaluation of the book at the end of the session. A week later, she explained their task to the other students: *we had to tell whether it was explained or whether the book would be good for a child.* The second GITA session with the heart text had no explicit instructions other than *just like we did it before.*

Analysis of the GITA protocols

The transcribed protocols were used to analyse metaphor processing and text processing under the GITA conditions. In analysing emergent interpretations of text and metaphors, the data were approached from two complementary perspectives. First, all protocols were analysed using a problem-based approach that identified sources of problems in text processing and the processes used to resolve those problems (Coté *et al.* 1998). Second, protocols of sentences containing linguistic metaphors were analysed for metaphor processing, and the interaction between participants in the metaphor processing was analysed. While this second procedure identifies what did happen, the first procedure works with what did not happen or did not happen as effectively as the writer might have expected. In line with Vygotsky's 'genetic' method (Vygotsky 1962), problems that arise in text processing and that are talked about in order to be resolved, are likely to generate the use of a wider range of internal and interactional resources, including those that are not yet established as stable. A problem-based analysis also offers more generalizability to this type of qualitative research that works in great detail with a small number of participants. While the processes observed may or may not be generalizable, the problems are generalizable, in that what goes wrong for Louise or Ellen may well go wrong for other readers. Each procedure is now explained and linked to the research questions.

Problem-based analysis of text interpretation

Text processing problems in sentence protocols were identified by instances, or combinations, of:

- a direct request from the participants for clarification of part of the text
  what has four chambers?
- explicit statement of doubt or disagreement
  I thought gases were meant to be harmful
- a response to a question from the researcher that demonstrated problems in understanding
  do you know what hormones are? No
- explicit negative evaluation
  it's very hard to understand for even us

The textual and conceptual sources of the problems were then identified, using information in the protocol and from the pre-GITA discussion. Sources of problems in the text were classed as:

- a word or phrase
- the structure of the sentence being discussed
- reference across sentences.

Any processing problem might have one or more textual sources, and might be confounded by missing or inaccurate previous knowledge.

The processes adopted for problem resolution were analysed. They included mediation (by peer or researcher), using knowledge of language, using background knowledge, or using information from elsewhere in the text.

Categories of metaphor processing

Metaphor processing in protocols was analysed using an adaptation of a system designed by Steen (1992) for a study with adult readers. The original system included ten categories relating to the processes of metaphor identification, metaphor processing and metaphor appreciation. It was modified for this study by recursively moving between the data and the categories. An additional process was evident in the GITA protocols – participants made explicit links between their own knowledge or experience and the Vehicle term of a metaphor. For example, when discussing the metaphor *the atmosphere is a blanket of gases*, Louise produced

> *when you're in bed you've got a blanket sort of protecting you from the cold*

This type of utterance was labelled 'Vehicle Contextualization' to link with the teacher's use of personal experience in the classroom discourse (Chapter 5). Contextualization was observed in analysis of the lollipop trees episode and of the volcanic lava episode (Chapter 5). It seems to be an important support for understanding metaphor.

Steen's category 'Vehicle Construction' was re-labelled 'Vehicle Development' and sub-divided to take account of the processes discovered in the first investigation (Chapter 5) by which metaphor Vehicles are explicated and elaborated within Metaphor Framing Episodes. Topic Development could also have been broken down in this way, but there were insufficient instances to warrant this. Contextualization was distinguished from Development through lexical content and/or pronominal reference (*you/your*). Steen's 'Metaphor Refunctionalization', which categorizes reference to metaphors used previously in the text, was re-labelled 'Metaphor Reference'. The final categorization system used in the protocol analysis is given in Table 7.2, illustrated with examples from the data.

Dynamic analysis of Topic and Vehicle interaction in metaphor processing

Analysis of the GITA protocols aimed to be 'dynamic', i.e. concerned with the process of understanding and interaction as well as the products (van Lier 1988). The use of the system for categorizing the metaphor processes described above produced an initial picture of metaphor interpretation through the interaction of text and discourse context, including participants' activated Topic and Vehicle knowledge. This category analysis had a static product orientation but it also offered the possibility of capturing the shifts between Topic and Vehicle domains that occurred in the talking-and-thinking. A dynamic view was obtained by examining the move between categories as the discourse proceeded. The content of each categorized utterance was analysed for its relation to the concept domains of Topic and Vehicle, and for whether the content came from inside or outside the text. Each utterance was examined for its sequential relations to other utterances in the protocol.

Summary: addressing the research questions

The data collection and analysis address the research questions as follows:

> RQ2-1 How do the students make sense of the linguistic metaphors they encounter in a text?

Table 7.2 *Categorization system for metaphor processing used in GITA protocol analysis*

1. **Evaluation of use of metaphor**
   The subjects express an opinion as to the value of using a metaphor.
   it's quite a good way of putting it
   it's helping us understand

2. **Restatement of metaphor**
   The metaphorical piece of language is restated immediately after the first reading, using the Topic and Vehicle terms, together with metalanguage indicating a restatement
   is sort of like saying it's like a blanket
   that's telling you about the atmosphere and the shield of air surrounding the earth (.)
   it's like a shield

3. **Vehicle Development**
   The Vehicle term is developed in several ways:
   3.1 **Vehicle Explication**
   Expansion, elaboration or exemplification of Vehicle term
   that protects it
   a good type of gas
   invisible (.) no one can really see it

   3.2 **Repetition**
   Vehicle term is repeated in identical or transformed form
   a blanket round our earth
   so shields and blankets

   3.3 **Relexicalization**
   A near synonym or equivalent of the Vehicle term is used, working at the same level of generality
   squeeze. . ...more like pump blood out

4. **Vehicle Contextualization**
   The Vehicle term is related to something outside the text, in participants' knowledge or experience
   when you're in bed you've got a blanket sort of protecting you from the cold

5. **Topic Development**
   Additional information (from elsewhere in the text or from previous knowledge) about the Topic domain is stated
   blood ..to take it to your arms and fingers and things
   it's a body

6. **Metaphor Construction**
   The Topic term is re-juxtaposed with the developed or contextualized Vehicle term to reformulate the metaphor
   and then there's another type of blanket which is of gases surrounds the earth

7. **Metaphor Reference**
   A reference to a metaphor encountered previously in the text
   he's already said something like that when he was on about (.) the blanket

Questions about Topic–Vehicle interaction and the interaction of previous knowledge with textual information were investigated through the categorization of metaphor processing and the dynamic analysis of Topic and Vehicle interaction in the protocols of sentences containing linguistic metaphors.

> **RQ2-2** How do encounters with metaphor affect conceptual alterity?
> Do the metaphors prompt processes that lead to new understandings?
> Do the metaphors assist recall of new information?

The content of the metaphor interpretations was examined for factual accuracy, and interpretations were compared with previous knowledge as demonstrated in the pre-GITA discussion or in sentence protocols. The post-GITA discussions were analysed for mention of linguistic metaphors from the texts and for accuracy in recall.

> **RQ2-3** What is the role of mediation in interpreting metaphors by text/writer? by peers in interaction?

Research Question 2–3 was investigated by bringing together findings from the metaphor processing analysis and mediation in problem resolution.

Having set up the background to the studies aimed at investigating metaphor understanding, described the procedures of data collection and analysis, and how the analysis addressed the research questions, we now need to consider the findings of the GITA tasks. We will see how the participants made sense of the texts and linguistic metaphors, drawing on their previous knowledge to make sense of new information. As the role of the metaphors in this process becomes clearer, we will see how metaphor both contributes to and limits understanding and learning.

8 Metaphors in text 1: 'The Ozone Layer'

Introduction

In this chapter, we see what happened when the young readers tackled 'The Ozone Layer' text under the conditions of the goal-directed interactive Think-Aloud procedure. Their interpretation of metaphors is investigated within the larger interpretative context of making sense of the text in the light of previous knowledge. We begin with the analysis of the metaphors found in the text, and their contribution to its informational content and structure.

Metaphors in the text

From the Ozone Layer text (Figure 8.1), I identified 12 items as Vehicle terms of linguistic metaphors, using the identification procedures set up in Chapter 3. To cross-check metaphor identification, the text was presented to groups of adults, containing a mix of native speakers and non-native speakers (N = 25). The results are summarized in Table 8.1. Column 1 shows the words that were underlined by respondents; the number of the sentence in the text is given in brackets. Columns 2 and 3 show how many of the respondents underlined a particular word or phrase, as a raw figure and as a percentage of the total number of respondents. One metaphor, *useful* energy, was added as a result of the cross-checking.

The gradedness of the results in Table 8.1 demonstrates the gradedness of metaphoricity for readers (Grady *et al.* 1999: 117), and the greater recognizability of the nominal metaphors. A discourse effect may be needed to account for the different rates of identification of the two verb metaphors that occur twice in the text, *escape, protect*, but which received different identification scores. This may, as Low (1999) suggests, be due to features of layout, e.g. the position of the second instance (sentence 9) of *escape* immediately below *traps* may add to its noticeability. The second instance of *protect* may also be rendered more obvious by the large sub-heading 'Protecting Earth' which is just above it in the text. In both cases, the second instance may be made more noticeable by the cumulative effect on the reader of the text already processed.

Introduction

1
2 It may seem strange that the liquid used to cool the air in a fridge could be harmful to
3 life on Earth. However, when old fridges are destroyed, harmful gases can escape into
4 the atmosphere. The atmosphere is the
5 blanket of gases that surround the Earth. It is
6 made up of several layers. One of these layers contains ozone, a gas which protects us from the Sun's harmful ultraviolet light.

Dangers and benefits

7
8 The Sun and the atmosphere make life on
9 Earth possible. The Earth is kept warm by the Sun's heat, and the atmosphere traps some of this heat so that it doesn't escape into
10 space. But not all the energy made by the
11 Sun is safe. Dangerous forms of radiation called ultraviolet, or UV, light are also given out, and these can be harmful to life.

12 The Sun is just the right distance away from Earth to warm us.   Animals cannot use the energy from the Sun directly, and so have to depend on plants for food.

Protecting Earth

13
14 The atmosphere is like an invisible shield of
15 air surrounding the Earth. It contains different
16 gases which protect life on the planet. The atmosphere lets useful energy through, but reduces the amount of harmful energy
17 reaching the Earth's surface. At a height of 10 to 30km above us, there is a layer in the atmosphere containing ozone. This stops
18 some of the harmful UV light getting to Earth.

Figure 8.1 Text 1: 'The Ozone Layer'. From M. Bright (1991), *The Ozone Layer*. London: Gloucester Press.

Table 8.1 Linguistic metaphors identified in 'The Ozone Layer' by adults

Linguistic metaphors		Number of subjects identifying this as metaphor [N=25]	%
(3)	the atmosphere is the blanket of gases	25	100
(10)	the atmosphere is like an invisible shield of air	25	100
(7)	the atmosphere traps	21	84
(7)	it doesn't escape	16	64
(12)	atmosphere lets...through	7	28
(11)	gases...protect	5	20
(7)	Earth is kept warm	5	20
(2)	gases can escape	5	20
(5)	a gas...protects	4	16
(12)	useful energy	4	16
(18)	This stops some of the...light	2	8
(10)	the energy made by the Sun	1	4
(11)	forms of radiation...are...given out	1	4
(8)	Sun and atmosphere make life possible	1	4

Of the final set of 13 linguistic metaphors in the Ozone Layer text, two have noun Vehicle terms and so are nominal metaphors, the rest are verb metaphors. The phrasal verb metaphor *lets ... through* is indexical, while the rest are more schematic, i.e. use words with high lexical content (Widdowson 1990). Unlike the metaphors found in spoken discourse, most have single word Vehicle terms.

Ten are verb animating metaphors in which non-animate entities, such as *the Sun* or *the ozone layer*, are made the agents of actions that are typically intentionally carried out by people.

The conceptual content of the text

The conceptual information in the text can be summarized in terms of the entities mentioned, the properties attributed to them, and the relations between them. Key entities in the text are:

> the Earth – life – space – the atmosphere – the ozone layer – the sun

There are two other linked sets of entities, involving technical language:

> heat – energy – radiation – ultraviolet light
> fridges – liquid – gases

The {*fridges – liquid – gases*} set occurs in the opening two sentences, linking the main topic (the atmosphere) to an everyday non-scientific context.

The properties and relations mentioned include the relative position of atmosphere, earth and sun; relations, including cause and effect; and 'explanatory theory', which sets out how the radiation from the sun is filtered by the atmosphere on its way to earth, and how this protects the earth.

Some conceptual information is implied rather than made explicit in the text. In sentence 2, the word *gases* refers to the vaporized *liquid* in sentence 1. The reader needs to bring to the text the knowledge that *liquid* turns into *gas*, and, more specifically, that fridge coolant vaporizes at relatively low temperatures. In the middle section (sentences 7–12), the items *heat, energy, forms of radiation, light* are used as related terms, without the hyponymic relationships between them (that radiation is a form of energy; that light and heat are forms of radiation) being made explicit. These implied links are also needed to make 'global coherence' of the text (van Dijk and Kintsch 1983), since *energy* and *light* are used interchangeably in sentence 16, which refers back semantically to sentence 9.

We should note also that the same lexical item *gases* is used in sentences 3 and 5 with very different referents: CFC gases and atmospheric gases. In this case, the reader needs to know the difference rather than the connection between concepts.

The analysis of the conceptual content of the text gives us one side of the conceptual alterity that participants are intended to reach.

The information and thematic structures of the text

The Flesch Grade Level score of the Ozone Layer text is 7.8, and the Gunning-Fog Index is 10, indicating a reading age of around 13, higher than the large print and short sections suggest. Analysis of the text in terms of given and new information showed that every sentence contains at least one information unit, reflecting the dense information load of the text. The thematic structure changes from section to section. In the first section, the theme begins with the link to the non-text world of *liquid in fridges*, and then follows *the atmosphere* and *its layer of ozone* as theme. *The atmosphere* is also the theme of each sentence in the last section. In the middle section, however, the theme changes with each sentence, *the sun – the Earth – the atmosphere – energy – radiation*; the last two sentences (17, 18) can be read as having a linked theme only if the reader knows the connection between *energy* and *radiation*.

Once past the opening sentence, a general pattern of movement from given to new information, mapped regularly onto theme and rheme, is found. Exceptions to this general pattern occur in places where the reader must use external knowledge, and following the two nominal metaphors.

The two nominal metaphors (sentences 4 and 14) switch the discourse topic to *the atmosphere,* and seem intended to act as introductory explanatory analogies in guiding or reinforcing the understanding of the structure, location and function of the atmosphere, similar to the explicatory deliberate metaphors in the classroom discourse (Chapter 5):

> The atmosphere is the blanket of gases that surround the Earth. It is made up of several layers. (Sentences 4, 5)

> The atmosphere is like an invisible shield of air surrounding the Earth. It contains different gases. (Sentence 14)

Both metaphors have the form:

> NP (Topic) *is* NP (Vehicle) *of* NP (Topic)
> [where NP = Noun Phrase].

The sentences (6, 15) that follow the metaphors both begin with an anaphoric pronoun *It*, which refers back to the first NP of the previous sentence. The 'given'/theme of the second sentence (*It*) is not the 'new'/rheme of the previous sentence or clause, nor is it the Vehicle item, but, in contrast with all the other sentences in the text, refers back to the theme/'given' of the previous sentence. The use of the nominal metaphors seems to disrupt the predictability of interplay of the informational and thematic structures of the text. In the second pair of sentences, a *shield* cannot *contain gases* and so there is a content mismatch between metaphorical rheme of the first sentence and theme of the second which may prevent the reader making an erroneous link. In the first pair of sentences, the parallel content-mismatch cue is disguised because, although a *blanket* cannot be made up of *layers*, it may, confusingly, be one layer of several on a bed.

The cyclical presentation of information on particular aspects of the topic across separate pages and sections of text constructs a 'spiralling' text structure, which, while appearing pedagogically sound, failed to help the student readers as much as it could, perhaps because of the amount and density of information included. The students commented explicitly on the structure of the text, Extract 8.1:

Extract 8.1 *Students' comments on text structure*

L:	it's good where it's going on bit by bit (.)
	but some of the sentences are quite hard to understand
E:	it's more like (.) spaced out (.) and it doesn't (1.0) do a lot on each (2.0) part
	it's just on about a certain thing and then it goes on to the next subject
E:	I think the writer's trying to .. remind you what he's written before so you don't forget

Mediational devices in the text that may support metaphor interpretation

1. Vehicle incongruity
The two nominal metaphor Vehicles are quite highly incongruous in the text. This should help them to be noticed. The verb Vehicles, although schematic, are less incongruous.

2. Use of tuning markers
Only the second nominal metaphor is explicitly hedged, by the use of *like*.

3. Modification of Vehicle
In no instances are Vehicle terms pre- or post-modified by other Vehicle domain items. The *shield* is pre-modified by a Topic domain term, *invisible*.

4. Metaphor clusters: repetition and relexicalization of Vehicle terms
The nominal Vehicle terms are not repeated. The *shield* metaphor can be seen as a relexicalization of the *blanket*.

Some of the verb Vehicles are repeated: *escapes, protects*, and relexicalized: *escapes → lets through; traps → stops*.

5. Development of metaphors
As noted above, the term *layer* might appear to be a Vehicle domain term, and thus to be developing the Vehicle *blanket*, but it is not intended as such. This, and the other nominal metaphor development in the sentences following the metaphors are Topic-related rather than Vehicle-related, as we might expect of explanatory analogies, given the classroom data. The failure to exploit the nominal metaphors contrasts with the use of metaphors in the geology lesson described in Chapter 5, where the use of a Vehicle term for volcanic lava, *melted butter,* was followed by further information that continued the Vehicle concept *butter* and linked it explicitly to the Topic.

Previous knowledge brought to the text

An indication of the conceptual alterity in this discourse can be estimated by comparing the content and assumptions of the text with participants' initial knowledge of the topic. From the discussion between participants and researcher before working on the text, an analysis was made of the subjects' previous knowledge about the ozone layer.

The reported sources of the children's knowledge about the ozone layer were primarily TV programmes, i.e. visual as well as verbal. The knowledge expressed by the children was non-specific, partial and uncertain. Their use of vague language to express their knowledge suggested uncertainty and incompleteness:

> R: *what is it?*
> E: *a big protective <u>thing</u> protecting the earth from the sun*
> E: *greenhouse effect <u>and everything</u>*

Uncertainty was also suggested by the children's use of questions in responses to my questions:

> R: *how did it get this hole in it?*
> L: *is it from the sun's rays?*

Partial knowledge was indicated by explicit reference to what was unknown:

> E: *I don't know much about it*
> L: *not really realizing what it's all about*

The specific knowledge about the ozone layer that was expressed by the children can be summarized, using their own words:

> Ellen: *the ozone layer is a big protective thing protecting the earth from the sun*
> *it's got a hole in*
> *there's a connection between the hole and the greenhouse effect*
> *pollution may have made the hole in it*
> *the earth is getting hotter*
> *if the hole gets bigger, it'll get hotter*
> *the ozone layer stops the sun*
>
> Louise: *it's a big hole*
> *the hole may be caused by the sun's rays*
> *the greenhouse effect might be connected with pollution*
> *greenhouses keep heat in*
> *the ozone layer could be trapping all the earth's heat*

In this discussion, the girls spontaneously produce the verbs *protect* and *trap* that were identified as linguistic metaphors in the text.

The potential of text and metaphors for learning

The participants do bring some knowledge about the ozone layer to the reading task; they have some basic acquaintance with key terms, and a beginning of understanding of relations between them, but there is clearly potential for growth in understanding through reduction of this alterity. Comparing the conceptual information activated in the discussion with that included in the text, we can see that the knowledge they bring to the text is incomplete and at a more general level than the text, in the following ways:

- Some entities in the scientific concept domain are not mentioned by the students:
  atmosphere
  space
  gases
  ultraviolet light
  radiation
  energy
- The ozone layer is said to *stop the sun*, rather than the more specific *radiation/energy/UV light* from the sun.
- The girls use the general term *pollution* rather than the more specific *harmful gases*.
- Although some properties of the ozone layer problem are suggested, and thus can be taken as known (*hot/protect/hole*), there is no indication that either girl understands the relational connections, e.g. how the hole was caused (Louise suggests it was made *by the sun*), or how the ozone layer works to protect.
- Participants mention *ozone* only inside the noun phrase *the ozone layer*, not that ozone is a gas, or that it is part of the atmosphere.
- *The greenhouse effect* seems to serve as a gross-level metaphor that, through frequent use, becomes familiar and is assumed to be understood. However, this is a false sense of understanding, since, when forced to explain it in detail, both researcher and children found themselves prevented by lack of specific understanding:

R: *when you try and understand it*
E: *it's when it gets all mixed up*

The review of the literature (Chapter 2) suggested a range of ways in which metaphor might contribute positively or negatively to understanding and learning. Applying these in a theoretical analysis of the text suggests the following points related to learning. Protocol analysis will allow confirmation or disconfirmation of these predictions:

- The two nominal metaphors appear to be potentially memorable through their incongruous Topic–Vehicle links, and may

as such assist recall of content. They are familiar to children and should thus help develop understanding of the function of the atmosphere.
- The lack of Vehicle development in the text may lead to difficulties in making use of the metaphor to restructure Topic knowledge.
- The metaphors may also be working at 'the wrong grain size' (Spiro *et al.* 1989: 507) in that they both take *the atmosphere* as Topic, whereas the major topic of the text is only one part of the atmosphere, the ozone layer.

The last two issues may lead to the metaphors being less than fully helpful in supporting cognitive change. In summary, the nominal metaphors seem likely to be accessible to the intended readers, but several discourse features may prevent readers from learning more about the ozone layer from the text. Non-metaphorical features of the text also seem likely to cause comprehension problems.

Findings: problems in text processing

The participants experienced problems in processing 7 of the 18 sentences or headings in the text, according to the criteria set out in Chapter 7 (p. 163). The textual sources of the problems lay in:

- words or phrases: 7
- sentence structure: 1
- across sentences: 3

The words or phrases (sentence number in brackets) that caused problems were:

liquid (2)
gases (4)
ultraviolet light (6)
benefits (7)
energy (10)
radiation (11)
harmful energy (16)

Two of the three cross-sentence problems were related: *energy* (sentence 10) was not linked to *heat* in sentence 9, and no sense could be made of it; *radiation* (sentence 11) was again not linked to either *energy* or *heat*. That all of these were related to and given out by the sun remained not understood. Previous knowledge about these conceptual entities and their relations was assumed by the writer, but was not available to the readers. The impact of this on interpretation will be seen later.

The causes of problems sometimes only became apparent as the participants attempted to resolve them. Resolution was sometimes clearly successful, sometimes clearly failed, and sometimes seemed likely to have been resolved but not clearly so. The resolution and causes of some of the problems repay closer study:

- *liquid* (sentence 2) caused a problem because the participants did not know that fridges contained coolant liquids, nor that these would turn into gases on being released into the atmosphere. The writer's attempt at starting the topic with a familiar example failed. The children came to understand it through researcher mediation.
- *benefits* (sentence 7) was an unknown word. It was resolved through linguistic comparison with *dangers* and the participants seemed to settle on a meaning 'what to do about dangers'.
- *ultraviolet* (sentence 11) was also tackled linguistically as meaning *extra strong, quite powerful*, an approximate meaning but without the key attribute of being harmful that would tie parts of the passage together.
- *energy*: When I enquired what meaning the participants had for *energy*, they explained in terms of their 'spontaneous' concept: *it's the thing we have, it's when you run*. This non-technical meaning of *energy* would not allow sense to be made of sentence 10, nor of the phrase *harmful energy* (sentence 16). It also does not prompt the cross-sentence link to *heat* (9) or to *radiation* (11).

Findings: processing of nominal and verb metaphors

The first finding from the application of the metaphor processing categorization system to the GITA protocols (Table 7.2) was that nominal and verb metaphors showed different patterns of comprehension and interpretation. Tables 8.2 and 8.3 show the number of instances of each category for each linguistic metaphor. The differing distribution of the categories is clear when the tables are compared.

The two nominal metaphors were explicitly and positively evaluated, indicating that they were noticed, whereas the protocols for the verb metaphors did not show explicit Evaluation of the metaphor Vehicle term. Where evaluative comments of verb metaphors were made, they concerned the larger phrase or sentence rather than

Table 8.2 Processing of nominal metaphors in the GITA protocols for 'The Ozone Layer'

Nominal metaphor processing	4. a *'blanket'* of gases	14. an invisible *'shield'*
1. Evaluation	3	1
2. Metaphor Restatement	1	1
3. Vehicle Development		
3.1 Vehicle Explication	1	3
3.2 Vehicle Repetition	3	4
3.3 Vehicle Relexicalization		
4. Vehicle Contextualization	1	1
5. Topic Development	5	1
6. Metaphor Construction	1	1
7. Metaphor Reference		4

Table 8.3 Processing of verb metaphors in the GITA protocols for 'The Ozone Layer'

Verb metaphor Processing	3. escape	6. protects	9. kept warm	9. traps	9. escape	11. given out	15. protect	16. lets through
1. Evaluation								
2. Metaphor Restatement		1	1	1	1	2		
3. Vehicle Development								
3.1 Vehicle Explication								
3.2 Vehicle Repetition	1	2	1	2	1		1	2
3.3 Vehicle Relexicalization	go into				get out			goes through
4. Vehicle Contextualization								
5. Topic Development	6 3	4	3	1	1		3	6 2
6. Metaphor Construction								
7. Metaphor Reference							2	3

being directly about the metaphor. There is thus no evidence that verb metaphors were consciously noticed. In fact, a stronger conclusion – that verb metaphors were not noticed – is suggested by the unmarked use of verb Vehicle terms in the protocols. For example, in talking about sentence 16, which contains the verb metaphor *let . . . through*, the girls used the verb as they made sense of the sentence:

Extract 8.2 *Unmarked use of verb Vehicle term*

L: well (.) it's <u>letting through</u> useful energy but then he's telling you about harmful energy (.) which is quite complicated to understand
E: oh I get it now. . .the shield is (.) um (.) <u>letting through</u> all the good kind of gases. . .

Applying the distinction set up in Chapter 1, it appears that the nominal metaphors are both linguistic metaphors and process metaphors, but the verb metaphors are not process metaphors by the GITA procedure.

Tables 8.2 and 8.3 demonstrate the different dynamics of Topic and Vehicle interaction in the talking-and-thinking about sentences with nominal metaphors and with verb metaphors. Nominal metaphors gave rise to more talk about the Vehicle, whereas verb metaphor protocols contained proportionately more talk about the Topic. Nominal metaphors were restated, explicated, contextualized and reformulated in Metaphor Construction, whereas verb metaphors were not. In contrast, verb metaphor protocols showed the verb Vehicles were not opened up for discussion, but were subjected only to repetition (as in Extract 8.2), and relexicalization, in most instances as phrasal verbs, e.g. *escape* relexicalized as *go into, get out; lets through* as *goes through*. The presence of the verb linguistic metaphors thus seemed to have little impact on patterns of sentence processing. The patterns in the protocols were similar to those of sentences without metaphors; the Vehicle terms did not become the theme of the talk at any point. The dynamic pattern of the talk in the protocols was mostly Topic-focused, as participants produced a succession of Topic Development statements. Within this sequence were embedded odd instances of Vehicle repetition and/or relexicalization.

Although the verb metaphors seemed to have little impact on the processing dynamics, there was evidence of possible influence on the outcomes of the interpretation process; as we will see on p. 184, there appeared to be a shift towards inaccuracy, that may, at least in part, be due to the use of metaphor.

A quite different dynamic pattern of Topic and Vehicle talk appeared in the protocols of nominal metaphors, with the metaphors themselves becoming the theme of utterances in the talk. In both instances, the metaphor was restated and evaluated immediately after it was read aloud. The participants then proceeded to, as it were, hold up the Vehicle term to the light, talk around it and dissect it a little, before fitting it back with the Topic term in an explicit reconstruction of the

Nominal metaphor processing	Verb metaphor processing
M → V → V → T → V → V → T → M	T → T → T → V → T → T

M = talk around the metaphor **T** = Topic
V = Vehicle

Figure 8.2 *The dynamics of metaphor processing in the GITA protocols*

metaphor. It seemed as if the metaphor Vehicle was incongruous enough to generate discussion, and the incongruity prompted the participants to work out how coherence with the ongoing text base could be rebuilt.

The different dynamics of nominal and verb metaphor processing can be visualized as in Figure 8.2. The figure shows the general pattern, rather than specifics.

We can see that talk around the nominal metaphors followed a similar pattern to teacher talk around the deliberate metaphors in the volcanic lava extract in Chapter 5. In the next sub-section the process of 'making sense' of the nominal metaphors will be considered at a more detailed level, showing how previous knowledge was brought to the interaction of Topic and Vehicle.

Processing the nominal metaphor: *the atmosphere is the blanket of gases*

Table 8.4 displays the categories of metaphor processing for the first nominal metaphor, *the atmosphere is the blanket of gases that surround the Earth*. Each turn, or part of a turn, that includes information about Topic, Vehicle or metaphor is categorized. The 'Metaphor process' column summarizes each category in terms of whether the focus of the talk is primarily the Topic or the Vehicle. An arrow (→) is used to imply a movement between Topic and Vehicle within a turn, so, for example, V→T represents a move in focus from a Vehicle theme to a Topic theme.

USE OF PREVIOUS TOPIC AND VEHICLE KNOWLEDGE

The Topic is developed first in this protocol after Ellen states a problem (line 1). It seems that the sentence has created some conflict of understanding, which becomes clearer as the protocol develops. The previous sentence had included the phrase *harmful gases*, referring to the CFCs emitted from fridges, and Ellen assumes that the *gases* referred to here are the same ones. This is a cross-sentence problem created by the writer. It is resolved by Louise bringing to the talk her previous knowledge of the Topic (lines 2, 4–6). In a successful piece of peer mediation, Ellen uses Louise's contribution to make sense of the metaphor in lines 3, 10–12. Louise's specific Topic knowledge of gases in the atmosphere is incomplete and inaccurate (*carbohydrate* in line 4) but it is still helpful in resolving Ellen's problem, because making sense is done at the more general level of *good and bad gases*. Vehicle knowledge (the positive connotations of *blanket)* prompts noticing of alterity between the text and Ellen's text-base; shared Topic knowledge works to decrease the alterity and solve the processing problem.

Table 8.4 GITA protocol and categorization of metaphor processing
Sentence 4: The atmosphere is the blanket of gases that surround the Earth.

	Sentence protocol	Metaphor process	Focus of talk
1	E: I thought gases were meant to be harmful	Topic Development	T
2	L: there's all types of gases though	Topic Development	T
3	E: one that protects the earth and one that	Topic Development	T
4	L: there's helium (.) there's (1.0) helium (2.0) carbohydrate (2.0)	Topic Development	T
5	um (5.0) but I can't remember it now		
6	R: no? (9.0)		
7	L: there's all different types of gases on different planets	Topic Development	T
8	L: though (2.0) in a way that does help a little bit though (.)	Evaluation	M
9	cos it sort of like (.) saying (.) it's like a blanket that protects it	Metaphor Restatement	V→T (M)
10	E: there's actually two types of gases (.)	Topic Development	T
11	there's a bad type of gas and a good type of gas	Topic Development	T
12	which is a (.) blanket around our earth	Vehicle Development: explication; repetition	→V
		Metaphor Construction	(M)
13	R: right (.) so the (1.0)		
14	E: it's quite a good way of putting it though	Evaluation	M
15	R: why?		
16	E: cos it's easy to understand	Evaluation	M
17	L: it's helping us to understand	Evaluation	M
18	E: cos when you're in (.) bed you've got a blanket	Vehicle Contextualization	V
19	sort of (.) protecting you from the cold		
20	L: yea (.) and then there's another type of blanket	Vehicle Development: explication; repetition	V
21	which is of gases (.) surrounds the earth . . .	Metaphor Construction	→T (M)

The Vehicle Contextualization, *when you're in bed you've got a blanket sort of protecting you from the cold* (lines 18 and 19), develops from the Evaluation (14) of the metaphor and the researcher's prompt (15); it uses previous Vehicle knowledge of how blankets function in everyday life. The contextualized Vehicle is then linked back to the Topic to reconstruct the metaphor (19). In this processing, participants' Topic and Vehicle knowledge has been shared and used to make sense of the metaphor and to resolve the cross-sentence referential ambiguity.

ACCURACY OF INTERPRETATION

The interpretation of the metaphor as summarized in lines 19 and 20 appears to match what the writer intended. However, along the way, an inaccurate interpretation appears. It is not temporary, but recurs in later protocols and in recall a week later. This is the slippage between *the atmosphere is a blanket* and **the ozone layer is a blanket*. The inaccuracy seems to develop through the distinction they make between good gases and bad gases, first appearing briefly in line 3, *one that protects the earth*, and then crystallized in lines 11 and 12, where being a blanket is assigned only to *the good type of gas*. Although the difference in meaning does not matter here, and the *blanket* Vehicle could apply equally well to both Topics (*atmosphere* and *ozone layer*), the shift will become significant in the larger picture of how linguistic metaphors contribute to the accuracy of interpretation of the text. The possibility of an inaccurate interpretation results from the writer's choice of Vehicle.

BRIDGING TOPIC AND VEHICLE DOMAINS

The shift is compounded by the content of the next sentence:

It is made up of several layers

It was noted in the text analysis that, whereas, in talk, utterances around a metaphor often provide further information about the Vehicle, in this written text, no further Vehicle-related information is given. The *'It'* in sentence 5 refers to *the atmosphere*, not to a *blanket*. However, *blanket* and *layers* are quite easily interpreted as linked, and the juxtaposition seemed to confuse the participants, who may also have been expecting Vehicle-related information. In the protocol of sentence 14, Louise recalled:

a layer like a blanket and now he's talking about it as a ..

This confusion can be described through the phenomenon of bridging in metaphor interpretation. Bridging terms are lexical items that can be used in reference to both Topic and Vehicle domains, and are potentially important in guiding interpretation of a metaphor (Kittay 1987: 166). In the metaphor protocol above, *protects* serves as a bridging term. In on-line processing, as opposed to theoretical analyses, participants may pick on other words and use them as bridging terms; depending on the accuracy of previous knowledge, the chosen bridging terms may vary in appropriateness. While theoretical bridges always lead happily from Topic to Vehicle domain and back, on-line bridges may lead to an inappropriate domain, or may not reach solid land at all. It seems that *layers*, although not intended as such, offers a bridging opportunity, applicable in both the Topic domain (*atmosphere-gases/ozone*) and the recently activated Vehicle domain, *blanket*. The *layers* bridge is crossed from Topic (*atmosphere*) to Vehicle (*blanket*) but the way back leads to a different Topic (*ozone*). Put less metaphorically, choosing this bridge seems to result in activated connections in the participants' minds of *blanket – layer –*

Table 8.5 GITA protocol and categorization of metaphor processing
Sentence 14: The atmosphere is like an invisible shield of air surrounding the Earth.

Sentence protocol		Metaphor process	Focus
1	L: (reads) the atmosphere is like an invisible shield of	Reading Aloud	
2	(.) air surrounding the earth (.)		
3	that's telling you about (1.0) the atmosphere (.) and	Metaphor Restatement	T→V
4	(.) the shield of air surrounding the earth (.)		(M)
5	it's like a shield protecting the (.)	Vehicle Development: repetition; explication	V
6	E: but it's invisible (.) nobody can really see it	Vehicle Development	V (→T)
7	R: do you remember what he said the atmosphere was	Researcher question	
8	like before? (2.0) at the beginning of the book? (2.0)		
9	L: oh		
10	E: I can't remember		
11	R: you said it was a good (.) a good (.) word that he		
12	used (.) it reminded you of when you went to bed (1.0)		
13	L: a blanket	(Metaphor Reference)	
14	E: a blanket	(Metaphor Reference)	
15	L: he he's talking about it was a shield (.) ?????	Vehicle Repetition	V
16	a layer like a blanket	Metaphor Reference	(V)
17	and now he's talking about it as a (.) invisible shield	Vehicle Repetition	V
18	E: [an invisible shield	Vehicle Repetition	V
19	R: mm		
20	E: so shields and blanket (*laugh*) (3.0)	Vehicle Repetition	V
		Metaphor Reference	(V)
21	L: that is quite a good way of putting it though	Evaluation	M
22	E: protecting (.)	Vehicle Explication	V
23	cos shields protect you when you're having (.) a	Vehicle Contextualization	V
24	war or something (.)		
25	and then (1.0) a shield protects you	Vehicle Repetition: Explication	V
26	L: [yea		
27	protects you (.)		
28	and also a shield (.) is protecting (.) the air	Metaphor Construction	V→T
29	surrounding the earth (6.0)		(M)

ozone, which influence interpretation of the text in later protocols and over the longer term.

PROCESSING THE NOMINAL METAPHOR: THE ATMOSPHERE IS LIKE AN INVISIBLE SHIELD

The second nominal metaphor occurs at the beginning of the third page of the text, after some explanation of how the atmosphere stops the dangerous ultraviolet light from the sun reaching the earth. As we noted in the Problems section, this page was not fully understood by the participants because they did not know the relations between *radiation – energy – heat – light*. The shield metaphor seems to refer both backwards, summarizing the action of the atmosphere, and forwards, establishing the theme of the page and of each sentence on the page. The categories assigned to the protocol are set out in Table 8.5. There is a similar distribution of tasks between the participants in this protocol and the previous one (Table 8.4), with Louise reading aloud, restating the metaphor, evaluating the metaphor, and constructing the metaphor at the end. Ellen performs the role of Vehicle Development and Contextualization. This may be due either to Ellen needing to do more unpacking of the metaphor than Louise, or to Louise adopting the more dominant role, perhaps because of her greater level of involvement in the research.

USE OF PREVIOUS VEHICLE KNOWLEDGE AND TOPIC KNOWLEDGE

The success of Vehicle Explication in this protocol was limited; most of the Vehicle-related processes in Table 8.5 did not develop the Vehicle, *shield,* very far beyond the general contextualization, *protect you when you're having a war or something* (lines 23 and 24). Possible reasons for this difficulty in resolving discourse alterity are suggested by later protocols, when the Vehicle *shield* is brought back into the discussion of sentence 16 by the researcher. This is discussed on p. 189, but we can note at this point that the problem in developing the Vehicle seemed to lie in the limited properties that can be activated for the Vehicle, given the Topic *atmosphere.* The *shield* metaphor re-emphasized the general point that the atmosphere protects the earth, but did not help with more specific understanding of how it protects, since there are no possible analogical links between *atmosphere* and *shield* (such as what they are made of) that might be helpful.

Although the choice of metaphor limited its contribution to new understanding, it is important to note that the processes of Vehicle Development and Contextualization still occurred. Choice of Vehicle influences the contextualization possibilities open to individuals. A week later when the metaphor was discussed by the group of five children, Dougal, the only boy, was more specific in his contextualization:

> *a shield protects you from swords*

The degree of specificity with which children are able to contextualize reflects their experience, previous knowledge, and level of involvement with the chosen Vehicle. These factors may in turn influence how successfully discourse alterity can be reduced.

ACCURACY OF METAPHOR INTERPRETATION

As with the *blanket* metaphor, the subjects had no difficulty in processing the metaphor, although again there was some inaccuracy and incompleteness of interpretation. The reformulation in the final Metaphor Construction (line 28) suggests a misunderstanding. In the original text sentence, *the atmosphere* is compared to *a shield of <u>air</u>*

surrounding the Earth. Line 28 suggests that Louise interpreted this differently, as the *shield is protecting* **the air**. This misunderstanding may be linked to lack of specific relational Topic knowledge that is displayed throughout in the connection between concepts of *atmosphere/gas/air/ozone*. While some of the utterances seemed to use the concepts and lexical labels unproblematically, others showed misunderstandings. In the protocol for sentence 16, Louise asks

> *is ozone a type of gas?*

An interpretation of this variability in understanding is that the domain linked to *atmosphere* is undergoing a process of restructuring towards a new level of understanding that will eventually show itself in more stable talk around the concept.

Processing of verb metaphors

Topic Reference Shift in the processing of verb metaphors

A repeated finding from the analysis of verb metaphor processing was that interpretations showed slight shifts from the writer's intended meaning. Topic Development was, in each case, related to the Subject or Object/Complement of the verb Vehicle, and for five of the seven verbs, this went slightly wrong for the participants, producing interesting evidence of co-occurrence of metaphor use and inaccuracy in the interpretation of the Subject or Object of the verb metaphor Vehicle. Whether there is a stronger causal link would need further investigation.

In the instances of inaccurate processing found in the protocols, some transfer of animacy from the verb to the Subject seemed to take place. The phenomenon of a slippage in the meaning of Subject or Object of the verb away from the intended meaning during metaphor processing is labelled **Topic Reference Shift**, and five instances are now described.

TOPIC REFERENCE SHIFT 1: *harmful gases* as Subject of *escape*

In the first two sentences of the text, the writer uses a concrete example of CFCs emitted when old fridges are destroyed to set the scene for topic of the book as a whole:

> 2. *It may seem strange that the liquid used to cool the air in a fridge could be harmful to life on Earth.*
> 3. *However, when old fridges are destroyed harmful gases can* **escape** *into the atmosphere.*

When processing sentence 3 in the Think-Aloud task, the girls are not able to reach an accurate understanding of *harmful gases*, because of a lack of relevant previous knowledge and the unhelpful inexplicit text. There is an (implied) anaphoric link between *the liquid* in sentence 2 and *harmful gases* in sentence 3, but there is no explicit statement that the liquid changes into a gas, or that the gases are/contain CFCs. As shown in Extract 8.3, questioning by the researcher revealed that the participants did not know that there is liquid in a fridge (lines 6 and 8). Furthermore, they did not make the connection between *liquid* and *gases,* but seemed to make sense of the Subject of *can escape* in sentence 3 without making a connection with *the liquid* (sentence 2):

Extract 8.3 *The link between liquids and gases in 'The Ozone Layer' protocols (sentences 2 and 3)*

```
1   R:   what's the ( . ) link between the liquid and the gases?
    E:   both bad for the ozone layer
    R:   mhm
    L:   yea
5   R:   where do the gases come from? (2.0)
    L:   is it (1.0) the liquid?
    R:   oh right
    E:   (whispers) I don't know
    L:   is it fuels and things?
```

Their lack of Topic-related knowledge, in particular that liquid in a fridge gives off CFC gases when exposed to air, leads to only a partial understanding of the Subject reference *harmful gases*. In this case, the problem of misinterpreting the Subject seemed to be caused by failure to link *harmful gases* to *liquid* in the previous sentence, and there is no evidence that the presence of the metaphorical *escape* contributed to the problem. The next sentence protocol to be examined is more suggestive of such evidence.

TOPIC REFERENCE SHIFTS 2 AND 3

> 9. The Earth **is kept warm** by the Sun's heat, and the atmosphere **traps** some of this heat, so that it doesn't **escape** into space.

The beginning of the protocol for this sentence is shown in Extract 8.4:

Extract 8.4 *From 'The Ozone Layer' GITA protocols: sentence 9*

```
1   L:   so that means the heat that comes in ( . ) it's (1.0) it's trapped by the atmosphere ( . )
         and then ( . ) so ( . ) none of the atmosphere can escape into space ( . ) so we can
         keep warm ( . )
    R:   mmhm
    L:   by the sun's heat ( . ) once it's been trapped in by the atmosphere
5   E:   and go lovely and brown
    L:   I can't stay in the sun long enough
```

This sentence contains three verb metaphors: *trap, is kept warm* and *escape*. *Trap* is unproblematically repeated and grammatically transformed to the passive voice. The Subject of *trap* remains *heat*, although reduced to pronominal form. However, when *is kept warm* and *escape* are repeated and transformed in line 2, the repetition is accompanied by two shifts in Subject reference, which can be set out formally as:

(i)	Text:	the Earth	is kept warm	by the Sun's heat
	Louise:	we	can keep warm	
(ii)	Text:	it (= heat)	doesn't escape	into space
	Louise:	none of the atmosphere	can escape	into space

In the first case, *the Earth* is replaced as Subject by *we* (line 2). *The Earth* becomes 'people on the Earth', with the last two lines in the extract suggesting that the girls are thinking about themselves in particular. I assume that the author's intended Subject was 'the Earth and everything on it', and suggest that the particular interpretation reached by the children may have been prompted or motivated by the animacy of the metaphorically used verb *kept warm*.

In the second case, we see, not a metonymic shift to a Subject that is a part of the intended Subject, but a misinterpretation of the anaphoric reference of the Subject *it* in *it doesn't escape into space*. Louise restated this, incorrectly, as *the atmosphere cannot escape into space* (line 2), although she repairs this almost immediately with *the sun's heat (.) once it's been trapped in* (line 4). Given her previous knowledge, this first interpretation is reasonable; after all, the atmosphere is made of gases, and in our real world experience, and in the second sentence of the text itself, *gases* do *escape*.

We see here how Topic-related knowledge was needed to disambiguate the reference, and how uncertain Topic knowledge can mislead interpretation, if only temporarily. Further difficulties were added by the complex sentence structure in which the verb metaphors occur, and possibly by the earlier use in the text of the verb metaphor *escape* with the same lexical item (*gases*) in Subject position, but with a different referent.

TOPIC REFERENCE SHIFT 4: Subject reference of **protecting/protect**

The heading of the middle section of text is 'Protecting Earth'. When the girls were asked to predict what the content of the section might be, they suggested:

Extract 8.5 Protecting Earth

E: how to stop all the (.) tion and things like that
L: [pollution
E: how we can help (.) protect the earth (.) *laugh*

The non-finite verb *protecting* was transformed into a finite form, with the human Subject *we*. However, two sentences later they encountered sentence 15:

> *It contains different gases which **protect** life on the planet.*

In discussing this sentence, Ellen comments that the heading does not appear to have been very suitable for the text:

Extract 8.6 From 'The Ozone Layer' GITA protocols: sentence 15

1	E:	this um protecting earth it isn't very good for this bit because it's the sort of (.) same thing we did before and it isn't telling you how (hh) to protect the earth which (*laugh*) we said it would be when it said protecting earth
	R:	right (2.0) who's doing the protecting here?
5	L:	it's the (.) shi (.) the invisible shield

In fact, the heading was suitable for the text underneath it, if the verb had been interpreted metaphorically. Again, the girls' reading of the earlier parts of the text about the dangers of ordinary things like fridges, seemed to create an expectation that later parts would link into this by showing how human behaviour could be adjusted. This led to an interpretation of *Protecting Earth* with an inappropriate Subject reference:

Ellen:	we	can help protect	the Earth
Text:	different gases	. . . protect	life on the planet

TOPIC REFERENCE SHIFT 5: Object reference of **lets . . .through**

In discussing sentence 16 (Extract 8.7), several problems seemed to coincide, all linked to lack of Topic knowledge, which prevented the girls from making sense of the sentence.

> 16. *The atmosphere **lets** useful energy **through**, but reduces the amount of harmful energy reaching the Earth's surface.*

Metaphor in educational discourse

Extract 8.7 From 'The Ozone Layer' GITA protocols: sentence 16

```
1   R:  well you tell her what you can understand and then maybe she'll be able to help you
    L:  well ( . ) it's letting through useful energy but then he's telling you about harmful
        energy ( . ) which is quite complicated to understand
    E:  oh I get it now (.) right (1.0)
5       the (1.0) shield (laugh) is ( . ) um ( . ) letting through all the ( . ) good kind of gases
        and ( . ) then it's not
    L:  it's reducing the amount of harmful energy ( . )
        the shield ( . ) must be reducing ( . ) the amount of harmful energy ( . )
        reaching the earth's surface ( . ) but there's still
10  R:                             [ how could it be doing that?
    L:  but there's still probably ( . ) harmful energy coming through ( . )
        it's just reducing
    R:  right
    E:  some of the harm ( . ) harmful harmful energy is ( . ) running out on the earth (laugh)
15  R:  so ( . ) how do you think the shield is ( . ) is doing this? (4.0)
    E:  I don't really know what it ( . ) like it's made (???)
        I don't really know what it's kind of meant to be ( . )
        I know what it is it protects us but
    L:                                      [ how (.) come (.) the shield is ( . )
20      reducing the amount of ( . ) harmful energy ( . )
        when it's just an invisible type?
    R:  mm
    E:  I don't know what it's meant to be=
    L:  that's quite complicated
25  E:  = I don't know whether it's like (1.0)
        I sometimes think of there being a big ball of glass ( . ) or something like that ( . )
        but I don't really know what it's ( . ) kind of of like made up of ( . )
        or is it made of gases (laugh)
    L:  it's not really ( . ) describing what it's made up of or anything ( . )
30      it's just telling you about it
```

Before the extract included here, Ellen had stated that she could not understand the sentence, and so I suggested (line 1) that Louise try to explain it to her, even though she herself was struggling. One of the basic problems here was with the contrasting pair *useful energy* and *harmful energy*, the first of which occurs as the Object of the verb metaphor *lets through*. Again, it is not clear whether, or to what extent, the misunderstanding was aggravated by the metaphor; certainly a number of factors, some of them related to metaphor, combined to create difficulties. In line 5, Ellen shifts the Subject of the verb metaphor from *the atmosphere* to *the shield*, and marked this reuse of the nominal metaphor with a turn-internal laugh. (Ellen's unmarked position for a laugh throughout the GITA protocols was at the end of her turns.) She reuses the verb metaphor as *letting through*, with the Object inaccurately relexicalized from *useful energy* to *the good kind of gases*:

> Text: *the atmosphere lets useful energy through*
> Ellen: *the shield is letting through all the good kind of gases*

It is clear, from this and other protocols, that the students did not know that *light* is a type of *energy*. The text does not explicitly state the relationship, nor is it clear that the writer does not intend readers to think of *gases* as a type of *energy*. For the readers, the *fridges* example in the opening sentences activated a household domain that may have affected this later interpretation.

Furthermore, the primary sense of *energy* for the participants is neither of these, but the non-technical sense: when trying to make sense of sentence 10 (*But not all the energy made by the Sun is safe*) the girls were asked what they thought of when they thought about energy, and they replied:

> L: *it's the thing we have*
> E: *it's when you run*

The sense of *energy* activated was thus quite distinct from the technical meaning intended in this text to include light and heat. The text provided no help with the intended meaning, and no explicit clue that a technical meaning was required, with the result that the girls worked with their existing, everyday meaning, or spontaneous concept, of the word. Ellen's interpretation here, that *energy* is the same as *gases*, seems an intelligent one, given the knowledge she brought to the text and given the earlier collocation in the text of *harmful* with *gases*. Louise continues to use the full phrase *harmful energy*, collocated with the verb *reduces*, throughout.

Lines 14–23 show, once again, how the metaphor of the *shield* could not be developed to help the participants understand the Topic more clearly. It seemed to be memorable – it was spontaneously brought back into the talk – but it was not very useful. The participants could not get past its basic function of *protecting* because they could not imagine how a *shield* can work to stop *energy/gases* coming through: *it's not really describing what it's made up of or anything* (line 29). A gap in Topic knowledge remained unfilled by the metaphor Vehicle, and their understanding of the topic remained limited to 'patches' of clarity in an overall mist of confusion that the text repeatedly failed to dissolve.

We can also note that Ellen's own metaphor for the earth and the atmosphere, *a big ball of glass,* presents the same problem. It helped her to imagine the general function, and perhaps too the appearance, of the atmosphere around the earth, but failed to help her understand the properties of *the atmosphere* that cause it to function protectively.

A further inaccurate interpretation occurs around the verb metaphor *given out* in the protocol of sentence 11. The main reason for the problem seems not to be the verb but the effect of the punctuation, together with lack of familiarity with the phrase *ultraviolet light.* In the text sentence the phrase *or UV* is inserted between *ultraviolet* and *light* and separated from the rest of the sentence with commas. The participants did not realize that *or UV* was anaphorically equivalent to *ultraviolet,* but instead saw the second comma as marking the start of a complete clause *light are also given out.* The grammar of this clearly did not feel right and they abandoned attempts to interpret it.

Reference Shift and sentences without metaphors

To develop the hypothesis that the use of metaphorical verbs increases the probability of Topic Reference Shift (TRS), evidence is needed, not only that TRS and verb metaphors co-occur, but that the absence of verb metaphors co-occurs with the absence of inaccurate interpretations or Reference Shift (RS). Examination of the full set of protocols shows that RS did not occur with nine non-metaphorical verbs (such as *stop* and *contain).* The pattern of co-occurrence is broken only once, by the metaphorical verb *trap,* which is processed accurately.

Explaining TRS: the centrifugal effect of metaphor

The verb metaphors appear to be processed differently from the nominal metaphors, with the major locus of processing being the Subject or Object of the verb. Misinterpretations often take the form of incorrect Subject/Object reference. These Topic Reference Shifts seem to co-occur with a metaphorically used verb, often compounded by other factors:

- partial or inaccurate Topic knowledge brought to the text
- earlier misleading collocations in the text
- complex reference within or between sentences

It is as if the use of a verb metaphor 'loosens' the Subject/Object reference, and that accurate Topic knowledge is required to 'fix' it and resolve the discourse alterity. When the text presents other difficulties, the risk of a shift in Subject/Object reference of verb metaphors increases. In some cases, the Subject/Object shift may be repaired; in others, it is absorbed into the processing and may mislead understanding.

The loosening effect of metaphor use was also observed with the nominal metaphors, principally in the re-alignment of the metaphorical Vehicles *shield* and *blanket* with *the ozone layer* in the participants' interpretation, rather than with the *atmosphere* as in the original text. The introduction of Vehicle terms into the text seemed to create a kind of centrifugal cognitive force that opens up potentially endless links to other concepts, and reduces the probability of successful reduction of discourse alterity. Working within Topic knowledge activated by the text provides a counter-balancing centripetal force that should constrain aspects of the Vehicle to those most relevant and useful to the Topic. The theoretically neat accounts of the Interaction theory or Conceptual Blending are, on-line and for real participants, much messier and more unpredictable.

Analysis of recalled knowledge about 'The Ozone Layer' in post-GITA discussion

Content of recalled information

Immediately after completing the GITA reading task, the participants evaluated the text and the 'useful' information they had gleaned. Extract 8.8 includes some of their comments, and shows that they were aware of their difficulties.

The two participants recall different types of content. Ellen recalls the two nominal metaphors (line 16); Louise recalls the non-metaphorical information about the height of the ozone layer above the earth (lines 15, 17, 19). Louise's preference for figures rather than the figurative recurs in the later discussion and in the next text GITA. In addition, in recalling the figures Louise also recalls accurately that they give the height of *the atmosphere containing the ozone*, in contrast to Ellen's Reference Shift from *atmosphere* to *ozone layer* in the recall of the *shield* metaphor in line 24.

The information recalled after the GITA task includes explicit mention of the two nominal metaphor Vehicles, and the fact of their protective function (line 22). The pre-GITA discussion had included reference to *protecting*. As seen in the analysis of the processing of the metaphors and the text, more detail about how the ozone layer protects the earth was not accessible.

Extract 8.8 *'The Ozone Layer': immediate post-GITA discussion*

```
1    E:    ??? not very good explaining for a younger child
     R:    why not?
     E:    because it's very hard to understand for even us (laugh) we're
     R:    how would you make it easier?
5    L:    by putting simpler words in ( . ) some of those words and =
     E:                                                          [ and it's
     L:    = describing the words that he put in ( . ) cos he put ( . )
           even if he did put smaller words ( . )
           the big words that he DID put in ( . )
10         he put he just put the big words ( . ) which meant nothing (.)
           well meant something but didn't mean anything to me and ( . )
           then he just carried on ( . ) and ( . )
           he should have explained what that word meant ( . ) and then ( . ) carried on
     R:    and did he do anything that WAS useful?
15   L:    yea ( . ) he ( . ) like he ( . ) told us the height ( . )
     E:                               [ the blanket and the shield
     L:    he told us like the height ( . ) where the atmosphere=
     R:                                               [ mm hm
     L:    = containing ozone is
20   E:    the shield is quite
     L:                  [ that's quite interesting to know
     E:    the shield was quite helpful because it ( . )
           you know that a a shield is protective ( . )
           and so that was telling you that the ozone layer was protective
25   R:    right ( . ) okay ( . ) this is the book then ( . ) you can see
```

One week after reading the text, the participants' recalled knowledge was assessed from transcription of a discussion with three of their peers, in which they were invited to retell what they had found out. The following extract from the transcription has participants' contributions placed in columns to facilitate reading of individual contributions. The numbers in brackets indicate the sequential order of turns.

The recalled information seemed more evenly shared by the two girls than in the pre-GITA discussion. When asked directly (9) about the ozone layer, there is a contrast with the pre-GITA discussion in that the language used was much less vague, statements were used rather than questions, with more precise technical terminology. (Ellen and Louise encountered information about chemicals and CFCs after the GITA task, when they looked at the rest of the book.) We can see then some reduction in conceptual alterity after the talking-and-thinking around the text. The changes are summarized in Table 8.6.

The Ozone Layer

Extract 8.9 *'The Ozone Layer': delayed post-GITA discussion*

Researcher's query	Louise's response	Ellen's response
(1) . . .explain to the others what they found out last week		(2) . . .it was about the ozone layer
	(3) learned about chemicals and gases	(4) what's harmful to the ozone layer
	(5) what's harmful. . .the ultraviolet rays. . .about fridges. . .	
(6) what did you find out about it?	(7) if people don't stop using CFCs the ozone layer will be getting thinner and thinner (.) it will be letting in more ultraviolet rays	(8) and we learnt that when like cans of CFCs could still be affecting the ozone layer a hundred years later
(9) what <u>is</u> the ozone layer?	(10) it's it's it's	(11) it's the thing that protects the earth
	(12) it's a type of gas	(13) gas
	(14) it's like an invisible shield around the earth	(15) or blanket (.) as the book put it
	(16) and it's protecting us from getting too much UV	(17) made of lots of different gases
	. . .	(18) it lets some of the sun's rays in but not all of them
	(19) the ozone layer's only 10 to 30 kilometres high	(20) . . . that's why she remembered it (.) she was so amazed about that

Inaccuracies in recalled information

Not all the changes in conceptual alterity are fully accurate, and Topic Reference Shift is again evident in long-term recall. The two nominal metaphor Vehicles reappear more or less verbatim, but with a different Topic from that used in the text. Louise uses the metaphor of the *shield* to apply to the ozone layer, whereas the text applied it to the atmosphere. Ellen picks up the turn and recalls *blanket*, also originally applied to the atmosphere. With the metaphor she seems to transfer the layered nature of the atmosphere and states that it is *made of lots of gases*, apparently contradicting Louise's earlier statement that she had echoed, *it's a type of gas*. From her elliptical statement, it is not clear

Table 8.6 *Reductions in conceptual alterity*

Before reading	After reading
Entities mentioned	
sun	UV rays, some of the sun's rays
pollution	chemicals, gases, fridges, CFCs
Properties	
it's a big protective thing	• it's a type of gas • it's like an invisible shield around the earth • or blanket • it's protecting us from getting too much UV • (it's) only 10 to 30 kilometres high
Relations	
the hole in the ozone layer was made by the sun's rays	• if people don't stop using CFCs the ozone layer will be getting thinner and thinner
it's a big protective thing	• it lets some of the sun's rays in but not all of them

whether she is referring to the atmosphere or to the ozone layer. Either the metaphor Topic reference is slipping, or her understanding of the distinction between the atmosphere and the ozone layer is not yet fully established, and the attractor is not stable. Despite her re-allocation of the metaphor *shield*, Louise makes and maintains the distinction between the atmosphere and the ozone layer in her contributions.

Discussion of results of GITA 1, 'The Ozone Layer'

Results so far are now discussed in terms of the research questions set out on pp. 164–6. In the next chapter the results of the second GITA task will be reported, and findings will then be discussed across both sets of results.

2-1 How do the students make sense of the linguistic metaphors they encounter in a text?

Discourse alterity around nominal metaphors was resolved through processes of Topic and Vehicle Development and recombination in Metaphor Construction. The processes in the children's protocols were very similar to those of the adults in Steen's 1992 study. Verb metaphors were processed less explicitly, with some repetition and relexicalization but much less Vehicle Development.

Evidence of temporary or longer lasting inaccuracies in interpretation points to the dangers of using metaphor. Introducing metaphorical language into a text has been described in terms of centrifugal forces; the choice of a Vehicle term brings with it a range of mental connections that can be made around it, potentially blowing apart the text base constructed up to that point. The alterity is suddenly increased. To rebuild coherence in the face of a metaphor requires discourse participants to select and constrain inferences from among the range of the possible. It is Topic knowledge, both that brought to a text and that taken from the text, that plays a major role in this constraining process. Although the literature on children's understanding of metaphor suggests that Vehicle knowledge is very important in the success or otherwise of making sense of metaphor, it is clear that Topic knowledge plays an equally crucial role in making sense of the metaphors in their discourse context. Topic knowledge in interaction with Vehicle knowledge is needed:

- to disambiguate pronominal and other anaphoric references, particularly around verb metaphors;
- to prevent the Vehicle being associated with the wrong aspect of the Topic, or the wrong Topic altogether, in interpretation and in recall;
- to prompt participants to access the appropriate property of the Vehicle to map the Topic domain.

Vehicle knowledge was not a problem in this particular text, since the nominal metaphors were quite simple. Even so, it played the following roles in interpretation:

- to signal an incongruity and thus prompt metaphoric processing;
- to identify the key properties and relations to transfer from Vehicle to Topic, through Contextualization in terms of the participants' life experience and through Vehicle Development;
- to provide sufficient transferable properties and relational connections at appropriate levels of specificity.

TOPIC REFERENCE SHIFT

Several instances of misinterpretation occurred in the talking-and-thinking about the text sentences and in recall. In fact, the metaphor Vehicles could apply quite appropriately to alternative Topics (e.g. the ozone layer rather than the atmosphere) and, in terms of knowledge development, the misinterpretations were not important. However, as a reminder of how loosely information is connected to language form, they were significant. A match between words and one's knowledge structure seems more salient than careful attention to syntax and the logical relations encoded by it. Since metaphor forces a receiver to search for appropriate although approximate matches, it may be that such slippages are more likely to occur in metaphor processing than in the processing of non-figurative language. This suggests an interesting paradox or conflict between the needs of science texts to inform accurately, and the inaccuracy prompted by the use of metaphors employed to inform effectively.

DIFFERENCES BETWEEN NOMINAL AND VERB METAPHORS

The differences in Think-Aloud interpretation processes between nominal and verb metaphors probably follow from fundamental differences between nouns and verbs and in how they relate to our embodied existence in the world. Cross-linguistically, nouns are more stable in their reference than verbs (Gentner 1978, 1982b). In early first language acquisition, verbs present a more demanding task than nouns, with a small number of key verbs being used across a range of communicative contexts (Gentner 1982b). In Chapter 3, I mentioned the tendency for verbs to be extended through use with collocates that stretch their meaning, sometimes creating idioms through collocations with nouns, e.g. *cast a shadow* (Hopper 1997). The flexibility of verbs to accommodate (Langacker 1987) a wide range of collocated nouns was noted by Brooke-Rose (1958) in connection with metaphor. She suggests that the metaphorical uses of verbs may rapidly become accepted, just because we are used to verbs being extended. In a study on the interpretation of novel metaphors created by putting together pairs of nouns and verbs, Matic and Wales (1982: 254) showed that verb meanings were more likely to be extended than noun meanings to make sense of anomalous noun–verb pairs, such as *hint boiled* or *rocked freedom*.

These differences in flexibility and likelihood of being extended in use suggest that verbs are likely to produce different effects from nouns when used metaphorically. They are likely to be used differently, and, as the findings reported above demonstrate, are likely to be processed differently by users of English. The greater flexibility of verbs in use may well be linked with the greater inaccuracy found in verb metaphor interpretation.

MULTIPLE USE OF METAPHOR AND SHARED UNDERSTANDING

Multiple use of metaphor appeared in the writer's relexicalization of the Vehicle from *blanket* to *shield*, and in Ellen's use of an alternative metaphor for the ozone layer. The writer's use of two metaphors appeared to help understanding by providing two aspects of the atmosphere: protection and stopping harmful radiation. However, the second metaphor did not offer more possibilities for new information than the first. What was needed to prompt useful cognitive change was further information that might illuminate more precisely how this protection and stopping is brought about, and what precisely is being stopped.

Ellen's own metaphor, which she mentioned both in the GITA protocol (Extract 8.9) and in the recall discussion a week later, has similar drawbacks, although it is slightly more extended than the writer's:

Extract 8.10 *Ellen's metaphor for the ozone layer*

> I sometimes think of it as a marble cos some marbles have like (.)
> the glass um and they have like (.)
> that um picture inside and I always think it looks like a boat inside (.)
> and the I think of the ozone layer as being the glass on the outside

The link seems to be made principally on visual grounds: the earth and a marble are both spherical. The further attributional link is between the glass outer surface of the marble and the ozone layer around the earth. The link helps imagine how it is but not how it works.

2-2 How do encounters with metaphor affect conceptual alterity?

DO THE METAPHORS PROMPT PROCESSES THAT LEAD TO NEW UNDERSTANDINGS?

As summarized in the previous section, encounters with the metaphors within the text did seem to add something to participants' understanding. However, the full range of potential new knowledge was not constructed through processing, and some new knowledge was inaccurate. The reasons for the failure of the *shield* and *blanket* metaphors to add further to the participants' knowledge lay, not in their previous knowledge, but rather in the limitations of the chosen Vehicles (and Topics) at a detailed level in providing transferable relational connections. The chosen Vehicles were not sufficiently cognitively specific or complex to push conceptual development into a new attractor that would represent new understanding. To this extent, the writer may be said to have misjudged the needs of the intended readers.

The nominal metaphors prompted the process of Vehicle Contextualization that seems potentially important for linking new information into previous knowledge.

DO THE METAPHORS ASSIST RECALL OF NEW INFORMATION?

The selection of striking Vehicle terms assisted recall directly, both immediately after reading and a week later, although recall was not always precisely in line with the intended meaning of the writer. As Spiro *et al.* (1989) warned, misinterpreted metaphors may be as memorable as correctly interpreted ones. Indirectly, recall seems to be assisted through the deep and active processing prompted by inclusion of the metaphors in the text.

2-3 What is the role of mediation in interpreting metaphors?

MEDIATION BY THE TEXT

Information about the productive mediation of metaphor can be gathered from the gap between the assistance provided for metaphor comprehension in the classroom discourse analysed in Chapter 5, and the immediate linguistic context of the metaphors in the Ozone Layer text as set out on p. 172. It was noted there that the text did not provide very much Vehicle-related information in modification, relexicalization, or explication, and in fact offered Topic-related information where one might expect to find Vehicle-related information.

MEDIATION BY PEERS

In the protocols, discussion of the nominal metaphors revolved around the Vehicle term and seemed to provide just the kind of support that is missing in the text. Making sense of metaphor (or at least of nominal metaphor) seems to involve centrally these Vehicle-related processes, and in the classroom discourse, the teacher verbally provided these for the pupils as an inter-personal scaffold for understanding. In the GITA protocols, the girls provided them for each other and for themselves. An alternative, weaker, view might be that the pupils in GITA were replicating the teacher talk around metaphor they were familiar with. However, it is unlikely that they would do this unless it were also helpful in the task of making sense. From these observations, I hypothesize that helpful mediation of metaphor will generally include the Vehicle-related processes of Development and Contextualization.

The GITA methodology has produced detailed and fine grained information about the participants' processing of linguistic metaphors in an information text. Certain patterns of processing emerged for nominal and verb metaphors that will be looked for in the second GITA study, in which the same participants work on a different text.

Such patterns are only suggestive since they may arise from the idiosyncrasies of the particular participants. More importantly, this empirical study has shown how different factors interact in making sense of a text, and how Topic and Vehicle knowledge (both new and old) are drawn on. The range of problems experienced by Louise and Ellen in reducing discourse alterity around the metaphors is generalizable. They are problems that other readers could experience. Having isolated and described the problems, implications can be drawn about how to use metaphors more effectively in written and spoken discourse. But before doing that, I consider the results from the second GITA study.

9 Metaphors in Text 2: 'The Heart'

Four weeks after the Ozone Layer reading, Louise and Ellen undertook a further round of interactive thinking aloud, using a text on 'The Heart' (Figure 9.1). This chapter reports on the metaphors in the text and how they were interpreted in the talking-and-thinking process. We see replicated the distinction between nominal and verb metaphors in processing, and the phenomenon of Topic Reference Shift.

A key difference between the ozone layer and the heart, as content areas and as texts, is that the concept of the working of the heart is metaphorically structured, in terms of the metaphor THE HEART IS A PUMP. Metaphors are not only linguistic devices to help explain concepts, but actually structure the concepts themselves. We see how the students negotiated the gap between their existing conceptual knowledge and the scientific concept, and how the text failed to prompt revision of some of their spontaneous concepts.

As in the previous chapter, we begin with an analysis of the linguistic metaphors in the text, and how they contribute to information content and structure.

Metaphors in the text

The initial identification and the cross-checking produced 23 linguistic metaphors (15 types) (Table 9.1). Column 2 in Table 9.1 differentiates three types of metaphors: technical, technical + theory, and sub-technical. Nearly half (11 of 23) of the metaphors are 'technical'; they are conventionalized terms within the scientific domain. The text contains other technical terms that are not metaphorical, e.g. *arteries, veins*. Five of the technical metaphors derive from the conceptual metaphor THE HEART IS A PUMP. This metaphor structures the expert scientific concept and so is a 'theory-constitutive metaphor' (Boyd 1993). The five linguistic metaphors are labelled Technical + Theory. Eleven linguistic metaphors are 'sub-technical' (see Chapter 5), in that they use some Vehicle term in place of a technical Topic term, e.g. *tubes* for *arteries*. The two remaining metaphors, <u>*tells*</u> and *a* <u>*rest*</u>, are more everyday in content.

THE HEART

1 Blood is the body's transport system (*as*
2 *explained on page 16*). At the centre of this
3 system is your heart. It has four chambers
4 with muscular walls. About once a second,
   the walls contract and squeeze blood out of
   the chambers into strong tubes, called
5 arteries. The blood is pushed around your
6 body. As the heart relaxes again, its
   chambers fill with more blood brought
7 back to it by other tubes, the veins. This
   pumping, which we call a heart beat,
   happens every second of every day, for as
8 long as you live. You can feel blood surging
9 through the artery in your wrist. Each surge
10 or "pulse" is one heart beat. So your "pulse
   rate" tells you how fast your heart is beating.
11   No man-made pump is as reliable as your
12 heart. It can beat for 100 years or more
13 without a rest. Also, the heart is adjustable.
14 It can beat faster or slower, and change
   how much blood it pumps with each beat,
15 depending on how active you are. The
   adjustments are controlled by nerves from
16 your brain and by hormones. When you
   are resting your heart might beat 60 to 70
   times a minute, and pump about 70
   millilitres (one-eighth of a pint) of blood
17 each time. When you run a race it beats
   over twice as fast and pumps three times as
   much blood with each beat.

Figure 9.1 Text 2: 'The Heart'. From S. Parker (1987), *The Body and How It Works*. London: Dorling Kindersley.

Table 9.1 Linguistic metaphors identified in 'The Heart' text

Linguistic metaphor	Technical and sub-technical metaphors
(1) Blood is the body's transport system	Sub-technical
(2) the centre	Sub-technical
(2) of this system	Sub-technical
(3) It has four chambers	Technical
(3) with muscular walls	Technical
(4) strong tubes	Sub-technical
(4) the walls	Technical
(4) contract	Technical
(4) (the walls) .. squeeze blood	Sub-technical
(5) The blood is pushed around the body	Sub-technical
(6) the heart relaxes	Technical
(6) blood brought back to it	Sub-technical
(6) by other tubes	Sub-technical
(7) this pumping	Technical + Theory
(10) your pulse-rate tells you	
(11) No man-made pump	Technical + Theory
(12) it can beat . . . without a rest	
(13) the heart is adjustable	Sub-technical
(14) it pumps	Technical + Theory
(15) the adjustments	Sub-technical
(15) are controlled by the nerves	Sub-technical
(16) your heart might. . .pump	Technical + Theory
(17) it pumps three times as much blood	Technical + Theory

The first sentence is a classic *A is B* copular metaphor that is extended in sentence 2. Sentence 11, *No man-made pump is as reliable as your heart*, is a 'negative metaphor', in which a metaphorical comparison is implied through being denied.

The metaphor density of this text is very high, at about 101 per 1000 words in comparison with the 27 per 1000 words of spoken discourse and 36 per 1000 in the Ozone Layer text. The high density of metaphor reflects the combination of a technical metaphor in the scientific concept domain and the sub-technical metaphor used to explain it.

Grammatically, the text has eight nominal metaphors, one adjective metaphor, and 14 verb metaphors. The most reliably identified metaphor, *blood is the body's transport system*, is a variation of a nominal group metaphor, using the possessive rather than {NP *of* NP} form. As with the Ozone Layer text, and in contrast with the spoken classroom discourse, the verb metaphors are schematic rather than indexical.

Metaphors in the informational structure of the text

The text used in the Think-Aloud was extracted from a double-page spread where it was positioned to the left of a visual representation of the *transport system* metaphor, showing motorways and lorries. In a box below the extracted text was a more technical explanation of how the heart pumps, with diagrams of the heart. The extracted text (Figure 9.1) had the largest font, and this, together with its positioning on the page, suggests that it was intended to give an overview of processes and concepts that might be read before, and again after, looking at the diagrams and reading the other small parts of text.

The conceptual content of the text

The text supplies the reader with details about the structure and working of the heart:

Paragraph 1
    Metaphor of blood as transport system   1, 2
    The structure of the heart   3
    How the heart pumps   4–6
    Heart beats and pulse rates   7–10
Paragraph 2
    The reliability of the heart as a pump   11, 12
    The variability of the heart   13, 14
    How the heart adjusts   15
    An example of this variation in resting/racing   16, 17

Although the first metaphor, *the blood is the body's <u>transport system</u>*, looks like an introductory analogy in a topic sentence, it is actually a summary of assumed previous knowledge about blood. The topic of the text, The Heart, is introduced in sentence 2 through an extension of the *system* part of the metaphor. The *transport* part of the metaphor is not further developed in the text. The *transport system* metaphor is both abstract and general (compare a more concrete and specific relexicalization: *blood carries food around the body just as lorries carry goods to the supermarkets*). It is also complex, in the sense that there are many possible mappings from the domain of transport systems, from which a reader has to select the appropriate and relevant ones. The most relevant mappings are relational, i.e. about functions and processes, rather than about properties or entities.

The information and thematic structures of the text

After the first sentence, the text has a more linear structure than the Ozone Layer text, with each sentence developing the information given in the previous one. Several sentences have a pattern in which a sub-technical metaphor is used in advance of technical terms, e.g. *strong tubes, called arteries*. This pattern works on a larger scale in the metaphorical descriptions in sentences 3 to 5 which precede the first use of the technical + theory metaphor *pumping*.

There does not seem to be any potential problem with anaphoric reference of sentence-initial pronouns as there was after the nominal metaphors in the Ozone Layer text (p. 171).

The reading age of this text is lower than the Ozone Layer text, with a Flesch Grade Level score of 6.3 and a Gunning Fog Index of 7.2. These scores largely reflect the simpler sentence structure.

Mediational devices in the text to support metaphor interpretation

1. Vehicle incongruity

The initial metaphor has a reasonably high level of incongruity, whereas the others are much less obvious as metaphors. When first introduced as a deliberate metaphor by William Harvey in the early seventeenth century, THE HEART IS A PUMP would have had a high level of incongruity for users, between the part of the body and the machine used for pumping water from a well. We have since become so used to the metaphor that *pump* is now considered non-metaphorical by many people.

2. Use of tuning markers

The metaphors are unmarked by hedges or tuning markers.

3. Modification of Vehicle terms

All instances of pre-modification of the Vehicle term employ modifiers relating to the Topic domain:

> the body's *transport system*
> four *chambers*
> muscular *walls*
> strong *tubes*

Unlike the teacher's deliberate metaphors in Chapter 5, e.g. *sticky treacle*, these pre-modifiers do not pick out one aspect of the Vehicle domain which is relevant to the Topic, but rather provide additional Topic domain information.

4. Metaphor clustering: repetition and relexicalization of Vehicle terms

Four of the 15 Vehicle terms are repeated:

> *system*
> *tubes*
> *pump/pumping/pumps*
> *adjustment/adjustable*

One verb Vehicle is relexicalized:

> *squeeze* → *pump* → *push*

5. Development of metaphors

The *transport system* metaphor receives no Vehicle development in the text, although this is the main function of the picture next to the text which includes lorries driving along roads in different directions, road signs, junctions, over- and under-passes, and tunnels.

The absence of Vehicle development applies to all the metaphors in the text. All development is in terms of Topic domains:

> other <u>tubes</u>, the veins
> the heart is <u>adjustable</u>. It can beat faster or slower

The lack of Vehicle development may result from the metaphors being mostly technical rather than deliberate and imagistic. However, as we will see, the child readers might have benefited from more help in making sense of the Vehicle terms and concepts.

Previous knowledge brought to the text

The knowledge of the students about the heart and circulatory system was elicited through a pre-reading discussion between the researcher and a group of five children, including Louise and Ellen, around the topic of *pumps*. This discussion revealed that participants brought considerable subject knowledge to their Think-Aloud task in the form of concepts and explanatory theories (Carey 1985). However, as before, incomplete and inaccurately structured knowledge implied conceptual alterity between existing concepts and the fuller scientific concepts in the text. To reduce the alterity would require both additional information, and the restructuring of existing explanatory theories.

The group discussion was initiated by asking for examples of pumps. When one student mentioned the heart as a pump, the researcher guided the discussion on to how pumps work, what the heart does and why it is needed. The transcribed talk was divided into columns for each speaker, with turns placed from left to right across

Metaphor in educational discourse

Extract 9.1 From the pre-GITA discussion on 'The Heart'

Researcher	Ellen	Dougal	Heather	Louise	Marie
(1) so what about the heart then?			(2) it pumps blood... blood comes from all directions and it pumps it out again		(3) used blood comes in and it's reused again
(6) where does it send it to?			(4) in out in out ...it's like recycling it	(7) all parts of the body to keep the body moving	(5) it goes out that way and comes in this way
			(8) like petrol to keep a car moving like air to keep up bicycle tyres		
	(9) so when you die your heart stops beating and all the blood stops going round you			(10) then it's preventing you from moving .. people have to lift you up cos you just flop cos no blood's going round	
(11) why do you need blood to go round your body?				(12) cos if you didn't have it you'd just uuu while it's moving it's keeping	
			(13) feeds your bones		
		(14) has it got calcium in it?	(15) cos it mixes round with your food	(16) while it's going round it's helping you keep up	
			(17) it's warming you to move .. well .. not .. cos if you're freezing cold you can't move .. so it's warming you up	(18) it's like water when it's just come out of the tap it can move but if you freeze it it's just still	
(19) so it's like blowing something up?				(20) yeah .. it gets right confusing	
(21) why?		(22) we don't know how to explain it		(23) cos we keep going round in circles	
(24) metaphor-ically speaking		(25) oh no..I said a metaphor			

206

rows, (Extract 9.1). By looking down the columns, each student's contribution to the discussion can be seen, while the jointly constructed understandings emerge from the combined columns. We cannot tell how far the jointly constructed understanding was internalized by each individual. In terms of what an individual took from the discussion to the reading of the text, we can probably say that this was likely to include their own understanding as verbalized in the discussion, together with some form of the jointly constructed understanding. It must also be re-iterated that this method cannot claim to find out what the participants would have brought to the reading if the research was not taking place. It only reveals something of what was activated in this particular discourse (and research) event.

When asked for examples of pumps, the group produced six types: three related to air: *bicycle pump/car (foot) pump/shoe pump;* and three related to liquids: *pump n spray (perfume)/petrol pump/ water pump.* The bicycle pump was first mentioned and may thus be assumed to be particularly salient to the students. When asked what all the examples of pumps have in common, Louise replied:

> they all got air to .. it's all got to do with air

She is largely correct, since the first three pumps mechanically push the air, and perfume and water pumps work by removing air, thereby increasing pressure, which in turn causes the liquid to rise. However, this is the first hint of the source of confusion that later affected the Think-Aloud.

Extract 9.1 includes the part of the discussion on the functioning of the heart. It is used to support the claim that the students' concepts of the heart and the blood systems brought to the text are inaccurate. Exploring what this extract suggests about the students' awareness of the scientific concepts, we can see that the children know that blood is pumped through the heart (2–5), and that Louise seems to know that one of the functions of blood *is to keep the body moving* (7). However, how this actually happens is more of a mystery. Heather produces two further analogies (8), which merit close attention:

	(blood)	to keep	the body	moving
like	petrol	to keep	a car	moving
like	air	to keep up	bicycle tyres	
	X	Z	Y	(Z)

Heather's analogies are parallel in form and in lexis to Louise's original statement about the function of the blood. In each analogy, there is a substance X in an object Y with a function Z, expressed using *keep*. However, there is an important difference between *keep moving* and *keep up*. The *petrol/car* analogy retains the original idea of *moving*, whereas the function of *air* in *bicycle tyres* is not movement but inflation. Ellen then brings into the discussion the idea of death as the absence of heart beating and of movement of the blood. Louise seems to pick up the idea of inflation in her next turn (10) when she graphically comments on the floppiness of dead bodies and links this to the absence of blood flowing round the body. She maintains this train of thought in (12) and (16), even though Dougal suggests an alternative function of blood, *feeds your bones*. He is the only one who mentions the fact that the blood takes nutrients around the body.

Louise's stated explanatory theory for how the blood keeps the body going is that the moving of the blood helps *keep up*, i.e. she has again used Heather's *bicycle tyre* analogy. We can note that Louise's explanation makes coherent sense of her experiential knowledge that lack of blood leads to floppiness. The explanation is adequate, in that it accounts for all her knowledge, if she does not know that the blood transports oxygen and nutrients to muscles, which are what actually keep us upright. However, her theory makes an inaccurate, direct cause–effect relation between blood circulating and being upright, when in fact the link is indirect.

Although Dougal knows the missing piece of information, that the blood moves 'food' around the body, he also seems to have an inaccurate explanatory theory in (17): blood warms you up, so absence of blood makes you cold, and freezing cold means immobile. Again, this explanation is consistent with spontaneous or experiential knowledge about dead bodies being cold and frozen things not moving. The students agree in (22) and (23) on the existence of conceptual alterity.

For Louise, conceptual knowledge about the domain of pumps and the circulatory system taken to the text can be summarized as:
- pumps share the attribute of involving air
- one of the most salient pumps is a bicycle pump
- a function of the circulatory system is to keep the body upright.

Her explanatory theory makes coherent sense of her knowledge and is internally coherent, in spite of the missing knowledge about the blood transporting oxygen and nutrients around the body. Ellen's contribution to the discussion is limited. She was the first to mention the bicycle pump and brought in the notion of death when the heart stops.

The potential of text and metaphors for learning

The discussion suggests the presence of conceptual alterity between the scientific concept of the working of the heart and the students' existing concepts, which can be seen as the 'current attractor' of their conceptual systems. Reading the text may perturb the systems from this attractor, and we are interested to see whether the reading provides sufficient perturbation to send the systems into an alternative attractor that is closer to the accepted scientific concept.

As well as a conceptual gap, there also seems to be a lexical gap between the text and the readers, in that the students' talk about the heart does not use the technical language of the text. For example, they talk about blood *going in and out*, whereas the text is more specific about how the heart *contracts* and *relaxes* to bring about this movement. Understanding the technical and sub-technical metaphors is a task in its own right, and part of the process of adjusting conceptual alterity.

On p. 204, it was noted that the writer uses metaphors but does not develop them. The initial nominal metaphors are thus unlikely to help Louise and Ellen fill out their knowledge about how the blood transports oxygen and nutrients. Analysis of the GITA protocols will show how they make sense of the text without this piece of the conceptual puzzle.

Overview of findings

Analysis of the GITA protocols produced a detailed picture of the various factors affecting interpretation of the text and the roles of linguistic metaphors in reaching shared understandings. Before presenting the detailed findings, this section summarizes the results in comparison with the results from the previous reading. The first set of results is strengthened, and, in some cases extended, by the second set.

Similarities with findings from 'The Ozone Layer' text

- Interpretation problems again arose from unknown concepts and lexical items from the Topic domain, and from complicating aspects of text or sentence structure.
- The overall pattern of differences between the processing of nominal and of verb metaphors was replicated.
- Explicit comments on some of the linguistic metaphors provided evidence that they were also process metaphors.
- Topic Reference Shift was evident, and, as before, occurred more frequently with verb metaphors.
- Lack of Topic knowledge restricted the development of full shared understandings of some metaphors.

Differences with 'Ozone Layer' findings

- Metaphor was present, not only at the level of linguistic metaphors, but more systematically as metaphorical models or 'theory-constitutive metaphors' (Boyd 1993) that hold together scientific concepts. This applied to THE HEART AS A PUMP, which has already been discussed (p. 208) in relation to the students' previous knowledge, and to THE CONTROLLING OF THE BODY BY HORMONES, which emerged as a gap in knowledge during the Think-Aloud process. While the conceptual alterity around the second metaphorical model was resolved through mediation, the alterity around the underlying PUMP metaphor was noticed but remained unresolved. Protocol analysis revealed the permeating effect of this conceptual metaphor alterity across the whole text interpretation process.
- The abstract nature of the *transport system* metaphor caused a different type of interpretation problem, due to lack of both Topic and Vehicle knowledge.
- Further strategies for interpreting technical metaphors were found.

These findings are now reported in more detail, illustrated with extracts from the protocols.

Processing of nominal and verb metaphors

Tables 9.2 and 9.3 show the interpretation processes in the GITA protocols for nominal and verb metaphors. As with the metaphors in the Ozone Layer text (p. 176), there is an overall pattern of differences in processing. Verb metaphors generally receive less attention and less explicit metaphor processing through Evaluation or Metaphor Construction.

Table 9.2 shows that the first two nominal metaphors receive extensive attention of the same kind as the *blanket* and *shield* metaphors in the Ozone Layer text, while many of the other nominal metaphors are discussed using fewer processing categories. In the reading of both texts, these nominal group metaphors tend to be more strongly recognized by children and adults, and to be processed more extensively than other forms of nominal or verb metaphors.

Comparison of Tables 9.2 and 9.3 again shows that, overall, nominal metaphors receive more processing than verb metaphors, and that there is a tendency for different types of processes to be involved. Verb metaphors are much more likely to pass unnoticed in the talk about the sentences they occur in.

Table 9.2 Processing of the nominal metaphors in the GITA protocols for 'The Heart'

Processing	The body's transport system	The centre of this system	Chambers	Muscular walls	Strong tubes	This pumping	No man-made pump	A rest	The adjustments
1. Evaluation	3			1					
2. Metaphor Restatement	2	2	1	1					
3.1 Vehicle Explication	4		2	2			3	1	1
3.2 Vehicle Repetition	1	5	2	1	2	2		1	2
3.3 Vehicle Relexicalization	2			1				1	
4. Vehicle Contextualization							1		2
5. Topic Development	2	3		2		2	1	1	
6. Metaphor Construction	4	1		1			1	1	1
7. Metaphor Reference		1							
Problems in interpretation	*	*	*	*			*		*

Table 9.3 Processing of verb metaphors in the GITA protocols for 'The Heart'

Processing	Contract	Squeeze	Pushed	Relaxes	Brought back	Tells	Pumps	Are controlled	Pump	Pumps
1. Evaluation						1				
2. Metaphor Restatement				1						
3.1 Vehicle Explication			?2							
3.2 Vehicle Repetition							2	2		
3.3 Vehicle Relexicalization	break up lets it through	pump		stops						
4. Vehicle Contextualization										
5. Topic Development			2		1				1	1
6. Metaphor Construction		1	1		2					
7. Metaphor Reference										
Problems in interpretation	*						*			

Five of the metaphors receive some explicit comment on lexical choice in the protocols, providing evidence that they were 'noticed': *transport system, centre, walls, squeeze, man-made pumps*. For example, about *squeeze* Louise commented:

> squeeze blood out (.) I thought it would be more like (.) pump blood out

In the case of *squeeze*, there is no further evidence of metaphorical processing, so that it may be that the reader is processing the word without any mapping of a Vehicle and Topic domain. The other four metaphors also received Vehicle development, and so can be said to be process metaphors as well as linguistic metaphors.

An effect of linguistic form on metaphor processing is illustrated by the comparison between protocols for *No man-made pump* and those of the other metaphors related to *pump*: nominal form *pumping* in Table 9.2, and verb forms *pumps, pump, pumps* in Table 9.3. Whereas *no man-made pump* generated discussion around Vehicle domain examples of types of man-made pumps, the expression *this pumping* was not explicated or developed. Verb forms like *pump* were not only not noticed in any explicit way, but were also used as an alternative to metaphorically used items (as in Louise's comment above) suggesting that they were processed non-metaphorically.

The finding that verb metaphors are processed differently from nominal metaphors adds to the earlier finding of differences in frequency of use. If, as suggested in Chapter 6, verbs in use easily extend their meaning to accommodate colligating noun phrases, this could explain both differences in frequency and differences in processing.

The results of repeated slight extensions over time may, seen synchronically, look like metaphorical extension. This effect combines with 'real' metaphorical extension of verbs to produce the many instances of verb metaphor. We should note that in English the combining of verbs and prepositions vastly increases the numbers of permutations available and the shades of meaning that can be expressed. The language 'evolves' through use, and the possibility of extending verb and preposition combinations seems a rich 'affordance' of English that has been made use of.

From a processing point of view, the strategies of users of English are likely to be co-adapted to the regular extension of verb meaning that occurs in discourse, so that processing may be more automatic.

Sources of problems in metaphor interpretation

From the last rows of Tables 9.2 and 9.3, we can see that several of the metaphors presented problems in interpretation. The readers experienced more difficulty with the Heart text than with the Ozone Layer text, even though the text and sentence structure was more straightforward. As we will see in this section, the prime source of problems lay in lack of specific Topic domain knowledge.

Anaphoric reference across sentences caused a minor difficulty, which was resolved through researcher intervention (Extract 9.2).

As with the Ozone Layer text, unknown lexical items caused problems, and again these were all Topic domain words: *chambers, walls, contract, hormones*. We can note that these are all technical terms in the Topic domain, and the first three are also identified as linguistic metaphors.

However, the GITA interpretation of this text had problems not just with the surface of the discourse, but at a deeper level of the theory-constitutive metaphors that constitute Topic domain knowledge. While surface level Topic knowledge was needed to interpret specific linguistic metaphors, inaccuracies in the underlying meta-

The Heart

Extract 9.2 A problem with anaphoric reference

1	L:	(*reads*) it has four chambers with muscular walls (1.0) muscular walls
	E:	(*whispers*) ?????
	R:	what's what?
	E:	what has four chambers?
5	L:	it's not telling you what has four chambers and
	R:	well read the sentence before again and see if that helps
	E:	at the centre of this system is your heart (.) it has four chambers (.) oh th (.) does that mean the heart has four

phorical conceptualizations in the Topic domain affected interpretation of the whole text.

The abstract and general nature of the Vehicle terms in the first metaphor compounded the problems from the start. Conceptual alterity then affected interpretations all the way through the text. Towards the end of the text reading, a further conceptual alterity became apparent. Not only did the students not know the word *hormones*, they also did not have a conceptual understanding of how hormones work in the body.

The two deeper problems with underlying metaphorical conceptualizations will be examined in some detail after the processing of technical lexis is discussed in the next section.

Processing technical language

Metaphorical processing of technical language: walls

The expression *muscular walls* was included as a linguistic metaphor after 71 per cent of respondents in the cross-checking exercise identified it as one. Like *chambers*, *walls* is a technical term, extended from everyday language to the domain of human anatomy. The extension of the use of the term *walls* to refer to the heart can be seen as metaphorical since the walls are no longer typically rigid, or in the exterior world.

In Extract 9.3, we see Louise and Ellen struggling to make sense of the sentence: *It* [the heart] *has four chambers with muscular walls*. They have sorted out the anaphoric reference as in Extract 9.2, and now have to cope with an unknown word, *chambers,* and a Topic domain, *the heart*, that they are not very familiar with. The strategy they adopt is to process *walls* as an active metaphor, attempting Vehicle Explication and Metaphor Construction:

The metaphorical interpretation of *walls* begins in lines 2–7. In line 2, Ellen explicates the term with the idea of *protect it*. Louise then explicitly evaluates the choice of lexis, *a strange word to use for your*

Extract 9.3 *Four chambers with muscular walls*

```
1   L:   muscular walls
    E:   oh the heart has four chambers with muscular walls ( . ) to protect it probably
    L:   muscular walls ( . ) walls is ( . ) quite a strange word to use for your body ( . )
    E:   could be your ribs (laugh)
5   R:   mmm
    L:   cos your ribs ( . ) protect your
    E:                   [ your ribs aren't like a wall though
    L:   yea
    R:   what's a chamber?
10  L:   it's like ( . ) it sounds like a dungeon
    E:   I always think of a
    L:   things are stored
    E:   I always think of like a big ( . ) sort of ( . ) chamber y ( . ) ri ( . ) like Louise ca
    R:   like what?
15  E:   like Louise um thinks of it
    R:   like a dungeon?
    E:   yea ( . ) sort of sounds ( . ) like it
    R:   so what's muscular mean? (2.0)
    L:   sounds as though it's like all your ( . ) muscles and
20  E:        [ strong
    L:   things put together ( . ) it's a very strong wall
```

body. This is evidence that she has not met this anatomical use of *walls* before, and that it sounds incongruous to her. Ellen (line 4) suggests *ribs* as a referent for *walls*, in what looks like a metaphorical mapping from a Vehicle domain to the Topic domain. Louise develops the metaphorical mapping by stating the idea of *protect* again as a relational link. We can note that *ribs* also share with *walls* the feature of rigidity. The temporarily constructed metaphor is dismissed by Ellen in line 7 on the basis of differences between *ribs* and *walls*, possibly that *ribs* are not continuous and solid but more like a fence.

When asked later in the protocol (line 18) about *muscular*, the girls opt for a non-literal interpretation of the Topic domain adjective, producing *strong* and *a very strong wall*. Making sense of *wall* as a process metaphor has a knock-on effect to its pre-modifier *muscular*, which is assumed by the girls to be also metaphorical. The intended interpretation of the phrase *muscular walls* is as a conventionalized metaphorical extension of the noun to the technical domain, with a literal pre-modifier. The students' strategy to compensate for lack of Topic knowledge has led to *muscular walls* being interpreted as a noun phrase metaphor Vehicle, that actively maps from a Vehicle domain of strong solid walls on to the Topic domain of the heart.

The middle section of Extract 9.3 (lines 9–17) shows a similar process happening with *chambers*. Again, this is a conventionalized technical metaphor in the Topic domain that is not familiar to the students. They interpret it as a deliberate metaphor, *like a dungeon*, (lines 10, 15–17), with features, *things are stored* (12) and *big* (13).

The sense they make of *muscular walls* as *a very strong wall* is consistent with the idea of a *dungeon*. In many ways this interpretation is inaccurate: blood is not stored in the chambers of the heart, but moves through them; the walls are not particularly thick or solid, although they are strong. In both instances, an unfamiliar technical metaphor is interpreted as a deliberate metaphor, using what is known about Topic and Vehicle domains to construct a coherent but inaccurate understanding.

Abandoning interpretation of technical language: contract

The next sentence of the text develops the concept of *walls/chambers* and includes a technical word unknown to the students, *contract*. The sentence also includes the linguistic metaphors *squeeze* and *tubes*:

> About once a second, the walls contract and squeeze blood out of
> the chambers into strong tubes, called arteries.

Contract differs from *walls* and *chambers* in that its extension into the technical domain is hardly, if at all, metaphorical. What caused it to be included as linguistic metaphor is its use to animate, or to make the *walls* the agent of the action (Chapter 5). *Squeeze* is also an animating metaphor, but is not a technical term.

Extract 9.4 shows the protocol for this sentence. It is immediately apparent that the students do not know the word *contract* (lines 4, 6), although Louise attempts an interpretation in line 5, *break up,* that is consistent with their earlier interpretation of *walls* as solid or rigid. The word *squeeze* conflicts with this sense of *walls*, and Louise is perhaps referring to this conflict in lines 9 and 11.

When the researcher intervenes at line 13 to encourage them to work out the meaning of *contract*, Louise calls on the meaning constructed earlier, *blood is stored in the chambers* (line 14). When she re-states her current understanding of the text in lines 28 and 29, the conflict between the rigidity of *chambers* and the plasticity necessary to *squeeze* seems to have been buried or left on hold, and the unknown word *contract* is not mentioned.

The sense-making attempts in this extract demonstrate how a problem with one metaphor (*walls*) can have knock-on effects across the sentence and into the rest of the text. The student readers are aware of conflicts in their constructed textbase, but in this instance are unable to resolve them. The strategy of abandoning attempts to make

Extract 9.4 *The walls contract*

```
1   L:   (reads sentence in a whisper)
         it doesn't tell you what um the wa ( . ) it sort of just ( . )
         about once a second the walls contract (2.0) the walls contract
    E:   what does that mean?
5   L:   do they break up or something?
         don't know what contract means
    R:   you don't know what contract means?
    E:   no (laugh) and squeeze blood out of the chambers into strong tubes (1.0) called
         arteries
    L:   squeeze blood out ( . ) I thought it would be more like ( . ) pump blood out ( . )
10  R:                                            [ ahaa
    L:   rather than squeeze blood out
    E:   still don't know what the um (laugh)
    R:   can you guess what contract means?
    L:   out of the chambers ( . ) that means ( . ) that means the blood ( . ) is stored in the
         chambers
15  E:                              [ lets it through
    R:   mmhm ( . ) and it squeezes it out when
    L:              [ into strong into strong tubes ( . ) called arteries (4.0)
    R:   that make sense?
    E:   no (laugh)
20  L:   it's (1.0) it's a bit ( . ) it would make sense
    E:                  [ it's ok for someone that ( . ) understands it (laugh)
    L:   it's a bit hard to understand ( . ) but if you knew ( . ) what you were doing ( . )
         then it ( . ) would be ( . ) alright
    R:   ok ( . ) so what picture have you got so far the ( . ) of what's going on in the heart?
25  E:   well ( . ) I was alright on that first
    L:                      [ it's ( . ) it's
    E:   but ( . )
    L:   blood's all stored in er chambers that's being protected and then it's squeezing blood
         out into strong tubes ( . ) so it can go right round your body
30  R:   do you know what arteries are?
    E:   no (2.0)
    L:   is it the tubes (1.0) to let ( . ) is it like ( . ) lots of tubes to let the blood go through?
    R:   mm
```

sense of the new word works in this instance because an alternative, *squeeze*, is available.

TOPIC REFERENCE SHIFT IN INTERPRETATION

The phenomenon of Topic Reference Shift (TRS) observed in the Ozone Layer protocols is again apparent in these data. Four instances of TRS were found, and Extract 9.4 includes one of them around the verb *squeeze*. (The other instances of TRS will be noted in following sections.)

In the original text sentence, the Subject of the verb *squeeze* is *the walls*. This plural Subject becomes singular (*it*), with the researcher responsible for the first shift in line 16, *it squeezes it out*. This formulation is repeated by Louise in her re-capitulation in line 28: *it's squeezing blood out*. No explicit referent noun is stated for the pronoun, although *the heart* would be an obvious candidate.

The TRS is metonymic, from the more specific part (*walls*) to the more general whole (*the heart*). Together with the non-understanding of *contract*, the shift contributes to a loss of conceptual precision, namely that, because the walls of the heart are made of muscle, they can contract and relax, and the result of the contracting is squeezing out of the blood.

Interpreting metaphorical technical language: discussion

Extracts 9.3 and 9.4 illustrate two strategies for making sense of unknown conventionalized metaphors used as technical language. In the case of *muscular walls*, lack of knowledge of the Topic domain led the students to process the conventionalized technical metaphor as deliberate metaphor. Previous research into children's understanding of metaphor (summarized in Chapter 7) has shown that they have a problem recognizing the need for metaphorical interpretation. This exchange demonstrates the converse problem: children need to learn to recognize when a metaphorical interpretation is <u>not</u> appropriate. Learning the meaning and use of metaphorical extensions of everyday words into technical domains is an area of language development particularly relevant to children in the middle of formal education who are learning the formal language of various disciplines as part of conceptual development.

With the word *contract*, there was no cue in the text that opened up the possibility of successful interpretation (contrast this with the very obvious and successful cue given in the text to the meaning of *arteries* processed in line 32 of Extract 9.4). Although text processing could continue after abandoning attempts to make sense of *contract*, the resulting interpretation was likely to be impoverished and a chance to reduce conceptual alterity was missed.

The underlying metaphor of the pump

In this section, we trace the multiple misunderstandings that occurred in the protocols and these can be traced back to incomplete conceptualizations of the heart domain. In the pre-GITA discussion, it was revealed that Louise and Ellen did not know the part of the concept which concerns the role of the blood in transporting oxygen and nutrients around the body. Furthermore, in talking about the metaphor of the heart as a pump, the bicycle pump was the most familiar.

Processing the 'transport system' metaphor

Extract 9.5 shows the analysis of the protocol of the first sentence in the text, the metaphor *Blood is the body's transport system*. Although a cognitive function is often attributed to metaphor, explaining the unfamiliar in terms of the already known, we see here how interpretation of a metaphor can require a threshold of knowledge about the unfamiliar Topic domain, as well as about the Vehicle domain.

In this metaphor, the Topic is the blood in the body, and the Vehicle is *transport system*. The intended interpretation is that the blood transports things around the body in a systematic way. The student readers come to the text lacking knowledge about the transporting function of the blood. In spite of their best efforts at unpacking the metaphor, they cannot make sense of it in the way intended by the writer.

The metaphor has further potential meaning in the Vehicle term *system*, with the implications of feedback, control and regulation that could be linked to the hormones released by the brain, mentioned later in the text. This protocol and that of the succeeding sentence show no indication of this sense of *system* being activated. This could be due to lack of Vehicle knowledge – the complex concept of a *system* – or to lack of Topic knowledge – their conceptualization includes the heart as central but does not appear to connect the brain with the circulation of the blood. Most likely, the failure to activate useful content arises from the combination of gaps in both Topic and Vehicle knowledge.

In the protocol, the students articulate two interpretations of the metaphor; neither coincides with the intended interpretation. The first (lines 16, 17) fits with their existing conceptualizations; the second (lines 30, 31) clashes with their understanding and is only put forward with some reluctance to take account of the constraints of linguistic form.

The first interpretation is reached through development of the Vehicle *transport system*, explicated as *lorry taking a load of bulls* (lines 3, 4), and then relexicalized in line 11 as *traffic driving about in you*. The general term *transport* is reformulated as the more specific and more familiar *traffic* and *lorries*. The missing piece of Topic domain knowledge means that a mapping cannot be made from *a load*

Extract 9.5 Protocol of 'Blood is the body's transport system'

	Utterance	Metaphor process
1	L/E: (*in unison*) <u>transport system</u>	Vehicle Repetition
2	(*laugh*)	
3	L: it sounds like it something like there's a <u>lorry</u> or something riding	Vehicle Explication
4	E: lorry taking like <u>a load of bulls</u> or something	Vehicle Explication
5	L: yea	
6	R: is that is that a good idea that it's (.)	Evaluation prompt
7	E: can we look at page 16?	
8	L: it's it's	
9	R: no (.) I haven't got page 16 at the moment	
10	L: it's it's a good way of explaining it (.)	Metaphor Evaluation
11	but it sounds as though there's like (.) <u>traffic driving</u> about in you	Vehicle Relexicalization
12	(*laugh*)	
13	R: and don't you like it to sound like that?	Evaluation prompt
14	L: it's a good way to explain it but	Metaphor Evaluation
16	E: it's a good way because like <u>traffic drives things</u> around (.)	Vehicle Explication
17	and that sounds like it's taking <u>all the blood round your body</u> (.)	Metaphor Construction
18	so that's quite a good way of (.) explaining it	Metaphor Evaluation
19	R: well it (.) right (.) so so (.) but it says blood is <u>the transport</u>	Direct intervention
20	<u>system</u> (.) so the blood is the lorries	
21	L: yea (.) blood is the body's <u>transport system</u> (1.0)	Metaphor Restatement
22	E: to keep your body going	Vehicle Relexicalization
23	L: so that means that <u>lorries and that are dri</u> (.)	Vehicle Explication
24	it sounds as though <u>lorries and things are driving</u> your blood	Metaphor Construction
	around	
25	to take it to like your arms and fingers and things	Topic Development
26	E: yea but	
27	L: although it's not really	
28	E: it doesn't say	
29	L: it's running through your veins and that	Topic Development
30	E: it says the (.) blood is (.) blood is <u>taking</u> the body round though	Metaphor Construction
31	(.) sort of thing (.) cos it's	
32	L: blood is	
33	E: blood is the body's <u>transport system</u> (.) so	Metaphor Restatement
34	R: mm (.) so?	
35	E: you put it in a different way there (*laugh*)	
36	R: so (.) what does that mean to you?	Understanding check
37	E: um (1.0) the blood's making the body go round instead of (.)	Metaphor Construction
	the	
38	body um (.) instead of the (.) <u>trucks taking</u> the blood around (.)	
39	R: right OK I see what you mean	

of bulls to oxygen and nutrients, and the students are forced to the metaphor construction that occurs in line 17: *it's taking all the blood round your body*. Aligning the metaphor, rewritten as a clause, and its interpretation shows the gap in the Object position:

blood	transports	?	round the body
traffic	*takes*	*blood*	*round the body*

At this stage the researcher intervened to point out that the first interpretation does not fit the form of the text sentence (lines 19, 20). Louise restates the first interpretation again (lines 24, 25) before regretfully putting it aside as not fitting the form. A second interpretation is then constructed, mostly by Ellen in lines 30–31 and 37–38: *blood's taking the body round*. This requires a different interpretation of the possessive form, *the body's transport system*, from a system inside the body to a system to transport the body. It now fits the form of the sentence but neither student is very convinced as to its appropriacy: Louise is uncharacteristically silent and Ellen hesitates more than usual in producing the metaphor constructions.

This protocol shows the loose connection between form and meaning that readers are happy to work with. In their first metaphor construction, the linguistic form seemed to act as little more than a guide to meaning. As expert users of language, the readers start with a rough but plausible match between their understanding and the sentence, using syntactic information at the level of clausal elements and using the nouns as lexical links to meaning. While the linguistic form encodes quite precisely the relations between items, the processing seems to work at a more approximate level. It is not until forced by a breakdown in processing that phrasal elements receive attention.

Without the researcher's intervention, the students would probably have remained with their first interpretation of the metaphor, which fitted their current understanding but not the form of the text. The readers failed to make sense of the metaphor as intended because of their missing Topic knowledge. The metaphor failed to develop their understanding by taking for granted what they, in fact, did not know about the Topic domain. In addition, the chosen Vehicle *transport system* seems to have little impact. The general term *transport* is reformulated in more specific terms; *system* remains undeveloped in this protocol. In the talk about the next text sentence, *At the centre of this system is your heart*, one property is activated, that of *controlling* (Extract 9.6).

However, this is again an incomplete understanding, since the brain in fact controls the heart and thus blood circulation.

Extract 9.6

```
1   L:   it's telling you that erm the heart is the centre ( . ) of ( . ) the system
    E:   which is making
    L:   which is your body
    E:   which is controlling ( . ) all the ( . ) blood going ( . ) round your body (2.0)
5   R:   mhmm
```

Pumps, air and the blood system

In this section, we move on through the processing of the text and see how the students' misunderstandings were further compounded by their confusion over the role of air in pumping. I hypothesize that the bicycle pump was serving as a prototypical example of *pump* for the students, underpinning their conceptual metaphor of THE HEART AS A PUMP in a systematic way, and helping them to retain inadequate concepts in the face of conflicting textual information. I suggest that the students used a conceptual metaphor – THE HEART IS A BICYCLE PUMP – whose main feature was a conflation of the respiratory and circulation systems. This hypothesis is supported and developed by evidence from across the protocols which is now discussed.

In the pre-GITA discussion, the bicycle pump was directly placed in analogy with the heart sending blood around the body. The analogy looked like this:

Vehicle		Topic
BICYCLE PUMP	⟺	HEART
pumps air in	⟺	pumps blood
to keep up a tyre	⟺	keeps up the body
(a flat tyre)	⟹	floppy when dead

It is easy to infer that the missing Vehicle aspect in the last line could be a flat tyre, although there is no explicit evidence of this in the discussion.

In the analogy between the bicycle pump and the heart, the substances pumped are domain specific, i.e. *air* belongs in the Vehicle domain of the *bicycle pump*, and *blood* in the Topic domain of the *heart*. In the protocol for sentence 5, we have the first intimation that Louise and Ellen may be connecting the bicycle pump and heart too closely, by using *air* as a bridging concept that is taken as salient in both Topic and Vehicle domains.

Extract 9.7 shows the first mention of *air* in the GITA protocols, in response to being asked what moves the blood around (line 3). Louise's initial reply in line 5 is that *air* or *oxygen* pushes the blood around. Ellen constructs what seems to be an alternative explanation (lines 7, 8 and 10) – that the pumping of the heart makes the blood move around. However, in the last line she brings the two possibilities together as: *it's giving it all <u>the air</u> to move around*.

Extract 9.7 *The blood is pushed around your body*

```
1   L/E: (read) the blood is pushed around your body
    E: we realized that (laugh)
    R: what's pushing it?
    (3.0)
5   L: is it air? oxygen
    R: mhmm
    E: it's the pumping
    L: yea the heart ( . ) sort of ( . ) um
    E: it's giving it all
10  L:            [action of your heart
    E: it's giving it all ( . ) s giving it all the air to move around
```

The explanation jointly constructed in this protocol seems to be that the pumping of the heart gives air that pushes the blood around. The substance *air* is apparently active in the domain of the blood circulation system.

When asked a similar question about how the heart pumps in the talk around sentence 7, the role of the air in pumping is made more explicit (Extract 9.8).

Extract 9.8 *Pushing and breathing*

```
E:   your heart pumping
L:   yea
R:   and what's ( . ) how's it doing it? (4.0)
     how's it pushing this blood around? (3.0)
L:   it ( . ) cos you breathe in air ( . ) and then breathe it out again
```

The linking of breathing in and out with blood being pumped may be made <u>contingently</u> rather than being a pre-established conceptual link that was merely voiced at this point. It is not possible to tell from the data. Whichever is the case, the linking is clear: Louise makes a connection between the movement of blood and breathing. The connection continues in the protocol of sentence 9 to account for an increase in heart beat when running. The students recall an incident when a visiting teacher had had the students compare their pulse rate when resting and after running. Louise explains the increase after running in Extract 9.9.

Extract 9.9 *Running and breathing*

R:	why was that? (2.0) why did you get an increase?
L:	because when you're running you're getting <u>more air</u> in you (.) which is making your pulse go faster and your blood run more

Text sentence 11 contained the negative metaphor *No man-made pump is as reliable as your heart.* As can be seen in Extract 9.10, this prompted two examples of man-made pumps to compare with the heart, both of which have air as a major component.

Extract 9.10 *Man-made pumps*

1	L:	no man made pump is as reliable (.) as (.) your heart (1.0)
		it's like (.) heh (.) um big <u>air pumps</u> (.)
	E:	[<u>bike</u>
	L:	that's not as (.) reliable
5	E:	[your bike (.) <u>your bike pump</u> might last longer than your heart but (.) it's
	L:	um (1.0) same <u>those bags of air type things</u> they put on you when you're in hospital (.)
		if you're having breathing difficulties (.)
		it's still not as (.) working as good as your heart (1.0)
		all that that it's (.)
10	E:	[it's just helping your heart
	L:	still <u>giving you air</u> but (.)
	E:	it's just helping your heart
	L:	[it's not giving you as much

Immediately after reading aloud the text sentence (line 2) Louise refers to *big air pumps*. Ellen then brings *bikes* back into the talk in line 3 and again in line 5. Louise's example is of pumps that help hospital patients to breathe. In line 8, she makes a direct comparison with the heart, as does Ellen in line 12, when she comments that the air bags are *helping your heart*.

In this extract, as in others, we see the students bringing their previous knowledge and experience to their reading and metaphor interpretation. The example comes as a concept with an explanatory theory or coherent system of relations. Where the underlying conceptualization of a domain is metaphorical, limited knowledge and experience may restrict the Vehicle knowledge that can be mapped. If, as here, Topic knowledge is also limited, the result may be an underlying conceptual metaphor that is systematically inaccurate.

The underlying metaphor of the pump: discussion

Extract 9.1 showed that the students did not readily talk-and-think about the blood as carrying oxygen and nutrients around the body. My hypothesis was that they did not know this. A weaker conclusion would be that they did know it, but it was not salient in interpreting the *transport system* metaphor. The accumulated instances of links made in the protocols between air going in and out and blood pumping round suggests a further strong hypothesis, that the students conceptualize a direct link between respiration and circulation. This would fit with the *bicycle pump,* where pumping harder automatically means going in and out more quickly. The strong hypothesis about the students' concepts would extend the earlier analogy to an underlying metaphor that looks something like this:

Vehicle		Topic
BICYCLE PUMP	⟺	HEART
pumps air in	⟺	pumps blood around the body
to keep up a tyre	⟺	keeps up the body
flat tyre?	⟹	floppy when dead
		HEART + BREATHING
pump by pushing air in and out	⟺	pump blood by breathing in and out
pump harder	⟺	puffing and panting co-occurs with pumping faster

Both the scientific concept and the students' existing concepts are metaphorically structured, and the two conceptual metaphors both include the idea of THE HEART AS A PUMP. The scientific conceptual metaphor is actually less extensive than the students' metaphor, in fact, since the mapping between HEART and PUMP relates the movement of the liquid in both domains through compression. The students' THE HEART AS A BICYCLE PUMP experiential conceptual metaphor makes more and tighter links, not by just mapping the presence of air and the pumping of air from pump to heart domains, but by including it in both domains. Both conceptual metaphors have explanatory theories that relate entities and properties in a logical and coherent way.

To reduce the conceptual alterity between the full scientific concept of circulation and respiration, and the students' current state of understanding would require a restructuring of the Topic domain of the HEART to include the information that:

- blood is pumped by the squeezing of the muscles of the heart;
- the blood system is separate from the respiratory system;

- the two systems connect when blood is pumped through the lungs where it collects oxygen;
- oxygen gets into the lungs through breathing;
- blood carries oxygen and nutrients around the body.

Whereas the Topic domain needs additional information, the Vehicle domain would need restructuring to <u>reduce</u> the properties and relations mapped, so that

- the metaphor of the pump applies to the outcome of the process but not to the mechanics of the process of pumping.

Such a process, which involves revising existing theories, dividing up existing categories or introducing new ones, as well as adding information, has been labelled 'strong restructuring' (Carey 1985). It is likely that such major changes in conceptualization would be resisted until the counter-evidence was overwhelming. In the processing of the *transport system* metaphor, we saw that, not only was the existing understanding unchanged, but the syntax of the text sentence could be misinterpreted to construct an understanding that <u>fitted existing ideas</u>. In the processing of the rest of the text, the incorrect conceptualization could continue to be used in interpretation without needing to be restructured.

The attractor of the students' conceptual system proved to be very stable and resistant to perturbation. We can speculate that metaphorically structured conceptualizations might be particularly coherent, and thus stable and resistant to change.

The data did produce an example of a metaphor prompting conceptual restructuring. However, in this case, it was not just text processing that led to conceptual change but interaction with the researcher and the mediating use of further metaphors. We examine this discourse next.

Mediation of metaphor

After completing the GITA task, Ellen offered an account of her restructuring of one part of the concept domain of the heart (Extract 9.11).

Extract 9.11 *Ellen's restructured concept of the heart and the brain*

> I've realized that it needs your brain to connect with your heart. . .I just thought your heart was a separate thing from your brain. . .that you didn't need your brain to like make your blood go round. . .I just thought your brain moved your arms and hands and everything.. and your blood just went round you and did nothing

The prompt for restructuring was the interaction between Ellen and the researcher over the text sentence 15:

> The adjustments are <u>controlled</u> by nerves from your brain and by hormones.

The interaction between researcher and participants is analysed here in order to isolate features that lead to successful use of metaphorical language in restructuring of incomplete and inaccurate concepts, and to show how adult mediation can play a role in this process.

The relevant exchange began in the middle of the protocol for sentence 15, when the researcher asks the participants about the word and concept *hormones*:

> R: *do you know what hormones are?*
> E: *no*
> L: *are they cells in the brain or something?*

The gap in knowledge prompted the researcher to explain. Analysis of the spontaneous explanation after the event showed the use of mediational mechanisms similar to those observed in classroom explanations, but generally absent in the written texts. The mediation continued (Extract 9.12), with talk between the researcher and Ellen proceeding through a series of metaphors that acted as conceptual stepping stones across the alterity between the full scientific concept and the student's starting point.

The mediation of concepts continues through negotiation and convergence of metaphors (Roschelle 1992), with Vehicles that are first simplified (line 5) and then gradually become more complex as the interaction proceeds. If we pull out of Extract 9.1, the metaphors used, the steps to complexification can be seen more clearly:

> Text: adjustments (to the heart) are <u>controlled</u> by nerves from your brain and hormones
>
> 1 R: hormones are like <u>switches</u>; they <u>switch things on and off</u>
> 2 E: your brain <u>communicates to</u> those; it can <u>say</u> ..
> 3 E: cos your blood's all <u>controlling</u> your body
> 4 E: your brain <u>sends messages to</u> your blood
> 5 E: then the blood <u>controls</u> the body

The researcher's explanation of *hormones* as *like switches* simplifies the biochemical definition to a Vehicle understood by the student and that focuses on a single functional feature. The communication metaphors (2 and 4) are introduced by the student, and extend the Topic domain by explaining how this function is performed. Her

Extract 9.12 *Conceptual stepping stones to mediate alterity*

	Researcher	Ellen	Categorization of utterance
1	they're chemicals go round in your blood		Topic development (definition)
2		oh	
3	come from different parts of your body		Expansion of definition
4	and do different things		
5	they're kind of like <u>switches</u>		Use of metaphor to explain function (Vehicle = switches)
6	they <u>switch</u> things <u>on and off</u> in your body		Vehicle Repetition + Development and link to Topic domain
7		oh right so your	E. introduces related metaphors
8		brain <u>communicates</u>	with relexicalized Vehicle
9		to those and then it	(Topic = controls; Vehicle =
10		can <u>say</u> =	communicates/say)
11	yea..if it releases some of these chemicals		Topic development – to explain function
12		= move my legs	Vehicle Contextualization by E.
13		really fast	
14	yea . . . if something scary's happening		Attempt by R. at contextualization
15	you feel . . .inside you..you go like that		including: use of new Topic term;
16	that's a hormone coming out (.)		repetition and relexicalization
17	a chemical going out in your blood		
18	stream (.) gets you ready to run away		End of contextualization
19		like yesterday when	Reciprocated contextualization
20		we did sports	
21		practice . . .	
22	. . .what are these adjustments (.) that		Question to check understanding
23	are <u>controlled</u>?	the adjustments for	
24		speed and resting	
25		and moving . . .	
26	. . . is it the speed of your body or the		
27	speed of your blood?	the speed of both	
28		really . . .	
29		cos your blood's all	Metaphor construction
30		<u>controlling</u> your	
31		body	
32		so when your brain	E. uses own metaphor to construct interpretation of role of hormones
33		sends messages to	and text sentence. Vehicle
34		your blood then that	Relexicalization
35		<u>controls</u> your body	Metaphor Construction

choice of metaphor is appropriate for the concept; the Vehicle is extended later in the talk as *sends messages to* (line 31).

There seems to be a drive towards contextualization in this interaction, as there was in the use of deliberate metaphors in the classroom talk. Ellen begins the contextualizing after her metaphor (2) at line 12 when she suggests the hormones might make her legs move fast. The researcher seems to pick up this context in her example *if something scary's happening . . . gets you ready to run away.* But we discover in lines 19–21 that Ellen was referring to a specific event, *sports practice,* that had happened that day. For the student, a concrete example helps by applying the new idea to something already known and familiar, pegging the new information more firmly into the familiar before proceeding to further extend the new. It is also likely to help recall and memory. For the adult, contextualization helps monitor the accuracy of the student's new understanding.

From line 22 on, the researcher is guiding Ellen back to the text metaphor *controlling*. The exchange ends with Ellen appropriating the metaphor of the textbook writer in a process of Metaphor Construction. From line 29 on, she summarizes her new understanding as having inserted a further stage into her earlier idea that *your blood's all controlling your body*. She now understands that the blood does this controlling through the intervention of the brain, which *sends messages to your blood*.

In fact, the two statements in Ellen's last utterance in Extract 9.12 include Topic Reference Shifts, which can be seen more clearly when the propositional information of the text sentence (i) and the researcher's reformulation (ii) is set out as Subject + Verb + Object + Adverbial:

(i) Text: hormones and nerves from your brain   <u>control</u>   adjustments
     Ellen: *your blood*   *'s <u>controlling</u>*   *your body*

(ii) Researcher: brain   releases   hormones   into the blood (to go around the body)
     Ellen: *your brain* <u>sends</u>   *<u>messages</u>*   *to your blood*

In TRS (i) the shift is from the specific of the text to the more general level of Ellen's statement. In TRS (ii) the researcher intended to explain that hormones <u>take messages</u> to other parts of the body, rather than that they <u>are messages to the blood</u> as Ellen's utterance implies. Given the lack of knowledge about the transporting function of the blood, this is probably as close as Ellen can get. It is, however, a major step in restructuring the concept by introducing new categories and dividing up an old one.

The mediating exchange about hormones includes many of the features of talk around metaphor found in the classroom discourse:

- repetition of Vehicle and metaphor (*switches*, lines 5, 6; *controls*, lines 23, 30, 35);
- use of a cluster of metaphors (*switch on and off – communicate – say – send messages*);
- tuning of Vehicle (*kind of like*, line 5);
- contextualization of the Vehicle (*something scary's happening*; *sports practice*);
- development of the Vehicle (lines 6, 9, 10, 33–35);

- relinking of developed Topic and Vehicle (lines 6, 29–31, 34–35).

Unlike the teacher-led classroom talk, both student and adult in this exchange offer and negotiate information through these mechanisms. The stepping-stone metaphors are negotiated between adult and student, and at each step the metaphors use familiar Vehicle terms to make sense of increasingly complex Topic domain content. The initial metaphor in the text could not reduce conceptual alterity and thus promote learning, because existing Topic knowledge did not allow it to be made sense of. The mediation of the metaphor, through a series of interim metaphors, provided both Vehicle and Topic domain information at an accessible level. Comparison of the fine-tuning of this interaction to the student's current conceptual resources with the (unmediated) struggle to make sense of the text metaphor of the *transport system* has implications for textbook writers and for spoken mediation of metaphor. These are set out in Table 9.4.

Interpreting metaphors in texts: summary discussion

The goal-directed interactive Think-Aloud tasks were designed to investigate the impact of metaphors in texts on the understanding of the student readers. The two studies have shown the potential of GITA for investigating the on-line processes of talking-and-thinking with children of 9 and 10. The data obtained were very rich, and revealed the participants making sense of text sentences and linguistic metaphors. The protocols could be analysed using metaphor processing categories (Table 7.2), very similar to those used by adults in previous metaphor Think-Aloud studies (Steen 1992), a result which supports claims for validity. It seems likely that the same method, with appropriate goals, could be used with even younger children.

In this section, I bring together the outcomes of the two readings to discuss what they tell us about the processing of metaphors. In the complex systems perspective, the talking-and-thinking of the two students is seen as a complex system that is continuously adapting to the input of each new text sentence, some of which contains linguistic metaphor. If a text sentence creates alterity with the students' current understanding, the protocol should show how the students attempt to resolve or reduce it. The research questions asked how linguistic metaphors were made sense of and how they impacted on understanding.

2-1 How do the students make sense of the linguistic metaphors in the text?

The impact of metaphor on discourse

In Chapter 8, the use of linguistic metaphor was described as the introduction of a centrifugal force into the dynamics of the discourse. This tries to capture the idea that the use of a Vehicle term from an incongruous domain may increase the risk of misunderstanding by diverting attention away from the ongoing text and Topic domain in some way.

When the students talked about the nominal metaphors, they unpacked and explained them. In restating the metaphors later in the discourse, they sometimes made errors, such as linking the Vehicle *blanket* to the wrong Topic. There was evidence of small slips of reference in talk around verb metaphors in the phenomenon called Topic Reference Shift.

A further type of loosening of the connections between talk and meaning occurred in the discourse around the problematic *transport system* metaphor, when the students were happy to work with an interpretation that did not fit the logic of the syntax.

There is then evidence in discourse around metaphor of the students making approximate connections between the intended meanings in the text and the interpretations in their talking-and-thinking. How far this is a phenomenon of on-line discourse and how far it affects deeper sense-making processes needs further investigation. Certainly, in the Ozone Layer text, the inaccurate interpretations voiced in the GITA were restated a week later in the recall.

The effect of linguistic form on processing

One theme of this book is the need to pay attention to the language of metaphors, as well as to their conceptual underpinning, as has been emphasized in the cognitive paradigm of metaphor studies.

The protocols showed that nominal and verb metaphors were processed differently. As in spoken discourse, nominal metaphors were more likely to be deliberate metaphors; in reading the texts, they were also more likely to be noticed by the students and to generate more processes than the verb metaphors. The verb metaphors were more likely to be conventionalized in the language and to be used without any observable evidence that they were noticed. As discussed on p. 196, the source of these differences is likely to lie in the different potential for use attached to nouns and verbs in English.

While differences were clear at word class level, there were also differences between different forms of nominal metaphors. Nominal group metaphors (NP *of* NP) were always noticed, perhaps because this form offers an important way of combining Topic and Vehicle in deliberate metaphors. The negative metaphor *no man-made pump* produced far more processing and talk than another noun phrase metaphor *this pumping*.

The processing effect of form was compounded by the cognitive demand of lexical content. When the combination of form and content presented too high a demand, form seemed to take second place to content, and acted only as a weak guide to finding a meaning for a metaphor.

Metaphor and simile

In the protocols of all three nominal group metaphors, the process of Metaphor Restatement moved between including and omitting the word *like*; for example, *the atmosphere is the blanket of gases* was restated as *it's like a blanket*. The *shield* metaphor which included *like* was processed in the same way as the *blanket* metaphor which did not. We can conclude that the two forms, in this discourse context, are equivalent for the readers. This supports the argument, made in Chapter 1, that a distinction between metaphors and similes made at the level of surface linguistic form ignores or cuts across a more fundamental distinction between metaphor and non-metaphorical comparison. The word *like* is better seen as one of a number of possible tuning devices that can be used with metaphor (Deignan and Cameron submitted).

The interpretation of deliberate metaphors

The scheme categorizing utterances in terms of aspects of metaphor processing (Table 7.2, p. 165) was applied to the sentence protocols. Three processes co-occurred with active metaphor processing, and so may be taken as necessary for a linguistic metaphor to be counted as a process metaphor: Vehicle Development, Topic Development and Metaphor Construction. Vehicle Contextualization also seemed to be important in active processing, but how far this is age-related remains to be investigated.

The process of successfully making sense of deliberate nominal metaphors followed much the same course in all instances, with the middle stages (2, 3 and 4) being revisited, sometimes several times, and in different orders, as needed:

1. Explicitly notice the metaphor through the contrast between Vehicle and Topic.
2. Develop the Vehicle term: use connotations, semantic features and synonyms to find a way in which to link Topic and Vehicle terms.
3. Develop the Topic term, drawing on existing knowledge and information from elsewhere in the text.
4. Draw on personal experience or knowledge to contextualize the Vehicle and highlight certain features of it.
5. Put the Topic and Vehicle terms back together after development to make sense of them in combination as a metaphor.

(The processing stages do not represent a claim about metaphor processing in general, only about how metaphors were processed in the GITA tasks.)

Two further principles seemed to operate for the readers:

- Stay with existing conceptualizations of the Topic domain, using them to make sense of metaphors wherever possible, and ignoring some degree of misfit.
- Use linguistic form as a guide to word-meaning links; work at this approximate level unless forced to close scrutiny of form by failure to reach an understanding.

The interaction of Topic and Vehicle domains in processing metaphors

We now look more closely into processing stages 2, 3 and 4, to summarize the many ways in which Topic and Vehicle information were brought together in the search for meaning.

In metaphor theory (Chapter 1), Topic and Vehicle domains are considered as separate, but brought together in a metaphor that somehow maps between the two domains. Metaphor processing is seen as moving between the two domains, as in Black's Interaction Theory, or using domain knowledge to construct and blend 'mental spaces', as in Blending Theory. The protocol analysis shows that it is difficult to separate the effect of Topic and Vehicle knowledge in the thinking of participants as they process metaphor under GITA conditions. In processing, previous knowledge is not a static set of information, activated on demand, but is, as Rose (1993) reminds us, reconstructed or 're-membered' each time it is used. It is thus dynamic, sensitive to discourse context and has some flexibility. It can be made to accommodate new information found in a text to avoid strong restructuring. For example, when the Heart text presented information in conflict with existing Topic knowledge, both the constructed meaning of the Vehicle in the text and existing knowledge were adjusted slightly, so that sense could be made without the need for radical conceptual change.

In the talking-and-thinking around metaphors, Topic and Vehicle domains were interrelated in the following ways:

VEHICLE AND TOPIC CONTRAST TO SIGNAL METAPHOR

Highly incongruous Vehicles that contrast strongly with the co-textual Topic domain lexis can signal metaphorical use of language and prompt metaphorical processing.

VEHICLE KNOWLEDGE FOCUSES TOPIC INTERPRETATION

A writer's choice of Vehicle is extremely important when metaphor is used ideationally. It should activate and focus attention on relevant aspects of the Topic, while at the same time avoiding the activation of inappropriate aspects.

In the classroom discourse, Vehicle contextualizing and development was directed towards Topic domain understanding: the teacher chose to talk about specific Vehicle aspects in order to map these on to the Topic domain and increase understanding of that domain. In the Ozone Layer text reading, neither *blanket* nor *shield* was effective at taking the students beyond the very general protective function of the Topic, *the atmosphere*. The nature of the Vehicle could not help but complexify the students' understanding of how the atmosphere protects the earth. Alternative metaphors such as *the ozone layer works like a sieve* might have been more helpful in focusing Topic interpretation.

TOPIC KNOWLEDGE FOCUSES VEHICLE INTERPRETATION

When the Vehicle term *transport system* proved too difficult to use in interpretation, it was reformulated as *traffic/lorries*. The simpler form was not chosen independently of the Topic, but because it made sense of existing Topic knowledge. Even if a Vehicle domain is familiar and well developed, metaphors may still present problems of interpretation, and Topic knowledge will be required to isolate appropriate aspects of Vehicle knowledge to map to the Topic domain.

Topic knowledge also acts as a safeguard against inappropriate interpretations of a Vehicle, as when Topic knowledge – *your ribs are not a wall* – led to the rejection of a mistaken interpretation of *walls*. A further role of Topic knowledge was to disambiguate reference around conventionalized verb metaphor Vehicles and prevent TRS.

Thus, while the literature on children's understanding of metaphor (pp. 148–50) suggests that gaps in Vehicle knowledge affect understanding of metaphor, we see that gaps in Topic knowledge also impact on interpretation.

TERMS BRIDGING TOPIC AND VEHICLE DOMAINS CAN HELP OR HINDER INTERPRETATION

Bridging terms (Kittay 1987: 166) are lexical items that are used in both Topic and Vehicle domains. They can be keys to an understanding of a metaphor because they can be understood in relation to both domains. An example is *protect*, used in relation to the ozone layer in the pre-GITA discussion and in relation to a *blanket* and *shield* in the protocols.

Words may be wrongly assumed to be bridging terms and result in inaccurate interpretations, as happened in the same text with the word *layers*. The students made a link between *layers* of blankets on a bed and *layers* of gases in the atmosphere; this may have contributed to their inaccurate processing of the Topic of *blanket* as *the atmosphere*.

These various types of language and conceptual interplay between Topic and Vehicle in producing and interpreting discourse highlight the simplification involved in constructing theoretical views of metaphor processing. Positing bounded conceptual spaces idealizes away much of the messiness and approximation of real, on-line processing. Instead of a tidy theoretical account with predictable outcomes, in real talking-and-thinking we have something that resembles a complex dynamic system, one that evolves and adapts as multiple variables interact in the specific environment of participants and the linguistic and cognitive resources that they bring to the task of making sense of metaphor.

Processing technical words metaphorically

Technical Topic domain vocabulary and concepts caused problems in both texts. Some words, like *energy*, were used with technical meanings but interpreted through their everyday meaning. Some technical words like *radiation* and *contract* could not be interpreted, while attempts were made to deal with *ultraviolet* by breaking it into morphemes.

It was found that another strategy for dealing with unknown technical vocabulary was to attempt a metaphorical interpretation, as with *walls (of the heart)*.

Studies of children's processing of metaphors have found that they sometimes do not recognize that a metaphorical interpretation is required. The inappropriate use of metaphorical processing inverts that finding, and suggests that a broader problem for children, or other non-experts in a technical domain, is distinguishing between deliberate metaphors and technical terms that may be conventionalized metaphors.

There are implications here too for students of English as a second language who may need to master technical language. In understanding technical discourse, it will help to know which words are technical terms and which are deliberate metaphors. In learning the technical language of a domain, making explicit the metaphorical roots of terms may be helpful in linking and organizing lexis, which will in turn assist memory and recall.

HOW DO ENCOUNTERS WITH METAPHORS AFFECT CONCEPTUAL ALTERITY?

The GITA studies aimed to find out how metaphors might lead to changes in conceptual understanding, both on the micro-level timescale of the GITA discourse, and on a longer timescale. Across the data, there have been instances where metaphors

- cannot be made sense of;
- are made sense of, but no new understanding is generated;
- lead to new, but inaccurate or unstable, understanding;
- lead to new, accurate understanding;
- lead to new understandings with the support of mediation from an adult.

In complex systems terms, the first two outcomes maintain the trajectory of the talking-and-thinking system in its stable attractor, while the other three move the system into a new part of phase space where new attractors represent new levels of conceptual understanding.

Previous conceptual knowledge proved resistant to change in the case of the *blood system*. The attractor was very stable, and the text and metaphors did not provide sufficiently strong perturbation to disturb the students' conceptualizations from the stable attractor. New information was made to fit existing theory rather than prompting theory change. This is probably a useful strategy for learners to adopt since it avoids too much variation or fluctuation in theories and concepts. When restructuring does occur, it will be significant, increasing the probability of conscious awareness (as in the case of *hormones*) and thus of the change being consolidated and effective.

The case of the *transport system* metaphor shows something like a shift into a chaotic attractor, when the students were pushed by the researcher to find an understanding that took account of the grammar of the sentence. This was very unstable and the students soon reverted to their original understanding by ignoring the alterity.

In both tasks, changes in understanding were mostly limited to weak restructuring, in which metaphors emphasized certain aspects of existing knowledge or added some details of information. The single instance of strong restructuring occurred when a metaphor in the text was further mediated by the researcher.

The metaphors of *blanket* and *shield*, although not very informative, were used in recall of the text content after a week, suggesting they did have some impact.

The last case, of *hormones* explained through mediating metaphors of *switches*, can be seen as shifting understanding to the 'edge of chaos' – in Vygotskyan terms, pulling the students into their zone of proximal development. On the edge of chaos, there was a sudden surge in metaphors produced and shared between researcher and students that led to a new and stable attractor of understanding.

WHAT IS THE ROLE OF MEDIATION BY TEXTS, PEERS OR ADULT IN REACHING SHARED UNDERSTANDING?

There are striking similarities in discourse around successful metaphor processing in GITA (stages 1–5, p. 232), in the mediation of the researcher in explicating *hormones*, and in teacher talk in the classroom discourse around deliberate metaphors (Chapter 5). The similarities in how metaphor is broken down, unpacked, expanded and then reassembled offer clues to effective mediation of metaphor.

Mediation is needed when the bridge offered by metaphor from familiar Vehicle to unfamiliar Topic concepts cannot for some reason be constructed. The GITA studies showed that metaphor may fail in this cognitive role for a range of reasons, often found in combination:

- Topic knowledge needed for interpretation is not known.
- Vehicle knowledge needed for interpretation is not known.
- Links between Vehicle and Topic, assumed to be obvious, are not available or made.

Mediation can help resolve problems by building smaller interim stepping stones that eventually lead the student across the original gap. This is done by

- assessing alterity, or gaps in knowledge;
- filling gaps in knowledge, often through related metaphors;
- making links between Topic and Vehicle explicit.

In spoken interaction, mediation can further include:

- negotiating understanding of the knowledge and the links (checking, clarifying and summarizing), often through converging metaphors.

In the process of mediation, clusters of metaphors are likely to be used. The empirical data suggest that multiple metaphors can be helpful if different metaphors

- involve relexicalization of the Vehicle for the same Topic;
- highlight particular key aspects of the Topic;
- work at different levels of generality or abstraction.

Mediation of metaphors can also be effected non-verbally, e.g. through the use of graphics, models and practical demonstrations.

In spoken face-to-face discourse, skilful mediation of metaphor has been shown to include sensitive fine-tuning to students and breaking down the task of understanding into manageable sub-tasks. Writers of texts do not have the presence of readers to help in tuning what they 'say', but are forced to estimate what will be brought to the text and how the text will be understood. The set of checking questions in Table 9.4 (p. 238) is compiled from the analyses of classroom talk and GITA protocols to help users of metaphor in educational discourse think about how to maximize conceptual intersubjectivity.

Table 9.4 *Checking questions for the use of metaphor to convey ideas in spoken and written discourse*

> Have you explicitly decided, in the light of your listeners' or readers' probable understanding of the topic, which particular ideas and explanatory information you want to get across through the use of metaphor?
>
> Have you included talk, text or graphics to ensure that the previous Topic knowledge you are assuming is established, summarized and activated?
>
> Have you selected Vehicle terms that will enable listeners or readers to focus on the key aspects of the Topics?
>
> Have you selected Vehicles for these metaphors that will be familiar to your listeners or readers, and that are not too abstract, general or complex?
>
> Have you chosen Vehicles that your listeners or readers will be able to contextualize to aspects of their everyday lives or experience?
>
> Have you chosen Vehicles that your listeners or readers will be able to develop – to find ways of relexicalizing them, give examples of them, elaborate them?
>
> Have you developed the Vehicle terms in the talk or text? Are they pre- or post-modified by Vehicle-related terms? Do you give examples of the Vehicle? Do you use both metaphorical and non-metaphorical language?
>
> Do you use clusters of metaphors for important or complex ideas?
>
> Do the talk, text or graphics illustrate the Topic–Vehicle links clearly?
>
> Have you taken precautions against Topic Reference Shift in processing, e.g. through careful use of anaphor and, in particular, of pronominal reference?
>
> Have you chosen a linguistic form for your metaphors that maximizes the probability of successful processing by setting out the T–V relation as explicitly and simply as possible, e.g. {NP *is* NP *of* NP}?
>
> Have you glossed or illustrated words likely to be unknown, to avoid inappropriate metaphorical processing?

10 Systematicity, metaphor and metonymy

Having analysed metaphor in the talking-and-thinking of teachers and students, in classroom discourse and in reading texts, this chapter brings together evidence of systematicity in metaphor use. The evidence is used to argue that a sociohistorical view of the development of metaphor can complement the cognitive perspective, and can explain how metaphor emerges in the gradual disembedding of talk from situated action over the years of schooling. On the way from 'talk about action' to 'disembedded language use', metaphor often works as metonymy.

Metaphors and minds

The cognitive theory of metaphor uses sets of related linguistic metaphors to claim an underlying conceptual mapping across domains. A foundational example of this type of analysis was Reddy's work on the conduit metaphor of language. The analysis of 'the metalingual resources of English' identified a large number of linguistic metaphors, including the following (Reddy 1993: 189–94):

> It's very hard to get that idea across in a hostile atmosphere.
> You know very well that I gave you that idea.
> Your real feelings are finally getting through to me.
> Insert that thought somewhere else in the sentence.
> I can't seem to get these ideas into words.
> The passage conveys a feeling of excitement.
> Mary has good ideas, but they get lost in her run-on sentences.

By generalizing across linguistic metaphors, Reddy and others (Lakoff and Johnson 1980; Grady 1998) suggest that language is conceptualized as providing containers for thoughts and feelings that are then transferred from one person to another. The conceptual metaphor LANGUAGE IS A CONDUIT is held to be conventionalized across the speech community and, according to contemporary metaphor theory, the conceptual metaphor has primacy over the linguistic expressions of it, both for language users and for analysts (Lakoff 1993). (Note: the constructivist metaphor of language and thought adopted in this book is a variant of Reddy's alternative conceptual metaphor, THE TOOLMAKERS' PARADIGM (Reddy 1993).)

Conceptual metaphors are, in the cognitive theory, part of our mental resources and, as such, may influence how we think about the world. An under-discussed issue for cognitive metaphor theory is the extent to which every individual is assumed to 'have' conceptual metaphors in their minds, and how those metaphors come to be there. The use of the first person plural pronoun in the title of Lakoff and Johnson's book *Metaphors We Live By* is both ambiguous and hegemonic: ambiguous, because it may refer to every individual or to the collective cultural group (Gibbs 1999b); hegemonic, as more and more studies claim to find evidence about how we think on the basis of metaphors in our discourse. It is likely that not all members of a discourse community will have the same set of conceptual metaphors, elaborated to the same degree of detail (Steen and Gibbs 1999). Furthermore, in the ontogenetic development of individuals it would seem possible that, in some domains, linguistic metaphors may be used in advance of conceptual development, just as children use words without full comprehension of their conceptual content (Locke 1993). In other domains, concepts may be well established in advance of linguistic development.

Using metaphor as a research tool

It has become quite fashionable to use metaphor as a research tool, often by collecting linguistic metaphors from participants, sorting the metaphors into groups by lexical connections, and giving conceptual metaphor labels to the groups. These labels may be 'pre-existing', i.e. conceptual metaphors identified in previous research and matched to the discourse data. For example, it would be possible to take a set of theoretically determined conceptual metaphors for emotions, identified in a scholarly study (such as Kövesces 1998), as the basis against which metaphors used by clients in therapeutic discourse will be matched. Alternatively, the conceptual metaphor labels may be selected by the researcher to suit what is found in the data, as is done in the applied linguistic studies of Cortazzi and Jin (1999), Oxford (2001) and Ellis (2001).

In either case, there are serious issues of reliability in using linguistic data as a basis for reconstructing conceptual content and processes (Semino *et al.* in press), and validity in ascertaining an appropriate level of generality for the conceptual metaphor label. For example, Oxford (2001: 98) chooses very emotive conceptual labels such as TEACHER AS WITCH or TEACHER AS HANGING JUDGE to generalize from the linguistic data. The linguistic data though show somewhat tenuous links with the concept: e.g. for witch: *demon-lady, torture, a great beast* from one student, and, from another student: *her breath smelled awful. The room was haunted by this awful stench . . . this woman is still allowed to cast her horrid lesson plans upon unsuspecting children.*

If linguistic metaphors are the basic data for inferring conceptual metaphors, then these perhaps offer evidence for LANGUAGE LEARNING (rather than teaching) AS TORTURE in the first instance, or BAD BREATH AS GHOST, LESSON PLANS AS SPELLS (or FISHING NETS?) in the second. The point is that very strong inferencing is often required to move from linguistic to conceptual metaphor when using metaphor as a research tool and this must be done cautiously, particularly if claims about participants' thinking or suggestions for future action are to be made (Vervaeke and Kennedy 1996; Cameron and Low 1999).

With an appropriate degree of caution then, I will proceed to describe three types of conceptual systematicity that emerged as particularly prevalent in the educational discourse data. The three types are animating and personification metaphors, journey metaphors and metaphors about literacy processes. The next section describes at the most general level how metaphors of animation and personification were used to describe natural processes. We then see how the well-established conceptual metaphor of JOURNEY can be applied to systematic use to describe classroom procedures. The next section pulls together systematically used metaphors of speaking that describe aspects of literacy processes, and suggests a sociohistorical explanation for this phenomenon that avoids the need to posit a pre-existing conceptual metaphor in the minds of students. Also extracted from the classroom data are metaphors used for mental processes. In this case, the lack of systematicity appears somewhat significant, pedagogically and theoretically.

Animating and personification metaphors

Personification metaphors use Vehicle terms from the domain of people to refer to Topics that are not human. Personification is one type of the broader category of animation, in which Vehicle domains are animate but not necessarily human. Examples of personification and animation from the classroom discourse are:

> the set square *gives* you a right angle
> where's my rubber (= eraser) *gone*?
> (german measles) can *kill* the baby

Commentary on the widespread use of animating (or 'animizing', Goatly 1997: 51) metaphors dates back to Quintilian, a successor to

Aristotle (Brooke-Rose 1958). The more recent conceptual metaphor approach describes personification as

> ontological metaphor(s) ... where the physical object is further specified as being a person. This allows us to comprehend a wide variety of experiences ... in terms of human motivations, characteristics, and activities. (Lakoff and Johnson 1980: 33)

Lakoff and Johnson point out that personification is not a unified process but highlights particular aspects of people and attributes them to physical objects. In the above examples, *measles* is personified as something akin to a murderer, whereas the *set square* is more like a donor, and the *rubber* is an independent being that can leave the student's desk.

In later work on metaphor in poetry (Lakoff and Turner 1989), personifications of *death* (e.g. as a *reaper*) are described in terms of a generalized conceptual metaphor, EVENTS ARE ACTIONS, in which the action serves as an analogy to the event, with parallel causal structure, aspectual structure and entities (Lakoff 1993).

Goatly, who examines linguistic metaphors in the COBUILD corpus, describes animating and personifying metaphors as conceiving of abstract entities in terms of four categories: life, survival, relationships and control (Goatly 1997: 52).

Conceptual metaphor theory explains personification as a mechanism that 'allows us to make sense of phenomena in the world in human terms' (Lakoff and Johnson 1980: 34). Cooper (1986) develops an alternative explanation in terms of 'intimacy', or the shared knowledge and concerns that tie together members of a sociocultural group. He suggests that a motivation to develop social intimacy leads to the use and conventionalizing of metaphor, and cites Hegel's views on personification as answering 'a need of the heart' to make the world seem less alien. As supportive evidence for the claim that intimacy sustains metaphor, Cooper offers the personification of threatening processes, such as disease, war and economic disasters, which play a role in uniting groups and motivating them to action.

The affective social explanation of Cooper can complement the conceptual dimension that cognitive linguists draw on to explain animating and personifying metaphors.

The linguistic form of animation metaphors in the data

Just over 10 per cent of the linguistic metaphors in the classroom discourse could be said to involve animation. The Ozone Layer text contained 10 (from a total of 13) animating metaphors, while the more technical Heart text contained 6 (from a total of 23). The much higher proportion in the texts than in the spoken discourse was due to their scientific content. Student talk in the pre- and post-GITA discussions also shows frequent use of animating metaphors.

The Vehicle terms of animating metaphors in the dataset are overwhelmingly verbs which animate the Subject, by using lexis characteristic of human or animate action:

the music <u>helps</u>	(teacher; dance practice)
16 <u>into</u> 124 doesn't quite <u>go</u>	(teacher; maths lesson)
where does the time <u>go</u>?	(teacher; general classroom talk)
a light to <u>call</u> him	(TV programme on deafness)
gases can <u>escape</u>	(Ozone Layer text)
the walls . . . <u>squeeze</u> blood	(Heart text)
I thought your brain <u>moved</u> your arms	(Ellen; post-GITA discussion)

The only nominal personification metaphors were used in relation to the *crinoids*, which are animate, but which were personified by being attributed *feet* and *arms*, and intentional activity to *catch food*, and in relation to the *heart*, which can beat *without a rest*.

Brooke-Rose's (1958) thorough study of the linguistic form of metaphor in English poetry also found that the most common grammatical way to animate was through a verb applied to a Topic domain Subject. She found several other forms of animating metaphors, not present in the spoken classroom discourse:

Direct address	sweet sleep, <u>Angel</u> mild	(Blake)
Copular verb	Pleasure is oft <u>a visitant</u>	(Keats)
Nominal group	the <u>steps</u> of the Sun	(Blake)
Possessive	the wind's <u>home</u>	(Eliot)
Owning verbs	For mercy <u>has a human heart</u>	(Blake)
Adjectives	your <u>blind</u> hands	(Browning)

The linguistic evidence from the texts, classroom and GITA talk, and Brooke-Rose's poetry corpus clearly locates the process of personifying or animating principally in the verb. Through the metaphorical verb Vehicle, the sense of the collocating Topic noun phrase shifts to become more animate or human.

The lexical/conceptual content of animating metaphors

When we turn our attention to the Topics of animating metaphors, we find that, although some of them were, as the literature suggests, abstract ideas (Brooke-Rose 1958; Goatly 1997), most were in fact physical or concrete entities metaphorically endowed with intentional or physical action. The abstract ideas included a small set of references to *time* as *going*, and a single reference to the *imagination* as *working*. Within the range of Topic domains talked about as animate, three particular groups stand out: technical, sub-technical and emphatic.

TECHNICAL METAPHORS

Examination of animating metaphors in the texts and talk reveals degrees of formality in technical language. The Ozone Layer text used much more informal animating metaphors than the Heart text, in which formal technical terms of the subject area were introduced to readers. Compare for instance the two technical terms for the action of muscles, *contracts* and *relaxes*, and the less technical verb *escape* used about gases. While *escape* seems to offer animating content from a human domain (e.g. links to prisoners escaping), *contracts* seems to have little to offer. If, as happened in the GITA talk, the term is unknown, it is not easy to infer a meaning for *contracts*. The third term *relaxes* is somewhere between these, since it is in everyday use with a somewhat different sense but is also a formal technical term.

Processing evidence from the GITA protocols showed that there was little explicit noticing of informal animating technical metaphors, and that the students used these metaphors in discussing the texts, but the use of such metaphors in the texts had a tendency to produce inaccurate on-line interpretations through shifts in Topic reference.

SUB-TECHNICAL METAPHORS

Informal animating metaphors use more common, more concrete verbs, whereas formal animating metaphors in technical discourse may be more opaque. Much of the technical discourse in the geology lesson and around the Ozone Layer text used informal, sub-technical animating metaphors with more familiar lexis. Mathematical operations were often animated through verbs of movement, with numbers *going up/into*. Table 10.1 lists some of the Topics and Vehicles.

Conceptually, we notice that the use of metaphor terms reduces the specificity with which the processes are described, and that there are more specific (and more technical) lexical verbs that could be used – *erupt, be extracted from, originate*. The Vehicle terms are animating, but not particularly human.

The Vehicle lexis in sub-technical animating metaphor is much more human and becomes even more so in the last group of animating metaphors.

Table 10.1 Informal sub-technical animating metaphors

Topics	Animating Vehicles
Geology lesson	
river	<u>bringing down</u> mud
volcano	<u>working</u>
minerals	<u>come out of</u> rocks
rocks	<u>are laid down</u>
where marble	<u>comes from</u>
it (rock)	<u>starts off</u>
crinoids	<u>catch/bring in</u> food
Ozone Layer text	
atmosphere	<u>lets . . . through</u>
forms of radiation	<u>given out</u>
Maths talk	
16, 12 (numbers)	<u>go into</u>
number patterns	<u>go up in</u>
Apostrophes	
apostrophes	<u>shorten</u> words
The Heart text	
the blood	<u>feeds</u> the body
the heart	<u>moved</u> the hands

EMPHATIC ANIMATING METAPHORS

A story read aloud by one of the students included 'poetic' metaphor in which *trees* and *fire* were personified through verb Vehicles:

> the fire began to <u>die</u>
> trees <u>hide</u> the fire

Students' experience of poetic metaphors was through external sources – the texts that they read, radio and TV programmes, religious services led by the local vicar – rather than through the teacher-led discourse. The spoken discourse parallel to poetic metaphors were 'emphatic' personification metaphors that occurred mostly in off-topic comments. The Topics are collocated with verbs that belong to the domain of humans, but they are also strong or emphatic in some way, either hyperbolic or dramatic:

> measles <u>kill</u> the baby
> my brain won't <u>manage</u> that
> this tape is <u>telling me something</u>
> this rash is <u>driving me insane</u>

This type of animating metaphor seems to aim to create empathy between participants. It is as if the dramatic Vehicle lexis creates a greater centrifugal force that opens up a wider space for sharing feelings among discourse participants.

Animating metaphors: discussion

The educational discourse data of different types showed widespread use of verb animating metaphors applied to processes and relational correspondences in a concept domain. The most human, personifying metaphors were used when the alterity in the talking-and-thinking was more to do with intimacy than conceptual content, when participants wanted to comment on something important to them and to arouse empathy in their listeners. When alterity was primarily conceptual, animating metaphors seemed to substitute for more specific, more complex and more abstract concepts. Using the meta-metaphor of *the stepping stone* from Chapter 6, animating metaphors act as conceptual stepping stones, whereas personifying metaphors act as affective stepping stones, to greater intimacy or empathy.

Pedagogically, the different levels of formality found in animating metaphors suggest different implications for the development of scientific concepts through discourse. Animating metaphors seem to help make formalized abstract concepts and explanatory theories more accessible through the activation of actions and relations in more concrete and familiar Vehicle domains. Some of the informal animating metaphors are used in the formal technical discourse, whereas in other cases they act as a step to different formal technical language. In the case where experts in a domain use the same informal animating metaphors as novices, e.g. *minerals come out of rocks*, we should be aware that the ideas underlying the language may not be the same; experts use the words with more developed concepts attached. Experts may revert to more informal animating metaphors and schemata to think about processes, as in the well-known example of the dream of a snake that produced the double helix form of DNA for Crick and Watson. What experts can do, and novices need to learn to do, is move back and forth between the informal and the formal in thinking, in language use and in metaphor.

Journey metaphors

In this section, the method for examining systematicity is to take a well-known and much discussed conceptual metaphor and examine how the linguistic metaphors in the classroom discourse data can be fitted into it. About 14 per cent of the linguistic metaphor Vehicles in the classroom set of linguistic metaphors could be seen as relating to a system of journey metaphors:

> let's just **go into** that a little bit more
> plan it out as you **go**
> you might do it **the long way**
> you'll <u>see</u> how **close** you were to getting them right
> <u>take it</u> **step by step**

This lexis was not necessarily characteristic of the school discourse community; it was more globally systematic (Cameron 1999b) across the wider speech community. In this section, I report on the use of this system of metaphors and discuss its relation to the conceptual metaphor explanation.

Journey metaphors have featured strongly in the literature on conceptual metaphor. Lakoff (1993: 207) describes the conceptual metaphor LOVE IS A JOURNEY as

> a set of ontological correspondences that characterize epistemic correspondences by mapping knowledge about journeys onto knowledge about love. Such correspondences permit us to reason about love using the knowledge we use to reason about journeys.

The journey metaphor is seen as a particular case of a more general 'event structure' metaphor, in which aspects of events, such as 'states, changes, processes, actions, causes, purposes and means, are characterized cognitively via metaphor in terms of space, motion, and force' (Lakoff 1993: 220). He describes the general mapping, as found lexicalized in English, as follows:

> States are locations
> Changes are movements
> Causes are forces
> Actions are self-propelled movements
> Purposes are destinations
> Means are paths (to destinations)
> Difficulties are impediments to motion
> Expected progress is a travel schedule
> External events are large, moving objects
> Long term, purposeful activities are journeys.

We might expect that the particular context of the classroom might lead to a greater focus on certain aspects than on others, and invoke particular lexical content. The linguistic metaphors in the data that relate to this conceptual metaphor are analysed in terms of the aspects of events that were metaphorized.

Classroom journeys

The classroom discourse used journey metaphors not to talk about long activities, such as a relationship, but short classroom activities such as stages of a lesson, writing, mathematical calculations and reading a book. They were however purposeful, and sometimes difficult. Some activities were shared class tasks, such as completing a worksheet, while others were individual tasks, such as writing pages of a diary.

Journey metaphors often occurred in clusters in Agenda Management sequences. Extract 10.1 comes from the beginning of a class work session, where the teacher asks students what they have finished and checks that they know what they will do next. *Diary for day one* refers to a written account of the first day of the school trip, and so on. In the above terms, this extract is a jointly constructed 'travel schedule'.

Extract 10.1 *Journey metaphors in Agenda Management*

```
1   okay ( . ) well you can see where you've got to go from ( . ) here ( . ) on can't
    you?
    what I'm trying to do is to get ( . ) diary for day one and an illustration ( . )
    day two and an illustration ( . )
    so you've got some writing and a picture to go into your personal ( . ) record ( . ) of the
    week (1.0)
5   alright? (2.0)
    some of it ( . ) at some point all of you will have done some computer work (1.0)
    for your writing (1.0) but a lot of it's going to be done by hand ( . ) isn't it? ( . )
    can you see where you've got to go from here? ( . )
    um we'll let Ellen and ( . ) Heather carry on with their writing now ( . )
10  but we must correct your work you two (1.0)
    to get that printed out (2.0)
    right ( . ) Marie's table ( . ) Marie you were doing your own work and illustrations ( . )
    how far ( . ) how far ( . ) on are you with that?
```

Progress with the writing and drawing pictures about the trip – the 'purposeful activity' – is talked about in terms of distance: *far*; travelling and direction: *where to go*; and location: *from here, at some point*.

The overlapping of the journey metaphor with the metaphor of UNDERSTANDING AS VISUAL PERCEPTION occurs in lines 1 and 8, when the students are asked if they can **see** where they've **got to go.** This overlapping of conceptual metaphors, manifested as combining linguistic metaphors with related Vehicle domains, was not uncommon. We now see how the linguistic metaphors map from the Vehicle domain of journeys to classroom action in the Topic domains.

GOALS AS DISCOVERIES, DESTINATIONS AND SIGHTS

In the maths lessons particularly, problems or test items were lexicalized as a kind of quest, through which something important would be discovered:

> how would you **find** an average?
> you **found** the difference
> how might you **find** some sort of agreement?

Other metaphors spoke of purposes or goals, not as discoveries, but as destinations, that might or might not be reached:

> how might we **arrive at** a fairly accurate result?
> that's (exact spacing in a dance) what we're **aiming at**
> you'll see how **close** you were to getting them right

Another way of speaking about purposes or goals was as something to be *looked at*, as if the journey was a tourist trip to important sights:

> two things we're going to **look at** this half term
> we'll have **a look at** why . . .
> you could **look at** it two different ways

INTERIM GOALS AS TEMPORARY STOPPING PLACES

Perhaps because much of the discourse was contingent management of events over time, final goals were much less talked about than interim goals. These were activities or topics talked about as temporary stopping places on the journey:

> I'd like to **get on to** that today
> you want to **get to a point**
> **where** are you **on to** with the writing?

Mapping interim goals as temporary locations underlies the many uses of *on*:

> that sentence you're **on**
> what page are we **on**?

Some interim goals are places worthy of closer investigation:

> let's just **go into** that a little bit more

STAGES OF ACTIVITIES AS PARTS OF A JOURNEY

Interim stages of activities were talked about as places passed through on a journey:

> let's quickly **go through** them
> **going on from** that
> some people had thought this **through**

RETURN TRIPS

Some classroom topics and activities were metaphorized as places that needed to be revisited:

> let's **go back to** these rocks
> we'll **come back** in a moment **to** how . . .
> you can **go back** and finish this later
> we're **going back to** possession

DIRECTIONS

The direction taken by the journey was described as a path:

> you're **on the right track**
> you might do it **that way**
> is there **a way**?

Some paths could be chosen by *looking* and *seeing* as mentioned in relation to Extract 10.1:

> **with a view to** sports
> **see how it goes**

EFFORTFUL JOURNEYS

Several metaphors emphasized the difficulty of the journey, implicitly describing it as a race or arduous:

> I think you all **deserve a medal**
> I'm really **pushing** you this afternoon
> I am **pressing** you
> let's do it **the long way**
> take it **step by step**

TEACHER AS GUIDE

A distinctive feature of the metaphorical journey of understanding a classroom topic or completing an activity is that the teacher helps the students:

> **I'm with** you now (= I understand your problem)

She selects the destinations, discoveries and sights that are the outcomes, topics and activities of the classroom journeys, and starts the students on their way:

> ***off*** you ***go***   (said to a student about to read aloud from a book)

She encourages the students to persist using both carrot and stick:

> I think you all **deserve a medal**
> I'm really **pushing** you this afternoon

However, the language around the Vehicle terms often reminds the students that they are not alone. For example, the inclusive *we* is used:

> **we're** going back to possession
> **we're** going to go over them now

or the teacher indicates how she will help:

> could **I** just go through what **you** managed to do

As we saw in Extract 10.1, the teacher also helps the students make their own decisions and plans by suggesting what is important and offering strategic advice:

> can you **see where you've got to go from here**?
> are you **clear** about who goes over (in a dance)?
> plan it out **as you go**
> take it **step by step**

In a Vygotskyan way, the guide is equipping the travellers with sufficient knowledge and skills to survive alone.

Journey metaphors: discussion

Undoubtedly the systematicity of these conventionalized linguistic metaphors can be fitted together into a mapping between journeys and classroom action. The learning that the students experience seems like a trek into unknown and sometimes difficult terrain. The journey is a kind of guided tour of concepts with stretches of intense, effortful activity. The ultimate goal remains unclear and achievement is mainly felt through interim goals. The guide is motivating and challenging, and will ultimately leave the travellers to their own devices.

Alternative metaphors for learning may be found for students at different stages of education and in different cultural contexts (e.g. Cortazzi and Jin 1999; Oxford 2001). The systematicity of such sets of metaphors may help us to understand the motivations and assumptions of teachers, but we must be careful about extending it across gaps in the linguistic data without further evidence. It would, for example, be impossible to say anything about what motivates students on this journey, or even whether they see themselves as travellers. We also can tell little about the balance between motivating and challenging just from the metaphor. Additional analysis of classroom action and talk is needed.

When using metaphor analysis as an investigative method offering access to underlying beliefs and values, it is tempting and enjoyable to construct a coherent story or systematic mapping from the bits of data. However, as in the previous section, the degree of inferencing required by the analyst must be acknowledged. The journey metaphors illustrate some of the issues of validity to be considered when constructing a conceptual mapping from linguistic evidence:

- How many instances of linguistic metaphor are needed to infer a particular mapping?
- What do we do with linguistic metaphors that do not fit the conceptual mapping? – some activities seem to be MYSTERIES TO BE UNLOCKED: *the* secret *to this skipping thing*.
- How far does the analyst's expectations about the conceptual metaphor shape the interpretations of linguistic metaphor? – *deserve a medal* could also be linked to FIGHTING IN A WAR; COMPETING IN AN ART SHOW, or A DOG SHOW.
- How do we decide the level of generality of the conceptual mapping? – is it a JOURNEY, a TREK or GUIDED TOUR, or A YOUNG PEOPLE'S ADVENTURE HOLIDAY?

There are also psycholinguistic issues around conceptual metaphor theory. How far does the use of systematic linguistic metaphors **come from** pre-existing conceptual metaphor in the way Lakoff suggests? Do discourse participants need knowledge about journeys to talk in these ways about classroom topics and activities? Certainly, the students who are expected to make sense of the language will know little about guided tours into difficult terrain. They are more likely to reason about classroom activities from the concrete actions and talk in the discourse context and from their previous discourse experience, than from their knowledge of journeys. While the conceptual metaphor is a convenient analytic device, we need to remain cautious about its existence beyond the mind of the analyst and its actual use by discourse participants.

Metaphors about literacy processes

There was evidence of systematic reference to skills and processes involving written texts through animating metaphors of speaking, which is of potential educational importance. Metaphors of literacy were extracted from the classroom discourse data, and from the GITA and pre- and post-GITA talk. In the classroom discourse, most examples were found in class work, when several students read aloud to the teacher or discussed their writing with her; other examples were scattered through the various discourse events. These metaphors were used mostly by the teacher. In the GITA data, the students themselves used metaphors when they discussed the meaning of text sentences or evaluated the text. Across these data sets, the Vehicle domain of 'speaking' was used systematically in talk about literacy, with very similar metaphor use by both teachers and students. This section reports the patterns found and suggests that the systematicity can be explained by the experiential basis of literacy in speaking.

The sociocultural context of learning to be literate

Before moving to the data, we should recall that the students in the study were between 9 and 11 years of age, that all of them had passed the basic stages of learning to read and write, and in their daily classroom activities were using written texts as sources of information and were writing their own texts, such as the diary of their trip and stories. In other words, they were competent readers and users of texts, who would soon, if they were not already doing so, be expected to expand their basic skills to include a range of academic study skills. This contextual information is relevant to interpreting the significance of the systematic use of metaphor around literacy skills and processes.

Oral skills form the basis from which reading and writing develop ontogenetically. A child trying to write will first say the words or sentence that she or he wants to capture in writing. A child trying to read will verbalize the written forms. The sociohistorical context of the teaching of literacy is also relevant. In UK schools, a principal technique in early literacy skills development is individual reading aloud to the teacher. The teacher monitors, guides and intervenes in the learning process through short spells of reading aloud by the child (for more details see Cameron 2001b). Even in their sixth year of school, the students in the study still read aloud to the teacher on a regular basis to monitor progress. Between reading aloud sessions, which might only take place once a week, the students spent time in class and at home reading their 'reading book'.

The skills and knowledge used in reading and writing are interdependent. For example, a child learning to write the genres of narrative and argument will make use of knowledge gained from reading as to the two genres make different use of language resources.

From metonymy to metaphor

When the teacher asked a child to read aloud a story, she used lexis from the oracy domain literally:

> I want to **hear** you read

At one point, she described one of her goals for the morning, in which *table* refers metonymically to the students sitting around the table:

> I'm supposed to be **hearing** a table read

As explained above, the process of *hearing (a student) read* refers to more than just listening; the teacher listens to the child and looks at the written text, and spots the differences between the two that she then uses as prompts for correction or explanation. Both student and teacher access written text through a spoken version of it.

In comments on texts being read, the same verb *hear* was used about a complete text rather than the process:

> I haven't **heard** this one before
> I've never **heard** a story before that . . .

This use of *hear* is metonymic because it is used to stand for the wider concept 'hear and understand'. Whereas metaphor maps across 'separate' domains, metonymy maps within one domain. However, this distinction rests on clear domain definitions, which is often tricky to establish. In the following example, the verb *talk about* is used metaphorically to mean 'includes as content', but metonymy is still present in that the child reader will *talk*:

> *it* (the story) does **talk about** racoons

Here, an encounter with written discourse is described metaphorically as both an aural and oral experience, but the metaphor is continuous and contiguous with experience, since once again the student read aloud and the teacher listened while reading the text silently. As we will see, other metaphors with Vehicle lexis from the oracy domain were used when oral production was no longer part of the process.

Oracy metaphors about written text

Examination of the datasets by hand, and then using a concordancing program, showed that the following Vehicle lexis was systematically used to refer metaphorically to the Topic domain of literacy:

> say
> sound
> tell
> talk about

SAYING

The verb *say* was used metaphorically to emphasize something about the surface level of the written forms, mostly at sentence level or below, and often contrasting actual words with their implicit meaning. In Extract 10.2, the teacher prompts a self-correction from a student who misreads the sentence *'I'll send it back'* during a read-aloud session. The self-correction is prompted in the second line of the extract through the contrast of *say* and *mean* that directs the students' attention to the actual words of the text. The self-correction, omitting the extra phrase *to you*, is spoken in the third line.

Extract 10.2 *Oracy metaphors about reading*

S: then I'll send it back to you (.) and you T: well (.) that's what it **means** (.) but it doesn't **say** that S: then I'll send it (.) back

The same teacher refers to other texts that are metaphorically held to speak:

    worksheet   *the next little bit of information* **says**
    slogan   *a sort of slogan and it* **said** *(.) no child is ineducable*

Oracy metaphors were also used to refer to word forms in the students' own writing when the teacher was discussing their diaries. Extract 10.3 shows the teacher giving a student Strategic Feedback to help decide whether she needs *bought* or *brought* in her text. (In a conversational disfluency, the teacher reverses the logic of her intended message in lines 3 and 4.)

Extract 10.3 *Writing as saying*

1   you BRING and you therefore BROUGHT ?????
     only way I can remember ????? whether I need to **say** brought or bought (.)
     if I brought it (.) I **say** bring????? br (2.0)
     and if I (.) bought it (.) then I **say** buy (.)
5   that's my memo ?????

Another student, writing about the school trip, had written: *I was so excited*. In Extract 10.4, the teacher is explaining that the *so* implies a statement expressing an outcome will follow. Again, in line 2, a contrastive link is made between *say* (in line 1) and *mean* (in line 2).

Metaphor in educational discourse

Extract 10.4 *Writing as saying*

---
1   if you **say** (.) so (.) excited (.)
    it **means** you're going to **say** (.) something else (.)
    so you'd have to put in something like (.)
    I couldn't wait (.) to get going (1.0)
5   or something like that (.)
    so you need another phrase (.) in there (.) clause

When the students talked about the GITA texts, they used metaphors of *saying* in a similar way about the specific form of words, usually at sentence level or below. The Subject of the verb *he* (the writer) or *it* (the text):

> he already **said** something like this
> it **says** the sun is just the right distance away

For both teachers and students, this verb was also used non-metaphorically with approximately the same frequency. In non-metaphorical use, there was often a focus on actual spoken words:

> I didn't **say** you could stand up
> don't **say** 'praise im' .. say your Hs

> Mrs C's going to ask who **said** that
> I can't **say** 'reliable'

It seems that the metaphorical use of the verb *say* mapped its reference to specific words and their form from its use in spoken discourse.

SOUNDS

The verb *sound*, usually in the simple present tense, had two metaphorical uses. One was in evaluating text:

Teacher	a sentence in students' writing	**sounds** lovely (.) real big family party (.) it **sounds** . . .
Teacher	explanation of apostrophe	it **sounds** terribly complicated
Student	choice of a word in a sentence	it makes it **sound** more interesting

It was also used to speculate about meaning, followed by *like, as though,* or *as if*:

Teacher	encyclopaedia extract	how many brontosauruses does that **sound** as if we could fit into our field?
Student	text sentence	that **sounds** like it's meant to be warming
Student	'chambers'	it **sounds** like a dungeon

The Subject of *sounds* was always inanimate, usually a chunk of text. The unit of text referred to could be a word, but was more likely to be sentence level or beyond.

TELLING

By far the most frequent of the four verbs, and used by the students in the GITA tasks, *telling* referred to the topic of a sentence or larger unit of text:

> it isn't **telling** you how to protect the earth
> then he's **telling** you about harmful energy
> it's not **telling** you what has four chambers

The Subject was mostly *it* (the text unit).

TALKING ABOUT

The previous sub-section included the teacher's uses of *talking about* to refer to the topic of a story. The students used it to refer to the topic of a part of the text they were reading:

> he's **talking about** it was a shield
> it's like **talking about** a pump there

Again, the Subject of the verb was mostly *it*, sometimes *he* (the author).

Other verbs used about writing

While there is heavy use of these 'speaking' verbs in the domain of writing, as well as consistency between teachers' and students' use of them, any claim that this is an important conceptual metaphor needs to be backed up by investigation of alternative lexis to see if other metaphors are used and how this compares with the use of non-metaphorical language. This was done by concordancing verb collocates of *he* and *it* in the GITA data, identifying verbs about writing, and then searching for all uses of these verbs. The list of alternatives includes both non-metaphorical verbs and other metaphorically used verbs. The most frequent were forms of *mean, put* and *explain*.

Non-metaphorical verbs used about writing
describe/describing
explain/explaining
mean/means/meaning
mention
write/written/writing

Metaphorical verbs used about writing
goes on (about)
was on about
put
use
carried on
make sense

The total number of uses of these verbs was roughly the same as the number of uses of 'speaking' verbs, although together they cover a much wider range of ideas. The significance of the systematicity of 'speaking' verbs is enhanced by comparison with other verbs used, and adds some validity to claiming an active conceptual metaphor.

Talking metaphors used about thinking

In a similar way to the slide from metonymy to metaphor in talk about written text, there seems to be a sliding between metonymy and metaphor in the use of the verb *talking about* and concepts to indicate the subject or topic of ongoing classroom discourse:

> we were **talking about** apostrophes/contractions

This expression is metonymic since they were indeed talking about apostrophes, although they were also thinking, learning and writing about them. It is metaphorical if we hold that *talking about* and *thinking about* signal different conceptual domains. While talking and thinking are interdependent, and talking probably doesn't often happen without thinking, it is certainly possible to think without talking.

Talking about is used with the sense of 'dealing with' for both large topics of lessons and more restricted topic reference, as in Explication about apostrophes (Extract 10.5). Before the talk in the extract, two boys have been asked to stand up holding their pencils, and the teacher uses them to explain the difference between the apostrophe in THE BOYS' PENCILS and in THE BOY'S PENCILS. She asks why, in the second case, the apostrophe comes before the S.

Extract 10.5 *Talking metaphors about thinking*

```
1   T:   why is that? (2.0)
         because we're talking about? (1.0)
         how many boys? (2.0)
    S:              [ one
5   T:   one
         what's the big long word ( . )
         beginning with S ( . )
         that we use when we're talking about ( . )
         one of anything? (2.0)
10       Hannah?
    H:   singular
    T:   sing ( . ) ular ( . ) when we use the noun in the singular ( . ) we're talking about
         one ..
```

In classroom discourse, the lexis of *talking about* seems to serve to refer to thinking as well – the process of talking-and-thinking is metonymically reduced to *talking*.

Metaphors of literacy processes: discussion

The four verbs from the Vehicle domain of speaking were systematically used by both teachers and students to talk about written text. The four verbs are not interchangeable, since each maps slightly differently onto the Topic domain in terms of the size of the text unit they are used about and their meaning in respect of it. Between them, they serve to describe a range of links between form and meaning in written text.

Vehicle lexis	Size of text unit	Use
says	specific words, sentence level or smaller unit	to indicate the precise meaning of specific words
sounds + *like, as though, as if*	sentence or larger unit	to evaluate a chunk of text to speculate about meaning
telling you	sentence or larger unit	to state the intended topic
talking about	sentence or larger unit	to describe the topic of the text

The verbs were mostly used with either *he* (the author) or *it* (the text) as Subject, so that either the author or the text is metaphorically speaking to the reader. Bakhtin (1981) developed a more abstract form of this metaphor in his notion of 'voice'.

The systematic set of linguistic metaphors may be considered from a cognitive theoretic perspective as indicating the existence of a conceptual metaphor. I have raised some of the problems in inferring conceptual metaphors from linguistic data, and I want briefly to discuss three issues in relation to this particular example:

- What is the conceptual metaphor? How should it be described?
- Where is the conceptual metaphor?
- What motivates the conceptual metaphor?

WHAT IS THE CONCEPTUAL METAPHOR?

There is evidence of metaphorical use of the four verbs related to speaking, so that a conceptual metaphor can be formulated as WRITING IS SPEAKING. The related use of *hearing* (p. 254) might tempt us to add the parallel conceptual metaphor, READING IS LISTENING, or a combined form such as WRITTEN DISCOURSE PROCESSES ARE ORAL DISCOURSE PROCESSES. However, the GITA data do not offer linguistic data to support this extrapolation. The only linguistic metaphor that hints at how the understanding of text is conceptualized is *telling*. When the discourse is searched for verb collocates of *you* or *we*, to try to find lexis use that refers to the readers' processes, there are very few active verbs (*you* mostly occurs in the Object position) and they are the non-metaphorical words *understand* or *know*. We should, I suggest, formulate this aspect of the conceptual metaphor as READING IS BEING TOLD. Other facets of reading might be investigated in other ways to elicit possible metaphorical conceptualizations.

The conceptual metaphor that these data suggest is then:

WRITING IS SPEAKING + READING IS BEING TOLD

WHERE IS THE CONCEPTUAL METAPHOR?

Where does such a conceptualization exist? It exists initially in the language use abstracted across the discourse. Whether it exists in the students' or teachers' minds is a difficult epistemological issue that begs the question of the existence of mental representations, denied by some, such as Thelen and Smith (1994), who take a complex systems approach. It also separates experience from language and from conceptualization, whereas the findings described in this section emphasize the continuity between talk, action and thinking in students' classroom experiences.

WHAT MOTIVATES THE CONCEPTUAL METAPHOR?

I suggest that the close, experiential and dynamic links between metaphorical, metonymic and non-metaphorical uses of language evidenced in the discourse data can adequately account for the systematic occurrence of linguistic metaphor in the metaphor dataset. The conceptual metaphor does have an experiential basis (Grady 1999) but this experience is situated action in real ontogenetic time, rather than the abstracted phylogenetic experience used in much cognitive linguistic theory of metaphor.

The basis for this argument lies in the metonymic use of Vehicle lexis alongside its metaphorical use in the actual spoken discourse. Examination of the metaphorically used lexis in its discourse context reveals the close links between metaphorical use and metonymic and non-metaphorical use. It seems highly possible that teachers, driven by an affective motivation to make new and difficult concepts accessible, might choose familiar lexis and concepts in their pedagogic interaction, and talk about thinking and reading in terms of speaking.

The data also show that students tend to use the same metaphors as their teachers. While teachers may have a range of other ways of talking about reading and writing, students are limited to those they encounter in discourse with other people. We can see how the cumulative effect of understanding through the metaphors of teachers and employing the metaphors in one's own discourse may have a strong impact on the construction of students' understandings of literacy processes.

Speaking metaphors for reading and writing appear to evolve from students' experiences in learning to read by reading aloud. As students progress to silent reading and to more advanced use of their literacy skills (for example to extract, compare, discuss and disseminate information) they will need metalanguage that is more precise and concepts that are relevant to written rather than spoken discourse. It may be that they will also need different metaphors, more suited to these advanced concepts.

We have here a further instance of the need for dynamic development in the choice of metaphors. While, in the contingency of moment-by-moment discourse, metaphors act as stepping stones from experience to more abstract academic concepts by making ideas more concrete, simpler or more familiar, over a longer timescale, metaphors need to become less concrete and more complex.

Systematicity in talk about thinking and learning

In this section, we look for systematicity in the data, not of Vehicle terms, but across Topic domains. In particular, we focus on discourse about cognitive processes of thinking and learning, to see how metaphor might offer metacognitive opportunities. Table 10.2 lists the Vehicle lexis used to talk about cognitive processes and states, grouped into the categories created from the data.

Some of the linguistic metaphors in Table 10.2 can be seen as expressions of common conceptual metaphors of mind (Barnden 1998; Gibbs 1994):

MIND AS PHYSICAL SPACE (NOTEBOOK)	*make a mental note*
MIND AS CONTAINER	*in your mind*
MIND AS BODY	*use your head*
UNDERSTANDING AS SEEING	*let's see*
IDEAS AS OBJECTS	*a bit of information, build information*

However, unlike the JOURNEY metaphors, or metaphors for writing and reading, there is little systematicity in the data, even though several of the classroom events involved teachers trying to help students think about ideas. Instead there are one or two linguistic metaphors that can be linked to each of several conceptual metaphors postulated by other researchers. We would need further evidence to claim that any of these conceptual metaphors of mind were active in this particular classroom discourse.

Table 10.2 Metaphors of cognitive processes and states

Topic	Vehicles
concentrated attending	use common sense think through use your head put your thinking caps on pay attention to look this way all eyes on the board
lack of attention	dreaming lazy
carrying conceptual information	says talking about tell a bit of information/history
finding meaning	make sense have a look at figure out
problems with finding meaning	muddled stuck
constructing shared understanding	give information build information I'm with you get it be clear let's see if
problems with shared meaning	a mystery I couldn't figure it out the secret
recall/use of memory	make a mental note ring a bell in your mind bear in mind go back to your memory you have a visual memory makes your imagination work know in your mind
calculating	find arrive at a figure say 16 into 2 look for do in your head gives you buying time
problems with calculating	my brain won't manage that hadn't been looking at what had been asked for
nature of underlying strategies	the first rule the secret the key

Systematicity, metaphor and metonymy

From the linguistic metaphors in Table 10.2, it seems that the affective over-rides the cognitive in the selection and use of metaphors of mind in teachers' talk. Many of the metaphors align teacher with students through non-threatening Vehicle lexis that tends to diminish the mental work that needs to be done, as was found in Chapter 6. While the metaphors of mind may help create a supportive classroom atmosphere, they do not appear to offer students anything very helpful metacognitively. The mind is some kind of container in which bells ring and notes can be made; information is stored visually and can be accessed visually too. Learning can sometimes be done by accretion of bits of information, but at other times is a more difficult process. Although students are exhorted to work, think and use their heads, they are not given more specific clues to how this might help. Some of the information they want to get may be hidden away from them as a mystery or a secret. If there is metacognitive help offered to students then, as in Chapter 5 or the Strategic feedback in Extract 6.7 (p. 135), it comes from the talk around metaphor rather than from the metaphors themselves.

Systematicity of metaphor in discourse: summary

In exploring the various types of systematicity in metaphor use, the usefulness and validity of constructing conceptual metaphors to describe and explain underlying mappings has been discussed.

Animating and personifying metaphors did occur across the data, both in technical talk and, more locally, in sub-technical talk. An interpersonal motivation for the use of personifying metaphors was inferred from the data, while animating (non-personifying) metaphors seemed to have a more conceptual motivation. Not only are animating metaphors widely used in all genres, but they also characterize talk with children, and so it is not surprising to find many instances in the discourse data.

Starting with an elaborated schema around a conceptual metaphor and using it to guide a search of the linguistic metaphors, it was possible to identify a systematic set of JOURNEY metaphors in the classroom discourse. Classroom processes, in teacher talk at least, were revealed as a journey of adventure through sometimes challenging terrain. A similar search for systematicity in metacognitive talk about thinking and learning processes showed that the metaphors themselves are neither systematic nor specific enough to be very helpful. It may be that a larger amount of data would reveal more systematic metaphor use.

The systematic use of lexis from the domain of speaking to talk about making meaning in written or spoken discourse suggests a very different type of conceptual metaphor, one that is actively shared by teachers and students, that links their talk with their classroom experience and action, and that is potentially important for teaching practice. This systematic mapping may be better described and explained as language in action rather than as thought. Its appearance in discourse can be accounted for as a result of shifts in prosaic language use rather than as a result of a pre-existing conceptual metaphor. From the perspective of language users, metaphors have come to exist in the shared discourse through gradual disembedding from previous non-metaphorical or metonymical use in situated action. Further examples of this process occurred in the teacher's use of *big circles* to refer to sets (Chapter 5), and in metaphors of mathematical operations that start from the concrete use of bricks or counters (Walkerdine 1982, 1984). This sociohistorical view of linguistic data offers an alternative explanation of systematicity in metaphor to the cognitive view, which places conceptual metaphor in the heads of language users, rather than in their shared social world.

11 Metaphor in educational discourse: review and discussion

How shall the heart express itself?
How shall another understand?
                    F. Tjutchev

Metaphor is terrifying because it presents to us the rivalry of likeness, the awful connectedness of everything.
                    James Wood

Metaphor has been explored in this book as a phenomenon of discourse, starting from the epistemic commitments set out in Chapter 1, that metaphor would be investigated as interactional, contextualized, prosaic and dynamic. To this end, a theoretical framework was constructed that combined Vygotskyan and more recent sociocultural theory with concepts from complex systems theory. The construct of 'alterity' was developed to capture the idea of an ideational space between discourse participants that they attempt to resolve and reduce through their contingent talking-and-thinking. Functional, linguistic and discourse analyses were employed for empirical investigation. In this final chapter, the findings and their interpretation are brought together to summarize what I have discovered about metaphor in use and to consider the implications.

Metaphor as prosaic

Bakhtin urged investigation of prosaic uses of language, the everyday and the ordinary. In the context of the classroom, we have seen how metaphor works to help the processes of everyday classroom life: managing lessons, and helping students articulate their ideas, expectations and values. In the talk of daily life, we constantly make metaphorical use of our language resources, particularly the short, simple words that extend the sense of lexical items to help communication across discourse alterity. Metaphor combines with our other prosaic communicative resources too: intonation, graphics and gesture (Cienki 1998).

Metaphor is not easily separated from other ways of using

language, including comparison, allusion, hyperbole, polysemy and metonymy. The continuity of metaphor in prosaic discourse has forced repeated analytical decisions to be made about category boundaries. One issue remains to be discussed: is prosaic metaphor continuous with creative poetic metaphor?

The answer depends on the direction of the question. If we start with metaphor as poetic, novel and creative, then we find more ordinary language making use of the same language and conceptual resources to produce conventionalized metaphors (for example Gibbs, *The Poetics of Mind,* 1994). However, we have started from the opposite direction, from the plains of the prosaic rather than the mountain tops of the poetic. When we look from this point at the skilful, artistic work with language that characterizes the most telling and creative poetic metaphors, we see that artists with language select and adapt from the metaphor resources offered by the language. They twist and mould and position the language in ways that make it special and out of the ordinary. Rather than trying to reduce alterity as happens in most everyday discourse, they may in fact deliberately increase alterity, to de-familiarize the language, slow down the interpretation and thereby create impact.

The data showed glimpses of creativity with metaphor, for example when students played with teachers' metaphors or, more rarely, created their own. Most of the time though, individuals used conventionalized metaphors from their existing resources to meet the contingent demands of discourse. While this process is, in some (prosaic) sense, creative, I want to retain the distinction between everyday creativity and the special skill of creating telling, poetic, metaphorical images and forms that have the power to move us emotionally.

Metaphor as language

This study of metaphor has used language both as starting point and as context. In doing so, it takes an applied linguistic approach fairly unusual in contemporary work on metaphor, which focuses more on the conceptual side of metaphor. To summarize what has been found:

- Every language has lexical and syntactic resources that can be used to bring together two ideas. In English, stretching the meanings of verbs and prepositions, and combinations of them, seems to generate the most frequently occurring forms of metaphor.
- On the other hand, nominal forms seem to produce the most noticeable, or strongest, types of metaphor, and are used

particularly for deliberate metaphors.
- The converse also applies: the form of metaphors affects their processing, and also whether they are noticed and unpacked.
- In the historical development of a language, particular forms tend to be selected for metaphorical use and other forms for non-metaphorical use. We saw this happen in the moment with the phrase *lollipop trees*, which emerged from the episode of talk as the preferred form to capture the idea of the round trees. A similar process appears to happen as metaphors are idiomatized over longer timescales (Deignan 1999b). That metaphors will settle into certain forms is predictable, but the precise form is not predictable. This kind of evolutionary co-adaptation between use and form is consistent with a complex dynamical view of language.

Metaphor as interactional

Metaphor has been investigated not just as monologic language use, but in use in social interaction between speakers. When we look at how metaphor works 'in the spaces between' people, and how it sometimes fails to work, we have a much richer picture of discourse phenomena driven by the goal of reducing alterity and managing communicative risk:

- Speakers repeat and reformulate their own and each other's metaphors.
- Speakers break down the meaning of deliberate metaphors to help listeners understand.
- Metaphors are 'tuned', through the use of hedges, to help direct listeners' interpretation processes. In a process of estimating alterity, speakers select tuning devices to meet their perceptions of listeners' understanding.
- Deliberate metaphors often occur in clusters of linked metaphors, presenting the same idea in different ways.
- Metaphors are used with simultaneous ideational and affective functions.
- Metaphors are used at a metacognitive level to organize discourse, often operating to frame events and episodes within events, and around topic shifts.
- The discourse alterity created by metaphor may sometimes be too large to cross. Failure to understand metaphor occurred if the Vehicle domain was in some way unavailable to discourse participants, and difficulty could be compounded by the use of

- demanding language structures.
- Metaphor sometimes created a centrifugal effect in the talking-and-thinking, loosening connections between meanings so that metaphors were inappropriately interpreted or recalled.

Metaphor as contextualized

We cannot, however, understand the interactional use of metaphor without looking at the sociocultural factors of the context of use. Information about the educational context of the studies reported here was used in several ways:

- To make a distinction between metaphors conventionalized within a particular sociocultural group, and metaphors used deliberately in the context. The deliberate/conventionalized distinction is a discourse equivalent of the novel/conventional distinction of traditional metaphor theory.
- To explain the development of a repertoire of shared metaphors within sociocultural groups, through the gradual disembedding of language linked in previous times with situated concrete action, or through the conventionalizing of initial deliberate use.
- To explain the affective impact of metaphor as teachers worked to express solidarity, to emphasize, and to evaluate across the power differential between themselves and the students.
- To identify special pedagogic uses of metaphor in which experts (teachers, researcher, peers) try to reduce conceptual alterity by offering a series of stepping stone metaphors between the known and the new concept, and by explicitly unpacking metaphorical meaning to explain it and then repacking it.

Implications

Educational implications

Understanding how metaphor works in reducing alterity can help improve the effectiveness of choice and use of metaphor in educational discourse. Issues of educational inclusion are implied by the findings. The use of metaphors in the technical language of disciplines means that they can, by accident or design, take on a gate-keeping role. We have seen that teachers make extensive use of sub-technical metaphor with young students. If these students are to become mature members of discipline areas, they will need to meet, understand and acquire the technical metaphors of the field. It seems important that teachers, or experts, see their sub-technical language as a stage towards this and not as an end in itself. The metaphors of educational discourse need to be made more complex as time goes by.

The prosaic use of metaphor to manage lessons implies that it may also play a gate-keeping role in classroom activity. Similarly, the use of indirect metaphors in giving feedback on student performance may affect access to teachers' meaning and the effectiveness of feedback for improving performance (Hampshire 1996).

Beyond education

Suggestions have been made about the choice and use of metaphors for textbook writers and teachers, but similar advice might be relevant for anyone involved in asymmetric discourse, including therapy and the workplace. The nature and functions of discourse in specific settings will give rise to roles for metaphor that may differ from their use in education. However, it seems likely that, as in classrooms, metaphor will be used affectively to express solidarity and to mitigate evaluative statements. Ideationally, exploratory talk in many settings might make use of the explicit unpacking, development, and re-assembling of deliberate metaphors in the process of building up shared understandings.

Metaphors can increase discourse alterity, as well as decrease it, and the use of metaphor to conceal information or highlight selected aspects of a domain may be deliberately exploited in some types of discourse.

The sociocultural analysis of metaphor in group discourse can be extended to other groups. We might look for the technical metaphors of groups and at how novices learn these as part of their developing expertise within the group. In school discourse, sub-technical talk was a rich site of metaphor use, and it seems likely that this would also be true in the discourse of other groups.

Analysis of metaphors used in discourse may reveal something of the values and ideas of groups. However, as we have seen, metaphors may occur in talk for many reasons: by chance, because of the nature of interactional talk, in sub-conscious accommodation with other speakers, or as deliberate tools for decreasing alterity. Researchers should be cautious in inferring underlying conceptualizations from metaphor analysis.

Implications for learning the metaphors of another language

The findings about metaphor in discourse allow a more detailed understanding of how learners and teachers might approach the metaphors in another language. The underlying mapping process of metaphor is a basic human skill but different languages construct linguistic metaphor differently. Learners should seek out the equivalent form–function matches, parallel, for example, to English nominal group metaphors used for deliberate metaphors, or verbs + prepositions for conventionalized metaphors.

Different languages have a different set of conventionalized metaphors, partly linked to formal constraints and affordances, and partly the result of historical accident. It is likely that basic or primary conceptual metaphors, such as EVENTS ARE ACTIONS, occur in all languages (Grady 1999), providing a helpful interpretation strategy for learners. However, the linguistic expressions of the conceptual metaphors are likely to differ and will need to be learnt for production. The systematicity of sets of linguistic metaphors can be used to help learning and recall. Conventionalized metaphors may best be learnt as vocabulary. Occasional review activities can bring together metaphors linked by content or form, using the links to reinforce learning.

Sociocultural factors are interwoven with language. Metaphor can be studied (not as a language phenomenon but as a sociocultural one) by examining how particular groups use metaphor. This may apply particularly to the learning of languages for specific purposes in which the use of metaphor by technical expert groups forms part of that learning (e.g. Charteris-Black 2000; Henderson 2000). The understanding of second language users can be assisted if producers of technical discourse make clear whether a particular term is a technical term or a deliberate non-technical metaphor.

The Vehicle domains of idiomatic metaphors may reflect the collective experience and possibilities of sociocultural groups, so that conceptual metaphors may be interestingly different and offer a starting point for culture and language awareness activities (e.g. Deignan *et al.* 1997).

Tuning devices differ across languages. Students should learn how to use the most unmarked of these as a communication strategy. For example, in English, using *kind of* in front of strong metaphors will mitigate the risk of choosing inappropriate metaphors. Metaphor clustering offers a further communication strategy in a foreign language. To have a greater chance of explaining an idea across languages, it may help to employ several different metaphors to express aspects of the idea.

In conclusion

After over a decade of research, metaphor in discourse continues to intrigue me. The quotation from the critic James Wood at the beginning of this chapter captures something of the complexity of metaphor: it is at once both true and false, both disjunctive and connecting, ordinary and yet surprising.

Appendix 1
Linguistic metaphors and grammatical analysis in the geology lesson

Noun
(crinoids wave their) arms
feet
a slate roof is quite something
is molten lava like wax?

it can be a bit like wax
we can put them in a big circle
put them into two smaller circles

Noun phrase
a bit depressing
a bit like wax
a little bit of information
a little bit more
the next little bit

a bit more
animal plants
rock becomes like sticky treacle
even like runny butter

Verb
(crinoids) bring it in
(crinoids) catch food
marble comes to be formed
the river deposited the mud
where's my rubber gone?
to give you a little bit of information
a classification helps classify
put your name
you need to put (= write)

a big circle that says
circles that say
the next little bit says
say that this is a rock
you see that
it won't take long
(crinoids) wave

(volcano) starts working
(volcano) working

Verb phrase
Mr C will come up trumps
the local rocks of Cumbria fit into the overall picture of the age of the Earth

we'll have a look at
have a little look at

Relative pronoun + verb phrase
where marble comes from
where these rocks come from

Phrasal verb
rain and temperature acts upon
(rocks)
the river was bringing down
information on which we can
build
build up heat
we'll come back to
it will come out in slices
minerals that come out of rocks
they keep coming up with ideas
to do with classes
let's go back to these rocks
steps that go down
let's just go into
rocks which are laid down
limestone is laid down
granite . . .laid down

laid down in shallow seas
layers are laid down
two things we're going to look at
they look at
Mr C's looking out a piece
rocks pressing down
we need to put in
it shades up to
it starts off as
it took up
isn't taking up so much room
that took up a lot of room

Adjective
a big word for
what's it a big word for?
high quality

Adverb
it won't take long

Preposition
in the compressing
in a group
in Italy
in Cumbria
in Wales

in the village
in slices
in the rain
on height
on the telly
on the news
under pressure

Prepositional phrase
for a long time
for too long
in actual fact
in fact
in mind
in comparison with

in other words
in a sort of way
in a moment
in use
on his own

Appendix 2
Linguistic metaphors and teaching sequences in the geology lesson

Number of 10-word blocks from start	Action	Teaching sequence	Metaphors
0–10	Ps put names and dates on worksheet	Framing – Organization	on the top line we need to put in you also need to put your name
11–20	T introduces topic and goal	– Agenda Management	give you a little bit of information on which we can build in other words minerals that come out of rocks rain and temperature acts upon two things we're going to look at
21–24	T addresses individual P about worksheet	Framing – Organization	it won't take long
25–29	T then P read aloud from worksheet		helps classifies
30–81	T explains *classification*	Explanation – explication	a big word for is it to do with classes? it is in a sort of way what's it a big word for?
	– verbal example of sorting marbles	– exemplification Framing – Agenda Management	let's just go into that a little bit more
	– moving children around into sets	– exemplification Summarizing – exemplification	a big circle that says circles that says on height you see that on his own

Appendix 2

Number of 10-word blocks from start	Action	Teaching sequence	Metaphors
82–83	T explains geologists' work introduces *igneous rocks*	Explanation – explication	they <u>look at</u> with three things <u>in mind</u>
84–103	Ps write on worksheets Topic shift from *igneous* to *sedimentary*	Framing – Organization – Agenda Management Explanation – explication	you need <u>to put</u> (= write) we'll <u>come back to</u> <u>in</u> a moment rocks which are <u>laid down</u> limestone is <u>laid down</u>
104–08	Sub-topic of *crinoid fossils in sedimentary rock* Back to *sedimentary rocks*	Explanation – explication Summarizing	<u>animal plants</u> <u>feet</u> wave their <u>arms</u> <u>catch</u> food <u>bring</u> it in
109–153	Shift of topic to *metamorphic rock* T squashes cup to show metamorphosis under pressure Return to real rocks *marble* as example of metamorphic rock	Explanation – explication – exemplification – explication Framing – organization – exemplification Summarizing	 <u>say</u> that this is a rock it <u>took up</u> it isn't <u>taking up</u> so much room x2 that <u>took up</u> a lot of room '<u>in</u> the compressing rocks <u>pressing down</u> you <u>build up</u> heat Mr C will <u>come up trumps</u> that's <u>where</u> marble <u>comes from</u>
154–74	Shift of topic to *igneous* again T helps Ps think about *volcanoes* and how *hot lava* becomes rock Back to *igneous rocks*	Framing – Agenda Management Explanation – exemplification – explanation – exemplification – explanation Summarizing	let's <u>go back to</u> these rocks igneous rock <u>comes</u> to be formed (volcano) starts <u>working</u> <u>on</u> the telly <u>on</u> the news <u>in</u> Italy <u>working</u> like <u>sticky</u> treacle like <u>runny</u> butter is molten lava like <u>wax</u>? it can be <u>a bit</u> like <u>wax</u> <u>where</u> these rocks <u>come from</u>

Linguistic metaphors and teaching sequences

Number of 10-word blocks from start	Action	Teaching sequence	Metaphors
175–213	Shift of topic to *Cumbria* and recall of examples of *3 types of rocks* seen there *sedimentary* *slate* as example	Explanation – explication – explication – exemplification	granites . . .laid down laid down in shallow seas the river was bringing down deposited the mud shades up layers are laid down it starts off as sedimentary it will come out in . . .slices really quite something in Wales very high quality in the rain a bit depressing
214–22	Back to filling in worksheet	Framing – Agenda Management – Organization	the next little bit says in Cumbria Mr C's looking out a piece in use
223–31	Recall of types of rock seen in Cumbria and locally	Explanation – exemplification	steps that go down from Binns
232–45	T states worksheet task Helps Ps decide on type of rock and complete worksheet	Framing – Agenda Management Explanation – explication	I'll have to find out a bit more
246–52	Summary of lesson: *rocks in Cumbria*	Summarizing	in Cumbria they keep coming up with new ideas
253–58	T tells what will happen the following day Closing of lesson	Framing – Agenda Management Organization	we'll have a look at how the rocks of Cumbria fit into the overall picture of the age

References

Abkarian, G., Jones, A. and West, G. (1990) Enhancing children's communication skills: idioms 'fill the bill'. *Child Language Teaching and Therapy*, **6** (3), 246–54.

Aitchison, J. (1987) *The Mental Lexicon*. Oxford: Blackwell.

Alexander, R. (1997) *Policy and Practice in Primary Education* (2nd edn). London: Routledge.

Arter, J. L. (1976) *The Effects of Metaphor in Reading Comprehension*. Unpublished doctoral dissertation. University of Illinois, Urbana.

Ausubel, D. (1960) The use of advance organizers in the learning and retention of meaningful verbal material. *Journal of Educational Psychology*, **51**, 267–72.

Bakhtin, M. M. (1981) *The Dialogic Imagination*. Austin: University of Texas Press.

Bakhtin, M. M. (1986) *Speech Genres and Other Late Essays*. Austin: University of Texas Press.

Barnden, J. (1998) An AI system for metaphorical reasoning about mental states in discourse, in J–P. Koenig (ed.), *Discourse and Cognition: Bridging the Gap*. Stanford: CSLI, 167–88.

Barnes, D. and Todd, F. (1995) *Communication and Learning Revisited: Making Meaning through Talk*. Portsmouth, NH: Boynton/Cook Heinemann.

Barsalou, L. W. (1989) Intraconcept similarity and its implications for interconcept similarity, in S. Vosniadou and A. Ortony (eds), 76–121.

Bateson, G. (1972) *Steps to an Ecology of Mind*. New York: Ballantine.

Battram, A. (1998) *Navigating Complexity*. London: The Industrial Society.

Billow, R. M. (1975) A cognitive developmental study of metaphor comprehension. *Developmental Psychology*, **11**, 415–23.

Black, M. (1962) *Models and Metaphors*. New York: Cornell University Press.

Black, M. (1979) More about metaphor, in A. Ortony (ed.), 19–41.

Block, D. (1996) Not so fast: some thoughts on theory culling, relativism, accepted findings and the heart and soul of SLA. *Applied Linguistics*, **17** (1), 63–83.

Block, D. (1999) Who framed SLA research? Problem framing and metaphoric accounts of the SLA research process, in L. Cameron and G. Low (eds), 135–48.

Boyd, R. (1993) Metaphor and theory change: what is 'metaphor' a metaphor for?, in A. Ortony (ed.), 481–532.

Breen, M. (ed.) (2001) *Learner Contributions to Language Learning: New Directions in Research*. London: Pearson.

Bright, M. (1991) *The Ozone Layer*. London: Gloucester Press.
Brooke-Rose, C. (1958) *A Grammar of Metaphor*. London: Secker and Warburg.
Brown, A. (1989) Analogical learning and transfer: what develops?, in S. Vosniadou and A. Ortony (eds), 369–412.
Bruner, J. (1990) *Acts of Meaning*. Cambridge: Harvard University Press.
Burke, K. (1945) *A Grammar of Motives*. New York: Prentice Hall.
Bütz, M. (1995) *Chaos and Complexity: Implications for Psychological Theory and Practice*. Washington, DC: Taylor and Francis.
Cacciari, C. and Glucksberg, S. (1995) Understanding idioms: do visual images reflect figurative meanings? *European Journal of Cognitive Psychology*, **7**, 283–305.
Cameron, L. (1996) Discourse context and the development of metaphor in children. *Current Issues in Language and Society*, **3**, 49–64.
Cameron, L. (1999a) Operationalising metaphor for applied linguistic research, in L. Cameron and G. Low (eds), 3–28.
Cameron, L. (1999b) Defining, knowing and describing metaphor, in L. Cameron and G. Low (eds), 105–32.
Cameron, L. (2001a) Talking and thinking with metaphor. Paper presented at the seminar on Spoken English, Grammar and the Classroom, QCA, London, 13 March 2001.
Cameron, L. (2001b) *Teaching Languages to Young Learners*. Cambridge: Cambridge University Press.
Cameron, L. and Deignan, A. (2001) Combining large and small corpora to investigate tuning devices around metaphor in spoken discourse. Paper presented at Interdisciplinary Workshop on Corpus-based and Processing Approaches to Figurative Language, University of Lancaster, 29 March.
Cameron, L. and Low, G. (eds) (1999) *Researching and Applying Metaphor*. Cambridge: Cambridge University Press.
Cameron, L. and Low, G. (1999) Metaphor. *Language Teaching*, **32**, 77–96.
Carey, S. (1985) *Conceptual Change in Childhood*. Cambridge: MIT Press.
Carter, R. and McCarthy, M. (1995) Grammar and the spoken language. *Applied Linguistics*, **16** (2), 141–58.
Casti, J. (1994) *Complexification*. London: Abacus.
Chandler, S. (1991) Metaphor comprehension: a connectionist approach to implications for the mental lexicon. *Metaphor and Symbolic Activity*, **6** (2), 227–58.
Chang-Wells, G. and Wells, G. (1993) Dynamics of discourse: literacy and the construction of knowledge, in E. Forman, N. Minick and C. A. Stone (eds), 58–90.
Charteris-Black, J. (2000) Metaphor and vocabulary teaching in ESP economics. *English for Specific Purposes*, **19**, 149–65.
Cienki, A. (1998) Metaphoric gestures and some of their relations to verbal metaphoric expressions, in J-P. Koenig (ed.), *Discourse and Cognition: Bridging the Gap*. Sanford: CSLI, 189–204.
Clark, A. (1997) *Being There*. Cambridge: MIT Press.

Cohen, T. (1979) Metaphor and the cultivation of intimacy, in S. Sacks (ed.), *On Metaphor*. Chicago: University of Chicago Press.
Cohen, J. and Stewart, I. (1994) *The Collapse of Chaos*. London: Viking.
Cooper, D. (1986) *Metaphor*. Oxford: Blackwell.
Cortazzi, M. and Jin, L. (1999) Bridges to learning: metaphors of teaching, learning and language, in L. Cameron and G. Low (eds), 149–76.
Corts, D. and Pollio, H. (1999) Spontaneous production of figurative language and gesture in college lectures. *Metaphor and Symbol*, **14** (1) 81–100.
Coté, N., Goldman, S. and Saul, E. (1998) Students making sense of informational text: relations between processing and representation. *Discourse Processes*, **25** (1), 1–53.
Coupland, N. and Giles, H. (1988) Communicative accommodation: recent developments. *Language and Communication*, **8**, 175–182.
Deignan, A. (1999a) Corpus-based research into metaphor and its application to language reference materials, in L. Cameron and G. Low (eds), 177–99.
Deignan, A. (1999b) Metaphorical polysemy and paradigmatic relation study. *Word*, **50**, 319–38.
Deignan, A., Gabrys, D. and Solska, A. (1997) Teaching English metaphors using cross-linguistic awareness-raising activities. *ELT Journal*, **51**, 352–60.
Dennett, D. (1991) *Consciousness Explained*. London: Penguin Books.
Dixon, K., Ortony, A. and Pearson, D. (1980) Some reflections on the use of figurative language in children's books. Paper presented at the 13th Meeting of the National Reading Conference.
Drew, P. and Holt, E. (1988) Complainable matters: the use of idiomatic expressions in making complaints. *Social Problems*, **35** (4), 398–417.
Drew, P. and Holt, E. (1995) Idiomatic expressions and their role in the organisation of topic transition in conversation, in M. Everaert, E.-J. van der Linden, A. Schenk and R. Schreuder (eds), *Idioms: Structural and Psychological Perspectives*. Hillsdale: Erlbaum, 117–32.
Drew, P. and Holt, E. (1998) Figures of speech: figurative expressions and the management of topic transition in conversation. *Language in Society*, **27**, 495–522.
Dreyfus, H. and Dreyfus, S. (1986) *Mind over Machine: The Power of Human Intuition and Expertise in the Era of the Computer*. New York: Free Press.
Duranti, A. and Goodwin, C. (1992) *Rethinking Context*. Cambridge: Cambridge University Press.
Edwards, D. (1997) *Discourse and Cognition*. London: Sage.
Ellis, R. (2001) The metaphorical constructions of second language learners, in M. Breen (ed.), 65–85.
Elman, J. (1995) Language as a dynamical system, in R. Port and T. van Gelder (eds), *Mind as Motion: Explorations in the Dynamics of Cognition*. Cambridge: MIT Press, 195–223.
Engeström, Y. (1996) Developmental studies of work as a testbench of activity theory: the case of primary care medical practice, in S. Chaiklin and J. Lave (eds), *Understanding Practice: Perspectives on Activity and Context*. Cambridge: Cambridge University Press, 64–103.

Ericsson, K. A. (1988) Concurrent verbal reports on text comprehension: a review. *Text*, **8**, 295–325.
Ericsson, K. A. and Simon, H. (1984) *Protocol Analysis: Verbal Reports as Data.* Cambridge: MIT Press.
Evans, M. A. and Gamble, D. (1988) Attribute saliency and metaphor interpretation in school-age children. *Journal of Child Language*, **15**, 435–49.
Evans, R. and Evans, G. (1989) Cognitive mechanisms in learning from metaphors. *Journal of Experimental Education*, **58** (1), 5–20.
Fairclough, N. (1989) *Language and Power.* London: Longman.
Fairclough, N. (1992) *Discourse and Social Change.* Cambridge: Polity Press.
Fauconnier, G. and Turner, M. (1996) Blending as a central process of grammar, in A. Goldberg (ed.), *Conceptual Structure, Discourse, and Language.* Stanford: CSLI, 183–203.
Fauconnier, G. and Turner, M. (1998) Conceptual integration networks. *Cognitive Science*, **22**, 133–87.
Fernandez, J. (ed.) (1991) *Beyond Metaphor: The Theory of Tropes in Anthropology.* Stanford: Stanford University Press.
Forceville, C. (1994) *Pictorial Metaphor in Advertising.* Unpublished PhD thesis, Vrije Universiteit, Amsterdam.
Forman, E., Minick, N. and Stone, C. (eds) (1993) *Contexts for Learning: Sociocultural Dynamics in Children's Development.* New York: Cambridge University Press.
Frawley, W. (1997) *Vygotsky and Cognitive Science.* Cambridge: Harvard University Press.
Freud, S. (1901/1975) *The Psychopathology of Everyday Life.* Harmondsworth: Penguin.
Frith, U. (1990) *Autism.* Oxford: Blackwell.
Galton, M. and Williamson, J. (1992) *Group Work in the Primary Classroom.* London: Routledge.
Gentner, D. (1978) On relational meaning: the acquisition of verb meaning. *Child Development*, **49**, 988–98.
Gentner, D. (1982a) Are scientific analogies metaphors?, in D. Miall (ed.), *Metaphor: Problems and Perspectives.* Brighton: Harvester Press, 106–32.
Gentner, D. (1982b) Why nouns are learnt before verbs: linguistic relativity vs. natural partitioning, in S. Kuczaj (ed.), *Language Development: Language, Culture, and Cognition.* Hillsdale: Erlbaum, 301–34.
Gentner, D. and Gentner, D. G. (1983) Flowing waters or teeming crowds: mental models of electricity, in D. G. Gentner and A. L. Stevens (eds), *Mental Models.* Hillsdale: Erlbaum, 99–129.
Gentner, D. and Toupin, C. (1986) Systematicity and surface similarity in the development of analogy. *Cognitive Science*, **10**, 277–300.
Gibbs, R. W. (1987) Linguistic factors in children's understanding of idioms. *Journal of Child Language*, **14**, 569–86.
Gibbs, R. W. (1994) *The Poetics of Mind: Figurative Thought, Language and Understanding.* Cambridge: Cambridge University Press.

Gibbs, R. W. (1999a) Researching metaphor, in L. Cameron and G. Low (eds), 29–47.

Gibbs, R. W. (1999b) Taking metaphor out of our heads and putting it into the cultural world, in R. W. Gibbs and G. Steen (eds), 145–166.

Gibbs, R. W. and Steen, G. (eds) (1999) *Metaphor in Cognitive Linguistics.* Amsterdam: John Benjamins.

Gick, M. L. and Holyoak, K. J. (1980) Analogical problem solving. *Cognitive Psychology,* **12**, 306–55.

Glucksberg, S. and Keysar, B. (1993) How metaphors work, in A. Ortony (ed.), 401–24.

Goatly, A. (1997) *The Language of Metaphors.* London: Routledge.

Goffman, E. (1974) *Frame Analysis.* London: Harper and Row.

Goodwin, B. (1997) *How the Leopard Changed Its Spots: The Evolution of Complexity.* London: Phoenix.

Goosens, L. (1990) Metaphtonymy: the interaction of metaphor and metonymy in expressions for linguistic action. *Cognitive Linguistics,* **1**, 323–40.

Goswami, U. (1991) Learning about spelling sequences: the role of onsets and rimes in analogies in reading. *Child Development,* **62**, 1–22.

Grady, J. (1998) The 'Conduit Metaphor' revisited: a reassessment of metaphors for communication, in J-P. Koenig (ed.), *Discourse and Cognition: Bridging the Gap.* Stanford: CSLI, 205–18.

Grady, J. (1999) A typology of motivation for conceptual metaphor: correlation vs. resemblance, in R. W. Gibbs and G. Steen (eds), *Metaphor in Cognitive Linguistics.* Amsterdam: John Benjamins, 101–24.

Grady, J., Oakley, T. and Coulson, S. (1999) Blending and metaphor, in R. W. Gibbs and G. Steen (eds), *Metaphor in Cognitive Linguistics.* Amsterdam: John Benjamins, 125–44.

Graumann, C. (1990) Perspective structure and dynamics in dialogues, in I. Markova and K. Foppa (eds), *The Dynamics of Dialogue.* London: Harvester Wheatsheaf, 105–26.

Halliday, M. (1985) *An Introduction to Functional Grammar.* London: Edward Arnold.

Hampshire, A. (1996) The development of sociolinguistic strategies: implications for children with speech and language impairments. *Current Issues in Language and Society,* **3** (1), 91–4.

Henderson, W. (2000) Metaphor, economics and ESP: some comments. *English for Specific Purposes,* **19**, 167–173.

Heritage, J. and Watson, J. (1979) Aspects of the properties of formulations in natural conversations: some instances analyzed. *Semiotica,* **30**, 245–62.

Hollingsed, J. (1950) A study of figures of speech in intermediate grade reading. Unpublished doctoral dissertation, Colorado State University.

Holyoak, K. J., Junn, E. and Billmann, D. (1984) Development of analogical problem-solving skill. *Child Development,* **55**, 2042–55.

Honeck, R. and Hoffman, R. (eds) (1980) *Cognition and Figurative Language.* Hillsdale: Erlbaum.

Hopper, P. J. (1997) Discourse and the category 'verb' in English. *Language and Communication,* **17** (2), 93–102.

Hopper, P. J. and Thompson, S. A. (1984) The discourse basis for lexical categories in Universal Grammar. *Language,* **60**, 703–52.
Huddleston, R. (1984) *Introduction to the Grammar of English.* Cambridge: Cambridge University Press.
Hunston, S. and Francis, G. (1998) Verbs observed: a corpus-driven pedagogic grammar. *Applied Linguistics,* **19**, 45–72.
Hymes, D. (1972) Models of the interaction of language and social life, in J. Gumperz and D. Hymes (eds), *Directions in Sociolinguistics: The Ethnography of Communication.* New York: Holt Reinhart and Winston, 35–71.
Janus, R. A. and Bever, T. G. (1985) Processing metaphoric language: an investigation of the three-stage model of metaphor comprehension. *Journal of Psycholinguistic Research,* **14**, 473–87.
Johnson, M. (1987) *The Body in the Mind: The Bodily Basis of Meaning, Imagination and Reason.* Chicago: University of Chicago Press.
Johnson, M. G. (1975) Some psychological implications of language flexibility. *Behaviorism,* **3**, 87–95.
Johnson, M. G. and Malgady, R. (1980) Towards a perceptual theory of metaphoric comprehension, in R. Honeck and R. Hoffman (eds), 259–82.
Kauffman, S. (1993) *The Origins of Order.* New York: Oxford University Press.
Kauffman, S. (1995) *At Home in the Universe.* London: Penguin Books.
Keesing, R. (1987) Models, 'folk' and 'cultural', in D. Holland and N. Quinn (eds), 369–93.
Keil, F. (1979) *Semantic and Conceptual Development: An Ontological Perspective.* Cambridge: Harvard University Press.
Keil, F. (1983) On the emergence of semantic and conceptual distinctions. *Journal of Experimental Psychology: General,* **112**, 357–89.
Keil, F. (1989) *Concepts, Kinds and Cognitive Development.* Boston: MIT Press.
Kelso, S. (1995) *Dynamic Patterns.* Cambridge: MIT Press.
Kintsch, W. (1988) The role of knowledge in discourse comprehension: a construction–integration model. *Psychological Review,* **95**,163–82.
Kintsch, W. (1998) *Comprehension.* New York: Cambridge University Press.
Kittay, E. F. (1987) *Metaphor: Its Cognitive Force and Linguistic Structure.* Oxford: Oxford University Press.
Knudsen, C. and Cameron, L. (2000) Simulated evolution in a linguistic model. *Discrete Dynamics in Nature and Society,* **5**, 189–201.
Kövesces, Z. (1998) *Metaphor and Emotion.* Cambridge: Cambridge University Press.
Kozulin, A. (1990) *Vygotsky's Psychology.* London: Harvester Wheatsheaf.
Lakoff, G. (1987) *Women, Fire and Dangerous Things.* Chicago: University of Chicago Press.
Lakoff, G. (1993) The contemporary theory of metaphor, in A. Ortony (ed.), 202–51.
Lakoff, G. and Johnson, M. (1980) *Metaphors We Live By.* Chicago: University of Chicago Press.
Lakoff, G. and Turner, M. (1989) *More Than Cool Reason: A Field Guide to Poetic Metaphor.* Chicago: University of Chicago Press.

Langacker, R. (1987) *Foundations of Cognitive Grammar.* Stanford: Stanford University Press.
Lantolf, J. (1996) Second language acquisition theory building?, in G. Blue and R. Mitchell (eds), *Language and Education.* Clevedon: B.A.A.L. and Multilingual Matters, 16–27.
Lantolf, J. (ed.) (2000) *Sociocultural Theory and Second Language Learning.* Oxford: Oxford University Press.
Lantolf, J. and Appel, G. (eds) (1994) *Vygotskyan Approaches to Second Language Research.* Norwood: Ablex Publishing Corporation.
Larsen-Freeman, D. (1997) Chaos/complexity science and second language acquisition. *Applied Linguistics,* **18**, 141–65.
Lazar, R., Warr-Leeper, G., Nicholson, C. and Johnson, S. (1989) Elementary school teachers' use of multiple meaning expressions. *Language, Speech and Hearing Services in Schools,* 20, 420–30.
Leont'ev, A. N. (1978) *Activity, Consciousness and Personality.* Englewood Cliffs: Prentice Hall.
Locke, J. (1993) *The Child's Path to Spoken Language.* Cambridge: Harvard University Press.
Long, M. (1983) Native speaker/non-native speaker conversation and the negotiation of comprehensible input. *Applied Linguistics,* **4** (2), 126–41.
Louw, B. (1993) Irony in the text or insincerity in the writer: the diagnostic potential of semantic parodies, in M. Baker, G. Francis and E. Tognini-Bonelli (eds), *Text and Technology: Essays in Honor of John McH. Sinclair.* Amsterdam: Benjamins.
Low, G. (1999) Validating metaphor research projects, in L. Cameron and G. Low (eds), *Researching and Applying Metaphor.* Cambridge: Cambridge University Press.
Low, G. and Cameron, L. (2002) Applied linguistic comments on metaphor identification. *Language and Literature,* **11**(1), 84–90.
Lowe, E. J. (1996) *Subjects of Experience.* Cambridge: Cambridge University Press.
MacCormac, E. R. (1985) *A Cognitive Theory of Metaphor.* Cambridge: MIT Press.
Mahon, J. (1999) Getting your sources right: what Aristotle didn't say, in L. Cameron and G. Low (eds), 69–80.
Mainzer, K. (1996) *Thinking in Complexity* (2nd edn). Berlin: Springer.
Marjanovic-Shane, A. (1989) Metaphor beyond play: development of metaphor in children. Unpublished PhD Dissertation, University of Pennsylvania.
Matic, M. and Wales, R. (1982) Creating interpretations for novel metaphors. *Language and Communication,* **2** (3), 245–67.
Maybin, J. (1996) Story voices: the use of reported speech in 10—12 year olds' spontaneous narratives. *Current Issues in Language and Society,* **3** (1), 36–48.
McCarthy, M. (1988) Some vocabulary patterns in conversation, in R. Carter and M. McCarthy (eds), *Vocabulary and Language Teaching.* London: Longman, 181–200.

Meadows, S. (1993) *The Child as Thinker*. London: Routledge.
Medin, D. and Ross, B. (1989) The specific character of abstract thought: categorization, problem solving and induction, in R. J. Sternberg (ed.) *Advances in the Psychology of Human Intelligence*, Vol. 5. Hillsdale: Erlbaum, 189–223.
Mercer, N. (1994) Neo-Vygotskian theory and classroom education, in B. Stierer and J. Maybin (eds), *Language, Literacy and Learning in Educational Practice*. Clevedon: Multilingual Matters: Open University, 92–110.
Morson, G. S. and Emerson, C. (1990) *Mikhail Bakhtin: Creation of a Prosaics*. Stanford: Stanford University Press.
Myers, J. and Simms, M. (eds) (1982) *A Dictionary of Poetic Terms*. London: Longman.
Nelson, K. (ed.) (1996) *Narratives from the Crib*. Cambridge: Harvard University Press.
Nippold, M. (1991) Evaluating and enhancing idiom comprehension in language-disordered children. *Language, Speech and Hearing Services in Schools*, **22**, 100–6.
Novek, E. (1992) Read it and weep: how metaphor limits views of literacy. *Discourse and Society*, **3** (2) 219–33.
Ortony, A. (1975) Why metaphors are necessary and not just nice. *Educational Review*, **2**, 45–53.
Ortony, A. (1979a) The role of similarity in similes and metaphors, in A. Ortony (ed.), 186–201.
Ortony, A. (1979b) Beyond literal similarity. *Psychological Review*, **86**, 161–80.
Ortony, A. (1980) Some psycholinguistic aspects of metaphor, in R. Honeck and R. Hoffman (eds), 69–83.
Ortony, A. (ed.) (1979) *Metaphor and Thought* (1st edn). New York: Cambridge University Press.
Ortony, A. (ed.) (1993) *Metaphor and Thought* (2nd edn). New York: Cambridge University Press.
Oxford, R. (2001) 'The bleached bones of a story': learners' constructions of language teachers, in M. Breen (ed.), 86–111.
Paprotté, W. and Dirven, R. (eds) (1985) *The Ubiquity of Metaphor*. Amsterdam: John Benjamins.
Parker, S. (1987) *The Body and How It Works*. London: Dorling Kindersley.
Pawley, A. and Syder, F. (1983) Two puzzles for linguistic theory: native-like selection and native-like fluency, in J. Richards and R. Schmidt (eds), *Language and Communication*. London: Longman, 191–227.
Petitot, J. (1995) Morphodynamics and attractor syntax: constituency in visual perception and cognitive grammar, in R. Port and T. van Gelder (eds), 227–82.
Pickens, J., Pollio, M. and Pollio, R. (1985) A developmental analysis of metaphoric competence and reading, in W. Paprotté and R. Dirven (eds), *The Ubiquity of Metaphor*. Amsterdam: John Benjamins, 481–524.
Pollio, H., Barlow, J., Fine, H. and Pollio, M. (1977) *Psychology and the Poetics of Growth*. Hillsdale: Erlbaum.

Pollio, M. and Pickens, J. (1980) The developmental structure of figurative competence, in R. Honeck and R. Hoffman (eds), 311–40.
Port, R. and van Gelder, T. (eds) (1995) *Mind as Motion: Explorations in the Dynamics of Cognition.* Cambridge: MIT Press.
Quinn, N. (1991) The cultural basis of metaphor, in J. Fernandez (ed.), *Beyond Metaphor: The Theory of Tropes in Anthropology.* Stanford: Stanford University Press, 56–93.
Quirk, R. and Greenbaum, S. (1975) *A University Grammar of English.* London: Longman.
Rampton, B. (1995) Politics and change in research in applied linguistics. *Applied Linguistics,* **16** (2), 233–56.
Reddy, M. (1993) The conduit metaphor: a case of frame conflict in our language about language, in A. Ortony (ed.), *Metaphor and Thought* (2nd edn). Cambridge: Cambridge University Press, 164–201.
Ricoeur, P. (1978) *The Rule of Metaphor.* London: Routledge and Kegan Paul.
Roebuck, R. (2000) Subjects speak out: how learners position themselves in a psycholinguistic task, in J. Lantolf (ed.), 79–96.
Rogoff, B., Mosier, C., Mistry, J. and Göncü, A. (1993) Toddlers' guided participation with their caregivers in cultural activity, in E. Forman, N. Minick and C. A. Stone (eds), 230–53.
Rogoff, B. (1990) *Apprenticeship in Thinking.* Oxford: Oxford University Press.
Romaine, S. (1984) *The Language of Children and Adolescents: The Acquisition of Communicative Competence.* Oxford: Blackwell.
Rommetveit, R. (1979) On the architecture of intersubjectivity, in R. Rommetveit and R. Blakar (eds), *Studies of Language, Thought and Verbal Communication.* London: Academic Press, 93–108.
Rorty, R. (1989) *Contingency, Irony and Solidarity.* Cambridge: Cambridge University Press.
Roschelle, J. (1992) Learning by collaborating: convergent conceptual change. *Journal of the Learning Sciences,* **2** (3), 235–76.
Rose, S. (1993) *The Making of Memory.* London: Transworld Publishers.
Ross, B. and Spalding, T. (1994) Concepts and categories, in R. J. Sternberg (ed.), *Thinking and Problem Solving.* San Diego: Academic Press, 119–48.
Rumelhart, D. (1979) Some problems with the notion of literal meanings, in A. Ortony (ed.), 71–82.
Sadock, J. (1993) Figurative speech and linguistics, in A. Ortony (ed.), 42–57.
Schiffrin, D. (1994) *Approaches to Discourse.* Oxford: Blackwell.
Schmidt, R. (1994) Deconstructing consciousness in search of useful definitions for applied linguistics. *AILA Review 11: Consciousness in Second Language Learning,* 11–26.
Schön, D. (1979) Generative metaphor: a perspective on problem-setting in social policy, in A. Ortony (ed.), *Metaphor and Thought* (2nd edn). Cambridge: Cambridge University Press, 137–63.
Scollon, R. (1998) *Mediated Discourse as Social Interaction: A Study of News Discourse.* New York: Longman.
Scollon, R. (2001) *Mediated Discourse.* London: Routledge.

Searle, J. (1993) Metaphor, in A. Ortony (ed.), 83–111.
Semino, E., Heywood, J. and Short, M. (in press). Methodological problems in the analysis of metaphors in a corpus of conversations about cancer. *Journal of Pragmatics.*
Siltanen, S. (1990) Effects of explicitness on children's metaphor comprehension. *Metaphor and Symbolic Activity,* **5** (1), 1–20.
Silverman, D. (1993) *Interpreting Qualitative Data.* London: Sage.
Sinclair, J. (1991) *Corpus, Concordance, Collocation.* Oxford: Oxford University Press.
Sinclair, J. and Coulthard, M. (1975) *Towards an Analysis of Discourse.* Oxford: Oxford University Press.
Slobin, D. (1996) From 'Thought and Language' to 'Thinking for Speaking', in J. Gumperz and S. Levinson (eds), *Rethinking Linguistic Relativity.* New York: Cambridge University Press, 70–96.
Smith, M. K., Pollio, H. and Pitts, M. (1982) Metaphor as intellectual history: conceptual categories underlying figurative usage in American English from 1675—1975. *Linguistics,* **19**, 911–35.
Smolka, A., de Goes, M. and Pino, A. (1995) The constitution of the subject: a persistent question, in J. Wertsch, P. del Rió and A. Alvarez (eds), 165–84.
Snow, C. (1996) Change in child language and child linguists, in H. Coleman and L. J. Cameron (eds), *Change and Language.* Clevedon: BAAL and Multilingual Matters Ltd, 75–88.
Sontag, S. (1991) *Illness as Metaphor: AIDS and Its Metaphors.* London: Penguin Books.
Sperber, D. and Wilson, D. (1986) *Relevance.* Oxford: Blackwell.
Spiro, R., Feltovitch, P., Coulson, R. and Anderson, D. (1989) Multiple analogies for complex concepts: antidotes for analogy-induced misconception in advanced knowledge acquisition, in S. Vosniadou and A. Ortony (eds), 498–531.
Steen G. (1989) Metaphor and literary comprehension: towards a discourse theory of metaphor in literature. *Poetics,* **18**, 113–41.
Steen, G. (1992) Metaphor in literary reception. Unpublished doctoral dissertation, Vrije Universiteit, Amsterdam.
Steen, G. (1994) *Understanding Metaphor in Literature.* London: Longman.
Steen, G. (1999a) From linguistic to conceptual metaphor in five steps, in R. W. Gibbs and G. Steen (eds), 55–77.
Steen, G. (1999b) Metaphor and discourse: towards a linguistic checklist, in L. Cameron and G. Low (eds), 81–104.
Steen, G. and Gibbs, R. (1999) Introduction, in R.W. Gibbs and G. Steen (eds), 1–8.
Sticht, T. (1993) Educational uses of metaphor, in A. Ortony (ed.), 621–32.
Strässler, J. (1982) *Idioms in English: A Pragmatic Analysis.* Tübingen: Gunter Narr Verlag.
Stratman, J. F. and Hamp-Lyons, L. (1994) Reactivity in concurrent Think-Aloud protocols, in P. Smagorinsky (ed.), *Speaking about Writing.* Newbury Park: Sage, 89–112.

Stubbs, M. (1996) *Text and Corpus Analysis*. Oxford: Blackwell.
Swain, M. and Lapkin, S. (1998) Interaction and second language learning: two adolescent French immersion students working together. *Modern Language Journal*, **82**, 320–37.
Tannen, D. (1989) *Talking Voices: Repetition, Dialogue and Imagery in Conversational Discourse*. Cambridge: Cambridge University Press.
Tharp, R. (1993) Institutional and social context of educational practice and reform, in E. Forman *et al.* (eds), 269–82.
Tharp, R. and Gallimore, R. (1988) *Rousing Minds to Life*. Cambridge: Cambridge University Press.
Thelen, E. and Smith, L. (1994) *A Dynamic Systems Approach to the Development of Cognition and Action*. Cambridge: MIT Press.
Toolan, M. (1996) *Total Speech*. Durham: Duke University Press.
van Dijk, T. A. and Kintsch, W. (1983) *Strategies of Discourse Comprehension*. New York: Academic Press.
van Geert, P. (1995) Growth dynamics in development, in R. Port and T. van Gelder (eds), 313–38.
van Geert, P. (1998) A dynamics system model of basic developmental mechanisms: Piaget, Vygotsky and beyond. *Psychological Review*, **105**, 634–77.
van Gelder, T. and Port, R. (1995) It's about time: an overview of the dynamical approach to cognition, in R. Port and T. van Gelder (eds), 1–44.
van Lier, L. (1988) *The Classroom and the Language Learner*. London: Longman.
van Lier, L. (1996) *Interaction in the Language Curriculum*. London: Longman.
van Lier, L. (2000) From input to affordance: social-interactive learning from an ecological perspective, in J. Lantolf (ed.), *Sociocultural Theory and Second Language Learning*. Oxford: Oxford University Press, 245–60.
Vervaeke, J. and Kennedy, J. (1996) Metaphors in language and thought: falsification and multiple meanings. *Metaphor and Symbolic Activity*, **11**, 273–84.
Vosniadou, S. (1987a) Contextual and linguistic factors in children's comprehension of non-literal language. *Metaphor and Symbolic Activity*, **2**, 1–11.
Vosniadou, S. (1987b) Children and metaphors. *Child Development*, **58**, 870–85.
Vosniadou, S. (1989) Context and the development of metaphor comprehension. *Metaphor and Symbolic Activity*, **4**, 159–71.
Vosniadou, S. and Ortony, A. (eds) (1989) *Similarity and Analogical Reasoning*. Cambridge: Cambridge University Press.
Vygotsky, L. (1962) *Thought and Language*. Cambridge: MIT Press.
Vygotsky, L. (1978) *Mind in Society*. Cambridge: Harvard University Press.
Waldrop, M. (1992) *Complexity*. London: Viking, Penguin.
Wales, R. and Coffey, G. (1986) On children's comprehension of metaphor, in C. Pratt, A. Garton, W. Tunmer and A. Nesdale (eds), *Research Issues in Child Development*. Sydney: Allen and Unwin, 81–94.
Walkerdine, V. (1982) From context to text: a psychosemiotic approach to

abstract thought, in M. Beveridge (ed.), *Children Thinking through Language*. London: Edward Arnold, 129–55.

Walkerdine, V. (1984) Developmental psychology and the child-centred pedagogy: the insertion of Piaget into early education, in J. Henriques, W. Hollway, C. Urwin, C. Venn and V. Walkerdine (eds), *Changing the Subject*. London: Methuen, 153–202.

Wells, G. (1999) *Dialogic Inquiry: Towards a Sociocultural Practice and Theory of Education*. New York: Cambridge University Press.

Wertsch, J. (1985) *Vygotsky and the Social Formation of Mind*. Cambridge: Harvard University Press.

Wertsch, J. (1991) *Voices of the Mind: A Sociocultural Approach to Mediated Action*. Cambridge, MA: Harvard University Press.

Wertsch, J. (1998) *Mind as Action*. New York: Oxford University Press.

Wertsch, J., del Rió, P. and Alvarez, A. (eds) (1995) *Sociocultural Studies of Mind*. New York: Cambridge University Press.

Widdowson, H. (1990) *Aspects of Language Teaching*. Oxford: Oxford University Press.

Winner, E. (1988) *The Point of Words: Children's Understanding of Metaphor and Irony*. Cambridge: Harvard University Press.

Wittgenstein, L. (1953) *Philosophical Investigations*. Oxford: Blackwell.

Wood, D. (1998) *How Children Think and Learn* (2nd edn). Oxford: Blackwell.

Index

Page numbers in **bold** indicate major discussions.

abstraction   131, 210
accommodation   110–11, 269
adaptive systems   42, 110
adjective metaphors   89, 95–6
advance organizer   128
adverb metaphors   89, 95–6
affect and metaphor   23–5, **139–40**, 263, 267, 268
affordances   40, 98–9, 143, 144
   see also opportunities
agenda management   79, 121–6, **127–9**
alterity   30–2, 45, 48, 229, 245
   conceptual   132, 143, 147, 172–4, 194, 197, 209, 235
   discourse   146, 194, 267
   management of   102, 104
   mediation of   107, 143
   reducing alterity   32, 132, 146, 199, 224, 267, 268
animating metaphors   67, 75, 169, 241–6
apostrophe lesson   55, 87, 88, 115,125
approximation   131
Aristotle   13–15
atmosphere, the   9–10, 25, **167–99**

Bakhtin, M.   6, 27, 30, 265
Black, M.   9, 16, 17, 60
blending theory   21–2
bridging terms   181, 234

centrifugal effect of metaphor   190–1, 230, 268
checking understanding   80

children and metaphor   37
class work   55, 122–3
clusters of metaphors   106, **122–3**, **137–9**, 159, 172, 205, 267, 270
collective variable   48
cognitive metaphor theory   18–22, 239–40, 252
comparisons as metaphors   74–5, 105–7, 131, 266
Comparison theory of metaphor   16–17
complex systems
   change in   44, 45–50
   discourse as   41–2, 44–5, 146
   learning as   47, 147, 235–6
   talking-and-thinking as   146, 229
   theory   28, 40–50
   view of conventionalized metaphors   116, 267
   view of volcanic lava episode   110
complexity of idea   131
concepts   144
   development   36, 39
   metaphorically structured   200, 224
   post-task   161
   pre-task   161
   scientific   32–4, 207, 224
   spontaneous   32–4, 200
conceptual metaphor   2, 25, 221, 239–40, 252, 259–60
context of research   51
contextual frames   4–5

Index

contextualization   107, 227, 228, 268
control sequences   81, 124, 126, **136**
conventionalization   116–9
conventionalized metaphors   100–1, 110–9, 270
corpus studies of metaphor   20
creativity and metaphor   1, 7, 266

'dancing'   3, 5, 55, 60, 88, 124, 128, 134, 135, 136, 137
degrees of metaphoricity   5, 69
Deignan, A.   20, 21, 109
deliberate metaphors   100–10, 231–2
density of metaphors   86–7, 201
discourse
    community   110
    context   4–6, 150
    dynamics   77, 104
    events   54, 78, 87–8, 120
    goals   34
    organization   267
    perspective   3, 265, 267
    and thinking   30
domain knowledge   38, 148
Drew, P.   24
dynamic analysis   164
dynamics
    of discourse   77
    of metaphor   8, 35
    of metaphor development   107, 267
    of metaphor processing   178–9
    of metaphor production   121–3
dynamic systems   43, 84

emergence   49, 75, 267
evolution of metaphor   71
exemplification sequence   80, 126, 130
explanation sequence   80, 126, 130
explanatory theories   33, 205, 208, 223
explication sequence   80, 126, **129–32**
extension, metaphorical   212

familiarity   131
feedback   125, **134–6**, 269
    evaluative   81, 126
    strategic   81, 126
focus and frame   9–11
framing sequence   79, 121, 124, 125, 267

Gallimore, R.   79
geology   55, 64, 84, 88, 102–8, 112, 120–2, 127, 128, 129

Gibbs, R.   1, 20, 21, 47, 149, 240, 266
Goal-directed Interactive Think-Aloud (GITA)   **153–7**, 229
gradedness of metaphoricity   167
grammar of metaphor   76, **86–99**, 266
    see also linguistic form

Heart   **200–38**
hedging   106, 108–9
Holt, E.   24
hyperbole   142, 266

identification of metaphor   **58–66**
    family resemblance approach to   61–2
idiomaticity   70
idioms   24, 57, 111, 267
information search sequence   82
Interaction theory of metaphor   17–18
internalization   28–9
interpretation of metaphor   149, 231
    accuracy   180–1, 183
    problems   212–13
inter-rater reliability   63–6
intersubjectivity   30–2
intimacy and metaphor   24, 111, 242

Johnson, M.   18, 239, 240, 242
journey metaphors   **246–52**

Kittay, E.   10, 181
knowledge brought to text   172, 205–8

Lakoff, G.   18, 19, 239, 240, 242, 247, 252
language
  learning   269–70
  as tool   28
  used in primary classroom   53–4
language of metaphor   22, 25, 98, 266
learning through metaphor   36–9
lexical content of metaphors   76, 243–4
linguistic form
  of animation metaphors   242
  of metaphor in poetry   243
  and processing   230, 267
linguistic metaphors   12, 25
  as category   59
  form   **86–99**
  as unit of analysis   78
literacy processes   252–61
'lollipop trees'   117–19, 267

'maths'   3, 4, 5, 55, 67, 68, 88, 112, 114, 124–5, 126, 135, 136
mediated action   34, 78, 107
mediation   28–9
  of affect   139–40
  of conceptual alterity   132
  of metaphor   225–9, 236–7
  by peers   198
  by text   198
mediational devices   172, 204–5
metacognitive opportunities   261
metonymy   69, 254, 260, 266
mind metaphors   261–3
multiple metaphors   39, 104, 196

nominal metaphors   77, 88–92, 196, 201, 266
  processing of   176–84, 209, 210–12
non-linearity   41–4

opportunities   31
organization sequence   79, 124, 126
ozone layer   3, **167–99**

personification   67, 241–6
poetic metaphor   1
preposition metaphors   73–4, 88–9, 96–8
primary conceptual metaphors   20
problem-based approach to protocol analysis   163, 175–6
problem setting   82
problem solving and metaphor   38
problems with metaphor   39
process analysis of metaphor   51, 75, 164
process metaphor   12, 25, 209, **231**
processing level analysis   23
processing of metaphor   21, 150, 163, **165**, 176–91, 210–12, 218–25
product analysis of metaphor   51, 75
prosaic approach to metaphor   6–8, 27, 265
protocol analysis   162

recall of information   191–4, 198
Reddy, M.   18, 30, 239
research aims, questions   50, 150, 164
research design   **150–7**
researcher's role   156
restructuring   33, 36, 225

Schön, D.   18
school talk   115
science, *see* atmosphere; geology; heart; ozone layer
scientific metaphors   148
sense   29, 35
  making sense   194
similes   231
Slobin, D.   27–8, 35
Smith, L.   34, 48
social inclusion   268
social interaction   267
sociocultural
  factors   270
  group membership   111–16, 269
  theory   28, 34

Index

Sperber, D. 7
Spiro, R. 39, 104
Steen, G. 152, 155, 163, 240
student use of metaphor 87, 112, **140–3,** 197, 266
Substitution theory of metaphor 15–16
sub-technical metaphor 113–15, 244–5
summarizing sequence 81, 126, **133–4**
systematicity 26, 144, **239–64**

talking-and-thinking 35, 47, 109–10, 146–7
teacher use of metaphor 54–8, 87
teaching sequences 78–85
    embedding 82–4
    metaphor in 84–5, 121–2, 126
technical language 66–7
    metaphorical processing of 213–14, 215–17, 234–5
technical metaphor 75, 112–13, 201, 210, 244, 269
texts
    metaphor in 56–8, 151–2, 198, 200
    structure 158–9, 203–5
Tharp, R. 79
Thelen, E. 34, 48
theory constitutive metaphor 210
theory level analysis 23
therapeutic discourse 269
Think-Aloud techniques 152–7
thought
    and language 27
    metaphor in 25

timescales
    interacting 84, 132, 146–7, 261
    of metaphor use 77, 132
Topic
    domain systematicity 261
    development 109, 163
    knowledge 179, 183, 190, 195, 210, 212–13, 233
    and Vehicle 11, 177–8, 232–4
Topic Reference Shift **184–91,** 193, 195–6
tuning 108–9, 159, 267
    markers 172, 204, 270
    mechanisms 109
types and tokens 76, 87

understanding of metaphor 145–8
    children's 148–50
validity 52
    in Think-Aloud 153–7
    in metaphor research 252
Vehicle 11, 159
    contextualization 107, 163
    development 106, 164, 205, 228
    incongruity 172, 195, 204, 233
    knowledge 150, 179, 183, 195, 233
    lexis 144
    relexicalization 106
verb metaphors 71–3, 77, 88–9, 92–5, 196, 201
    delexicalized 72–3, 94, 112
    processing 177–8, 209, 210–12
voices 142
Vygotsky, L. 27–35

Wertsch, J. 28, 31, 34
Wilson, D. 7